Practicing What We Teach

How Culturally Responsive Literacy Classrooms Make a Difference

Practicing What We Teach

How Culturally Responsive Literacy Classrooms Make a Difference

PATRICIA RUGGIANO SCHMIDT
ALTHIER M. LAZAR

EDITORS

Foreword by Patricia A. Edwards
Preface by Lee Gunderson

Teachers College, Columbia University
New York and London

Published by Teachers College Press, 1234 Amsterdam Avenue, New York, NY 10027

Library of Congress Cataloging-in-Publication Data

Practicing what we teach : how culturally responsive literacy classrooms make a difference / edited by Patricia Ruggiano Schmidt, Althier M. Lazar ; foreword by Patricia Edwards ; pref. by Lee Gunderson.
    p. cm.
  Includes bibliographical references and index.
  ISBN 978-0-8077-5220-3 (pbk. : alk. paper) 1. Teachers—Training of—United States. 2. English language—Study and teaching—United States—Foreign speakers. 3. Linguistic minorities—Education—United States. 4. Bilingual education—United States. I. Schmidt, Patricia Ruggiano, 1944– II. Lazar, Althier M.
  LB1715.P674 2011
  370.117′50973—dc22

                                                                          2011001179

ISBN 978-0-8077-5220-3 (paper)

Printed on acid-free paper

Manufactured in the United States of America

18 17 16 15 14 13 12 11   8 7 6 5 4 3 2 1

Contents

Foreword

This book resonates with me on so many levels. The first involves the notion of centering students in the classroom. As an African American woman, I grew up in a mid-sized southwestern Georgia community (Albany, Georgia), read Dick and Jane in primary school, and the literary canon in high school. These books had nothing to do with my life. Although I sometimes complained to my mother about this, I adjusted to the circumstances, primarily because of what she used to tell me. She would say, "Are you going to spend your time trying to change everything, or are you going to spend your time achieving so you can get to the point where you *can* change things?" I ended up following her advice and I mastered the game of school (see Edwards, McMillon, & Turner, 2010).

Unfortunately, some of my classmates did not take this path. Many of them resisted school because they felt it was culturally alien to them. They saw themselves as activists, fighting the injustices of the Euro-centered curriculum that did not include them. The problem was that they were not in a position of power that would have enabled them to take this kind of stand. These students eventually disengaged completely and failed to live up to their academic potential. They might have won the battle, but they lost the war.

I was fortunate to have a mother to set my priorities straight. Now I am in the position to advocate for greater inclusiveness in the curriculum. For example, I am a distinguished professor at Michigan State University and the 2010–2011 President of the International Reading Association. I firmly believe that children must be able to see themselves in the books they read and they must be able to write about their experiences and interests (Sims Bishop, 2007). Of course they can benefit from reading the canon and experiencing worlds beyond their homes and communities, but they also need to feel that they are valued. Not all children have caregivers like my mother—a person who helped me see that even though the books I was given had nothing to do with my life, I needed to read them to make things better for others. Without her guidance, I, too, may have been among the disenfranchised. We cannot do this to children. The stories in this book show many teachers who help children feel connected with school because they invite children's worlds into the classroom through literacy.

I also related to this book because of my work with parents. Several years ago I made an important discovery in the largely working class community of Ruston, Louisiana (Edwards, 1989, 1990a, 1990b,1995a, 1995b, 2010). I worked with parents of children in grades K–2 at a Head Start center. These children were struggling readers and I knew that unless they had exposure to print at home, they would be at great risk for failing in school. The teachers told me that these children "are not read to" at home. I spent time getting to know these children's parents, and many shared with me that they had difficulty reading. I learned that the majority of the parents were too frightened and embarrassed to tell their child's teachers that they could not read even simple picture books. The teachers in the school kept telling them: "You must read to your kids." To avoid the humiliation of being "found out" they distanced themselves from their children's teachers and the school. This experience made me very sensitive to parents who feel insecure about their own literacy abilities and how teachers think about these parents.

The problem lies in the assumptions made by both parents and teachers. From a teacher's perspective, it is easy to feel frustrated when parents do not seem to be supporting their children's literacy development. When children come to school woefully underprepared, teachers begin to wonder if parents care enough to support their children's academic learning. It is easy to make the assumption that they don't, but we have to question it. I learned firsthand that it is not that parents don't care, it is that they do not know how to implement what teachers are telling them to do. From a caregiver's perspective, the teacher should be able to support the literacy needs of all children regardless of the amount of support they get from home. After all, the teachers are the ones educated to do so. Here lies another assumption. Teachers have a very complex job. They must serve many children with a variety of learning and literacy needs. They often have to serve children from many different backgrounds, and, oftentimes, they do not have the answers when working with culturally diverse families.

These kinds of misunderstandings between parents and teachers do not have to exist. Teachers can listen to parents, and, in these exchanges, parents can learn about the complexities of being a teacher. This book features teachers who communicate successfully with their students' families and communities. Through their listening and conversations they know about their students' out-of-school lives and the challenges that they and their parents face. Teachers like this are much less likely to blame parents and much more likely to work with them for the purpose of helping children develop healthy emotional and social lives.

Finally, there is the issue of teacher education. In today's classrooms, multiple literacies and languages exist (see Edwards, 2004; Edwards, Mc-Millon, & Turner, 2010; Li & Edwards, 2010). The research on culturally responsive teaching suggests that teachers need to understand and build on the different linguistic and literacy capacities that children bring to school. Consequently, implementing culturally responsive teaching can be enormously complex. Presently, we are asking primarily White teachers, who often have very few experiences with diversity, to attend to all of their students' cultural needs. But many teacher education programs have not shown them how to do this. One problem is that teacher preparation programs and professional development programs are not unified in offering teachers the knowledge and support they need in order to teach in culturally responsive ways. For 30 years, we have had conversations about teaching to diverse groups of students, but we still don't have a unified set of objectives for making this happen. This is why the stories in this book are so important. They give us concrete examples of what it takes to build teachers' awareness of culture and culturally responsive teaching. They offer hope that this kind of growth can happen among all teachers.

The great challenge we face today is how to serve students whose literacy and language backgrounds are at odds with the literacy practices valued in schools. And too many are not achieving academically (Li, 2006, 2008, Li & Edwards, 2010). This is at a time when we still have many questions. This reminds me of the recent BP oil well disaster in the Gulf of Mexico. Everyone was screaming to stop the flow, but no one knew an easy way to do it. The same is true regarding the too many kids living in high poverty and in culturally diverse communities who are failing in school. As educators, we want to stop this, but are often unclear about how to do it, much less with the meager resources we have. However, the stories of the teachers profiled in this book suggest that there are important things we need to consider if we are going to have any success at helping students achieve. We need to focus students in the curriculum, build better relationships with students and parents, build on the linguistic competencies of students, and learn how to be more culturally aware. In a perfect world, all children should have a mother like mine—a mother who encouraged academic achievement no matter what the school taught, a mother who was confident about her own education and could successfully communicate with the teachers, a mother who could prepare her children for the language of school. However, it is not about what *should* be but what *can* be. With the resources and frameworks we have available to us now, this book moves us closer to bringing culturally responsive teaching to the forefront. The teachers profiled in this book keep the conversation alive and move us toward more just educational settings.

—*Patricia A. Edwards*

REFERENCES

Edwards, P. A. (1989). Supporting lower SES mothers' attempts to provide scaffolding for bookreading. In J. Allen & J. Mason (Eds.), *Risk makers, risk takers, risk breakers: Reducing the risks for young literacy learners* (pp. 222–250). Portsmouth, NH: Heinemann.

Edwards, P. A. (1990a). *Parents as partners in reading: A family literacy training program.* Chicago: Children's Press.

Edwards, P. A. (1990b). *Talking your way to literacy: A program to help nonreading parents prepare their children for reading.* Chicago: Children's Press.

Edwards, P. A. (1995a). Combining parents' and teachers' thoughts about storybook reading at home and school. In L. M. Morrow (Ed.), *Family literacy: Multiple perspectives to enhance literacy development* (pp. 54–60). Newark, DE: International Reading Association.

Edwards, P. A. (1995b). Connecting African American families and youth to the school's reading program: Its meaning for school and community literacy. In V. L. Gadsden & D. Wagner (Eds.), *Literacy among African American youth: Issues in learning, teaching and schooling* (pp. 263–281). Cresskill, NJ: Hampton Press.

Edwards, P. A. (2004). *Children's literacy development: Making it happen through school, family, and community involvement.* Boston: Allyn & Bacon.

Edwards, P. A. (2010). The role of family literacy programs in the school success or failure of African American families and children. In D. Fisher & K. Dunsmore (Eds.), *Bringing literacy home* (pp. 184–202). Newark, DE: International Reading Association.

Edwards, P. A., McMillon, G. M. T., & Turner, J. D. (2010). *Change is gonna come: Transforming literacy education for African American children.* New York: Teachers College Press.

Li, G. (2006). *Culturally contested pedagogy: Battles of literacy and schooling between mainstream teachers and Asian immigrant parents.* Albany: State University of New York Press.

Li, G. (2008) *Culturally contested literacies: America's "rainbow underclass" and urban schools.* New York: Routledge.

Li, G., & Edwards, P. A. (Eds.). (2010). *Best practices in ELL instruction.* New York: Guilford Press.

Sims Bishop, R. (2007). *Free within ourselves: The development of African American children's literature.* Portsmouth, NH: Heinemann.

Preface

A lot of people are convinced that teachers are responsible for many of the ills of society in North America and around the world. I've heard this in supermarket checkout lines and on city buses. I've heard a thousand prescriptions for making schools better from all kinds of people who don't know what they're talking about. Parents who have trouble controlling their two children complain about poor discipline in schools and grandfathers with high school educations lament that everything would be fine if teachers would only teach phonics. Most people simply do not know the difficulties teachers face. The worst views, however, almost always come from politicians who should know better. Even the authors of children's books are heard. Paten (2009), for instance, notes that Susan Hill, a well-known British author, complained that students are taught "so badly, so dully and so mechanically that many children were being turned off to literature altogether." Has she ever visited a secondary classroom?

Teachers are usually blamed for poor school achievement. However, students are also blamed. ESL students, for instance, are blamed for the sad state of affairs in schools. Reading scores in the 1990s in California fell dramatically. At first, teachers were accused of using bad practices, but soon students were also cited as responsible agents. Asimov (1997), for instance, reporting on a study conducted by *Education Week*, noted that it had been concluded that California's poor results were because, in part, "vast numbers of students speak little English, and one in four lives in poverty" (p. A2). Spanish-speaking students have been doing poorly since the 1960s (Gunderson, 2008). Interestingly, many ESL students are native born. African American and other groups of students continue to fail to learn in school.

"The achievement gap between English learners and their English-only counterparts can be attributed in part to a number of inequitable conditions that affect their opportunities to learn" (Gándara, Rumberger, Maxwell-Jolly, & Callahan, 2003, p. 9). They concluded that "these students appear to receive a significantly inferior educational experience, even when compared to other low-income students in the public schools" (p. 9). ESL and immigrant students have not done well in elementary and secondary schools. Their achievement is low and they drop out in huge numbers (Gunderson, 2007, 2008, 2009). These dismal results appear to be getting worse.

The promise of school has been and always should be that no matter what a child's cultural background or family income or what language is spoken, if the school is to serve all children, then all students should be taught the literacy skills needed to succeed in society. Gunderson (2007) notes, "Education in North America has been viewed by many as a system that has allowed human beings who would not otherwise have access to gain social capital" (p. 322). After the Second World War, for instance, hundreds of thousands of returning soldiers went back to school thanks to the GI bill. A high school diploma was viewed as a kind of entry-level ticket to employment. "Over the last twenty or thirty years, however, the system has seemed to change into one that does not provide students, especially those from diverse cultural and economic backgrounds, with the social capital it did previously" (p. 323). Indeed, the promise of inclusive and comprehensive education no longer appears to apply to poor students or those who speak a language other than English at home or come from a different culture. There is the view that the basic sink-or-swim approach should apply to students from different cultural and language backgrounds even though they have not done well in American schools for over a century. Indeed, in 1911, it was noted:

> Immigrant groups did much worse than the native-born, some immigrant groups did much worse. The poorest were Italians. According to a 1911 federal immigration commission report, in Boston, Chicago, and New York 80% of native white children in the seventh grade stayed in school another year, but 50% of Southern Italian children, 62% of Polish children, and 74% of Russian Jewish children did so. Of those who made it to the eighth grade, 58% of the native whites went on to high school, but only 23% of the Southern Italians did so. In New York, 54% of native-born eighth-graders made it to ninth-grade, but only 34% of foreign-born eighth-graders did so. (Olneck & Lazerson, 1974, in Foner, 2002, p. 259)

The "melting-pot" metaphor of American culture turns out not to be a particularly positive one for teachers or students. For the thousands who in the last 150 or so years entered the United States and benefited in various ways, there was an unseen toll. "The individuals of the third, fourth, and fifth generations are the lost ones whose first cultures like unsettled spirits haunt their angst filled reveries" (Gunderson, 2000, p. 693). Many of these individuals are teachers who "occasionally revel in the broken bits of culture that are the dwindling tokens of their lost identities like *lefsa, ufta, grapo, domathes, May 1, and May 5,* (emphasis in original) while passionately condemning new immigrants for their apparent reticence to lose what they themselves have lost, their languages and cultures" (Gunderson, 2000, p. 693). *Culture* appears to be a word with negative connotations for teachers. Culture is what "they" have. Ruggiano Schmidt (1999) quotes a teacher as saying "I'm an American, I don't have a culture." This statement is unfortunate testimony to the fact that many of us teachers have lost track of our own cultural backgrounds. We have become, the "shadow diaspora" (Gunderson, 2000). As teachers we should know about our own cultural backgrounds and the culture of our schools, and we should know about the cultures of our students (Gunderson, 2009). If we do not, "immigrant students will continue to fail because culture is part of identity, and identity relates to how well a student does in school and society" (Gunderson, 2000, p. 693). If we do not, students who come from different cultural groups will continue to fail.

In Canada, the metaphor used to represent culture has been "tossed salad" (Gunderson, 2009). In this metaphor diverse cultures are part of the whole, yet separate, recognizable, and distinguishable. The melting-pot metaphor was adopted to represent a united, single monoculture in the United States whereby different cultures were indistinguishable and combined to form a unitary whole. Unfortunately, individual cultures lost much of what distinguished them from one another. In this sense, the classrooms of the early 20th century could more easily be represented by the melting-pot metaphor, because many students were members of groups made invisible by the process of submersion. As the 20th century passed, the cloak of invisibility provided by the melting pot began to fail. Students from different cultures were, indeed, visible. It is ironic that teachers in many classrooms have become the "visible minorities" (Li, 2006).

The underlying model in this book is based on a notion mentioned by Li (2007) that a classroom is like a rainbow. It is a unitary entity, but its parts are clearly different and discernable. Classrooms are filled with human beings who bring different cultural backgrounds to the teaching and learning occurring there. It is clear that beliefs about the teaching and learning of literacy are deeply embedded in culture (Gunderson, 2009). Culture is a literacy variable.

Teaching students who are linguistically and culturally diverse is not, as some have said, simple, because the students vary so much in so many ways. They vary in how developed their first language (L1) is, what their first language is, how extensive their first language literacy background is, how developed their English ability is, how old they are, what their motivations are, what their first cultural views and expectations are concerning teaching and learning, and what their socioeconomic status is (Gunderson, 2008). All of these factors are true for children born in the USA (Purcell-Gates, 1995) as they are for children born in other lands (Gunderson, 2009). *Culturally responsive* (CR) pedagogy is the core concept of this book. Patricia Ruggiano Schmidt and Althier Lazar understand well the importance of culture as an integral part of literacy teaching and learning. CR teaching is complex, with ties to a variety of important concepts, notions, and disciplines such as anthropology, education, linguistics, and cultural studies.

Althier Lazar, in her introductory chapter, notes that CR pedagogy is "a mindset, a philosophy, of working in flexible practices, and a way of being, doing, and thinking." In addition to being complex, CR teaching is also, according to Lazar, "highly individual" and based on an individual teacher's social realities and school circumstances. It cannot be taught to teachers in a single in-service session because it is so complex. Literacy as a cultural practice is also intimately related to the notion of *funds of knowledge*, a notion developed by Moll, Amanti, Neff, and Gonzalez (1992). Successful teachers use their students' funds of knowledge to create learning experiences. In this respect, CR teaching connects literacy practices with school literacy practices. CR teaching also involves a knowledge of critical literacy and social equity. A particularly important aspect of CR pedagogy is the teacher's deep understanding and knowledge of critical race theory. This understanding begins to emerge when teachers explore the complexities of culture and implement classroom practices that connect students' backgrounds with the curriculum.

Ruggiano Schmidt and Lazar understand well that the complexities of CR teaching cannot easily be learned and appreciated through the pages of an academic text. Instead, the content of this book explains the intricacies of CR teaching in detail and in a contextualized fashion. Indeed, the book is filled with the real stories of teachers in their classrooms providing culturally responsive teaching to their diverse students. The contents of this book document and describe the work of thoughtful teachers who know about diverse students, classroom-tested teaching practices, and the importance of valuing culture as a feature of instruction. Their voices are authentic and they describe how they employ culturally responsive teaching approaches for students from all cultural, linguistic, socioeconomic, and ethnic backgrounds.

For instance, the teachers featured in Part II—Tara, Amelia, Jamie, Crystal, and Kristin—tend to focus on centering their students in the curriculum. This means that they all use materials, primarily literature, that reflects the students' lives and heritage. Often these materials are used to enhance students' engagement and to strengthen their literacy abilities. Woven throughout the teachers' stories is the need to have students see themselves in the curriculum as a way of celebrating their personhood. In Chapter 2, for example, Tara Ranzy describes how she helps children recognize the richness of their ancestry and the knowledge that literacy achievement is her students' rightful legacy. Her philosophy is partly a response to the racist curricula that she was exposed to as a youth. Tara also balances instruction in specific skill development with meaning-based approaches in order to give students the tools they need to gain access to the "culture of power" (Delpit, 1995).

The five teachers featured in Part III—Gurkan, Kevin, June, Ernie, and Fiona—also center students in the curriculum, but their stories emphasize how they build important relationships with students, caregivers, and the community, which is an essential tenet of culturally responsive–diverse constructivist teaching. An especially critical message in these chapters is how these teachers extend themselves beyond the classroom to connect with students and caregivers. In Chapter 7, for example, Gurkan Kose writes about being a 23-year-old, 2nd-year teacher who had the chance to build a relationship with one of the most disruptive students in his school. Without understanding how the boy felt about life, school, and other things, Gurkan would not have been able to help this student attain success in high school.

The need to validate students' home languages and support their acquisition of those languages while learning English are essential for academic success and are important dimensions of CR teaching. In Part IV, teachers like Harry, Sunita, Mario, Julie, Roseanne, and Maryellen describe their ways of paying close attention to issues of language, literacy, and identity. Harry Hughes, for example, demonstrates an ability to use his knowledge of hip hop to help his African American students recognize the legitimacy and beauty of their own language but, also, to support thoughtful discussions about the relationship between students' language and more standard ways of using language.

Across many of these stories, teachers revealed how they came to acquire these ways of thinking and acting. Tara's emphasis on centering students in the curriculum had much to do with her being culturally displaced as a student in school. For others, like Kristin, it was a graduate course that put her on the path to using critical literacy when she facilitated discussions about literature. The bottom line is that all of these teachers' ways of acquiring culturally responsive teaching practices were learned over time. In Part V, the chapters clarify how this kind of learning can happen. These last chapters address the infusion of culturally relevant teaching (the how) and social equity principles (the why) into the teacher education curriculum.

One of the themes that surfaces in these stories is the teachers' ability to enact CR teaching in the presence of scripted curricula and rigid testing schedules. All of these teachers have found room to negotiate the curriculum in ways that allow for CR practice. All have been able to recognize and build on the cultural capital children bring from home and to tap this knowledge in order to grow readers, writers, and thinkers. In Chapter 3, for instance, Amelia Coleman-Brown discusses how she was able to negotiate the literacy curriculum to infuse critical, culturally responsive teaching elements. She understands the consequences of not advocating for her students and realizes her own power to enhance their life opportunities.

Finally, at the end of each of Chapters 2 through 18 is a distinct section titled "Make This Happen in Your Classroom." These sections explain how to implement culturally responsive teaching in childhood, secondary, and higher education classrooms. These sections allow teachers to attempt these ideas. Additionally, the Appendix includes a means for teachers to evaluate their own progress in the creation and implementation of culturally responsive teaching and learning.

THE STATE OF TEACHING AND LEARNING in schools in the United States is at a crisis point. Schools increasingly fail to provide students with the teaching and learning they require for achieving and prospering in our competitive society. Reports of rising dropout rates and school failures are found in the media on nearly a daily basis. It is all too easy to blame teachers and students for this crisis. CR teaching provides teachers with the knowledge to connect home and school literacy within a framework that considers funds of knowledge, critical literacy, critical race theory, cultural practices, and teacher growth. Ruggiano Schmidt and Lazar have produced a book that provides future and practicing teachers, teacher educators, educational leaders, and school activists a thoroughly contextualized description and understanding of CR teaching. It will become a classic. I am convinced it will provide the background teachers need to begin to teach in culturally responsive ways. The classroom stories presented in this book will inspire and inform readers who have not previously considered the role of culture as being important to their literacy programs. The contents of this book will inform them in ways that will help them to improve dramatically the teaching and learning they design for all of their students and, in doing so, CR teaching will help to change the dismal conditions in our schools.

—Lee Gunderson

REFERENCES

Asimov, N. (1997, January 27). California schools rate D-minus in report: Exhaustive study blames Prop. 13 for the damage. *The San Francisco Chronicle*, A2.

Delpit, L. (1995). *Other people's children: Cultural conflict in the classroom*. New York: The New Press.

Foner, N. (2002). *From Ellis Island to JFK: New York's two great waves of immigration.* New Haven, CT: Yale University Press.

Gándara, P., Rumberger, R., Maxwell-Jolly, J., & Callahan, R. (2003). English learners in California schools: Unequal resources, unequal outcomes. *Education Policy Analysis Archives, 11*(36). Retrieved January 10, 2010, from epaa.asu.edu/epaa/v11n36

Gunderson, L. (2000). Voices of the teen-age diasporas. *Journal of Adolescent and Adult Literacy, 43*(8), 692–706.

Gunderson, L. (2007). *English-only instruction and immigrant students in secondary schools: A critical examination.* Mahwah, NJ: Erlbaum.

Gunderson, L. (2008, November). The state of the art of secondary ESL teaching and learning. *Journal of Adolescent and Adult Literacy, 52*(3), pp. 184–188.

Gunderson, L. (2009). *ESL (ELL) literacy instruction: A guidebook to theory and practice* (2nd ed.). New York: Routledge.

Li, G. (2006). *Culturally contested pedagogy: Battles of literacy and schooling between mainstream teachers and Asian immigrant parents.* Albany: State University of New York Press.

Li, G. (2007). *Culturally contested literacies: America's "rainbow underclass" and urban schools.* New York: Routledge.

Moll, L. C., Amanti, C., Neff, D., & Gonzalez, N. (1992). Funds of knowledge for teaching: Using a qualitative approach to connect homes and classrooms. *Theory into Practice, 31*(2), 132–141.

Paten, G. (2009, January 1). Poor teachers fuelling "loathing of books." Retrieved January 12, 2010, from http://www.telegraph.co.uk/news/4060267/Poor-teachers-fuelling-loathing-of-books.html

Purcell-Gates, V. (1995). *Other people's words: The cycle of low literacy.* Cambridge, MA: Harvard University Press.

Ruggiano Schmidt, P. (1999). Know thyself and understand others. *Language Arts, 76*(4), 332–340.

Editors' Notes and Acknowledgments

Unequal educational situations that currently exist provided the stimulus for our book. And the first people we consulted were Patricia Edwards and Lee Gunderson, both exemplary literacy researchers and presidential leaders in national and international literacy organizations. Dr. Gunderson's research on English language learners and Dr. Edwards' studies regarding home and school communication for literacy learning have served as foundations for our own work in teacher preparation for diverse literacy classrooms. Furthermore, Dr. Edwards and Dr. Gunderson have encouraged us as we presented and published our research. Therefore, it was natural to invite them to write the Foreword and Preface of this book. Reading about their ideas concerning culturally responsive literacy teaching and its significant connections to English language learning and parent/teacher relationships prepares readers for the wonderful teachers they are about to meet in this book.

We also owe debts of gratitude to the teachers represented in this book who have made a significant difference in the lives of the children and families in their classrooms and schools. Finally, we are grateful to Jean Ward, our acquisitions editor for Teachers College Press. She searches for researchers who are attempting to be heard in the myriad of voices proclaiming easy answers to complex human questions. She listened to us and gave us the opportunity to give wonderful examples of teachers who demonstrate compassion, connection, and commitment.

We hope our readers will be inspired to initiate new teaching practices, or continue their own successful ones, and adopt and adapt some of the exemplary, culturally responsive teaching practices found in this book.

Finally, we wish to dedicate this book to our families. Patricia is grateful to her husband, Tom, for his patience and carefully attentive friendship. Althier is thankful for her husband, Mitch, and sons Zach and Aaron for their loving support.

Practicing What We Teach

How Culturally Responsive Literacy Classrooms Make a Difference

Part I

THE NEED FOR CULTURALLY RESPONSIVE LITERACY TEACHERS

In the United States, factors such as language, skin color, and economic status often impact academic achievement. Those with lighter skin shades, those who speak Standard English, and those who understand middle-class values are better positioned to acquire the cultural capital needed to successfully negotiate the educational system and access mainstream opportunities. Unfortunately, there are vast numbers in this country who represent the culturally marginalized. They often attend underfunded schools with teachers who have not received the preparation necessary to understand and appreciate children and families from diverse backgrounds and experiences. Living on the edge, parents in these communities often work 70 hours or more a week in low-wage jobs, and far too many have difficulty finding gainful employment. Their children are left to deal with a school curriculum that has little relevance to their lives. Unless they are provided with committed teachers who can recognize their full potential and nurture their growth, it will be difficult for them to acquire the capital needed for academic success. As editors of this book, we believe that culturally responsive teaching can give teachers the necessary tools to help these children succeed in school, access mainstream opportunities, and add to the rich cultural mix that defines our nation.

CHAPTER 1

Access to Excellence

Serving Today's Students Through Culturally Responsive Literacy Teaching

Althier M. Lazar

The United States is a nation of many diverse heritages. Some of our grand-parents and great-grandparents traveled across an ocean to seek prosperity in this country. Some of us have ancestors who came here to escape religious persecution, poverty, or the political turmoil of their native lands. Some of us have ancestors who were brought here in chains. Others of us have ancestors who had lived here for thousands of years but were stripped of their lands within a span of one lifetime. Emerging from these different histories is a population of many hues, cultures, languages, faiths, beliefs, and experiences. Some have different kinds of privileges by virtue of their race, class, religion, gender, and language ability, and some are subjugated by these characteristics. Opportunities for those who came voluntarily, those who did not, and those who have been culturally displaced have been unequal despite our pledge of "justice for all."

This diversity is reproduced in many classrooms today, often with teachers representing the "culture of power (White, middle class, European American)" and a growing number of students representing the culturally marginalized. These students often come to school with different languages and print experiences and many have not had equal access to the literacies typically valued in school. As educators, it is our job to help these children attain academic excellence. This means recognizing and validating children's existing knowledge, languages, and experiences; criticizing deficit-based descriptions of students and their families; setting high expectations; building on students' knowledge; centering students in the curriculum;

teaching the culture of power through explicit and meaning-based experiences; building relationships with students and their families; and valuing the linguistic and literacy capacities that children bring from home. Underlying these practices is the notion that all children have limitless potential and that a teacher's central responsibility is to develop this potential. When teachers see children's potential, appreciate and understand their cultural capital, and use knowledge about children's everyday worlds to inform instruction, the teachers are better able to help them achieve in school (Cummins, 2000; Darling-Hammond & Bransford, 2005; Moll & Gonzalez, 1994; Nieto, 1999).

These ways of knowing and being are the basis of *culturally responsive teaching* (Gay, 2000; Ladson-Billings, 1992). Culturally responsive teaching has had a major influence on educational philosophy and research, but it is not the focus of every teacher's thinking and practice. Despite 3 decades of research that establishes the significance of culturally responsive teaching for engaging students and helping them achieve, our visits to schools suggest that it is practiced minimally. Scripted curricula and high-stakes testing have made it more challenging for teachers to enact culturally responsive teaching practices. Yet the stories in this book show that teachers can meet the needs of students who possess diverse languages, cultures, and economic situations by validating and building on their culture, even when they teachers are working with a prescribed curriculum.

These teachers' work needs to be shared if we want to make culturally responsive teaching a reality in all schools. We need more explicit examples of how successful teachers engage in these practices and how it matters in terms of students' engagement and achievement. It is especially important to understand *why* teachers engage in these practices. What often drives these teachers is a strong sense of social equity—the knowledge that there are differences of power and privilege that need to be rectified, and giving their underrepresented students access to excellence in the classroom is one part of leveling the playing field.

In this chapter, I present a rationale for why culturally responsive teaching needs to become a priority and provide an overview of the perspectives associated with culturally responsive practice, all of which are exemplified by the teachers profiled in this book. First, I will provide some information about the demographic shifts that have taken place over the last few decades that have made it necessary to focus on how teachers successfully serve the needs of children in nondominant communities.

WHO WE SERVE NOW

"Rainbow" is an apt way to describe classrooms today (Li, 2007). Most teachers fit a middle-class demographic and are often cultural outsiders with respect to the culturally and linguistically diverse populations they serve. Most teachers in the United States are White and monolingual, but they now serve a growing population of children of color, many of whom speak languages other than English. The percentage of English language learners has grown precipitously in the last 2 decades. Twenty percent of children ages 5 to 17 speak a language other than English in their homes (U.S. Department of Education, 2008). Hispanics and Asians are among the fastest growing groups of English language learners. These growth trends mean that classrooms will likely be filled with children raised in homes where English is not spoken, or where African American Language and Spanglish are used. Unfortunately, our schools have been largely unsuccessful in meeting the needs of children in these communities, as indicated by their abominably high school dropout rates (Gunderson, 2007).

The other major difference between children and many of their teachers is one of class. Poverty negatively impacts academic achievement because of diminished options for housing, health care, and education. Even in the best of times, many working-class families live paycheck to paycheck, but the deep and prolonged economic recession in this country has left millions of Americans unemployed. These job losses mean that families of formerly middle- or working-class status are now considered poor according to the 2008 federal standard of $21,200 for a family of four (U.S. Department. of Health and Human Services, 2008). The recent financial crisis has also resulted in increases in homelessness. Teachers will see more of their students living in temporary housing and shelters, and this means higher levels of student mobility, absenteeism, and stress. The United States has the highest rate of childhood poverty among Western democratic nations (Corak, 2005). In 2007, 24.5% of Blacks and 21.5% of Hispanics were poor, compared to 8.2% of non-Hispanic Whites and 10.2% of Asians (National Poverty Center, 2006).

These realities result in growing numbers of children who are coming to school with different experiences, understandings, literacies, and ways of using language. They enter classrooms in which their ways of knowing, communicating, and behaving may be misunderstood and or devalued. This can negatively impact students' ability to access the literacies associated with school achievement. It is imperative that we reconceptualize literacy teaching through the lens of culturally responsive teaching. Next, I will define culturally responsive teaching and provide some insights about the challenges of enacting it in schools.

PERSPECTIVES OF CULTURALLY RESPONSIVE TEACHING

Culturally responsive pedagogy has been defined and redefined over the last 30 years. The term morphed from *culturally appropriate* (Au & Jordan, 1981) to *culturally congruent* (Mohatt & Erickson, 1981) to *culturally responsive* (Cazden & Leggett, 1981). In her groundbreaking study of successful teachers of African American students, Ladson-Billings (1994) used the term *culturally relevant* to describe how teachers took responsibility for their students' achievement, drew upon their knowledge of students' cultures to teach, and helped students develop a *sociopolitical consciousness*, the ability to think critically about social injustice.

Gay (2000) defined culturally responsive teaching as that which "uses the cultural knowledge, prior experiences, and performance styles of diverse students to make learning more appropriate and effective for them; it teaches to and through the strengths of these students" (p. 29). She asserts that culturally responsive teaching includes the following five characteristics:

- It acknowledges the legitimacy of the cultural heritages of different ethnic groups, both as legacies that affect students' dispositions, attitudes, and approaches to learning and as worthy content to be taught in the formal curriculum.
- It builds bridges of meaningfulness between home and school experiences as well as between academic abstractions and lived sociocultural realities.
- It uses a wide variety of instructional strategies that are connected to different learning styles.
- It teaches students to know and praise their own and each other's cultural heritages.
- It incorporates multicultural information, resources, and materials in all the subjects and skills routinely taught in schools. (p. 29)

Gay further explains that CR teaching is multidimensional (involving a mix of attributes like learning contexts, relationships, teaching strategies, different academic disciplines), empowering (valuing self-efficacy, academic competence, and personhood), transformative (fostering social critique), and emancipatory (emphasizing liberation of thought and action).

In the last 20 years, English language learning research has recognized the significance of culturally responsive teaching (Cummins, 2000; Fitzgerald & Noblit, 1999; Gunderson, 2009; Nieto, 1999). Studies suggest that students who are literate in their first languages appear to grasp their English language learning more quickly. Additionally, students who cannot read or write in their first languages find it easier to learn English by associating spoken first languages with English. Therefore, teachers who are culturally responsive draw upon these home languages to teach English. This practice validates the children's family and community cultures while introducing English language learning. Such experiences give the English language learners control over their learning, thus empowering them academically and socially.

Over the last decade, CR teaching principles and practices have been described and demonstrated in books, articles, videos, Web sites, blogs, professional conferences, and teacher workshops. Scholarly reviews of the theories and practices associated with culturally responsive literacy teaching are available (Morrow, Rueda, & Lapp, 2009) as are specific recommendations for practice (Ruggiano Schmidt & Ma, 2006). Over the last few years, presentations on or associated with CR pedagogy have had a dominant presence at major research conferences. While information about CR instruction is pervasive, not all students have benefited from it.

VARIATION IN CULTURALLY RESPONSIVE PRACTICES

Our visits to schools suggest that some children are exposed to CR instruction and some are not. One reason seems to be that many school districts, pressured to show academic achievement as a result of the No Child Left Behind federal law, have redirected teacher practice and professional development toward the goal of raising test scores, primarily in the areas of reading and math. The teachers I speak with describe their professional development as involving "how to prepare students for standardized tests," "how to use standardized test results to inform instruction," or how to "teach according to the curriculum guide." This emphasis on testing and scripted teaching has eclipsed a focus on teacher reflection and decision making. Teachers often feel there is little room for exploring issues like teachers' own cultural awareness or the kinds of cultural capital that children bring from their homes and communities. Teachers have been asked to *do*, not to *think*. Given these constraints, it has become difficult for many teachers to enact CR practices.

This doesn't mean that CR teaching doesn't happen. Many teachers today make instructional decisions based on CR teaching principles, perhaps because they were exposed to them in their teacher preparation programs or because they attended professional workshops or read books or articles on the topic. Some teachers have studied their own CR-based practices and have added to the archive of professional articles and books on the topic. Still, though, many teachers have not had the opportunities and tools needed to carry out CR principles. Since CR teaching is complex, it cannot be reduced to a daylong workshop or a litany of practices (even though many practices are associated with it). CR teaching is a mindset, a philosophy, a set of working and flexible practices, and a way of being, doing, and thinking. It is not just what we do and how we do it, but *why we do it*. It is highly individual, informed by one's own social realities and school circumstances.

In the remaining pages of this chapter, I highlight the various theories and practices associated with CR pedagogy. This will help you to interpret the teachers' stories you are about to read, and it will help you construct your own unique vision of CR teaching for the benefit of your own students.

LITERACY AS CULTURAL PRACTICE

Culturally responsive teaching is informed by research in the combined areas of anthropology, education, and linguistics, which finds that learning is socially mediated, constructed, and culturally situated (Rogoff, 1990; Scribner & Cole, 1981; Vygotsky, 1978). What we know is mediated by others through language, and language is shaped by culturally defined practices. Literacy, then, is framed as a set of culturally situated practices that are determined by the needs and goals of particular social communities.

Literacies valued in children's homes and communities may not be the same as those valued in school, but this does not mean that they are *less than* or *inferior to* those valued in school. Brian Street's (1995) *autonomous* view of literacy assumes that school-based literacies are value neutral and disconnected to culture. Yet literacy standards are molded around the lifestyles and expectations of the mainstream White middle class. The object of schooling is to master these literacies, with the assumption that doing so will enable success within the dominant culture.

In contrast, an *ideological* approach to literacy sees literacy as inherently entwined with culture and heritage. This view recognizes that all literacy practices serve legitimate communicative purposes for all families, but their value is determined by the power that specific communities hold in society. This view acknowledges that power relations exist in society and determine how different literacies are valued. It is often assumed that the literacies of nondominant or underrepresented groups are nonexistent or inferior to those of middle-class, White, Western societies, but dozens of ethnographic studies have exposed the literate practices of nondominant groups as aligned with cultural practices and serving purposeful functions (Au, 1981; Heath, 1983; Taylor & Dorsey-Gaines, 1988).

Cultural conflict in the classroom exists when the expectations of schooling are out of sync with the discourses that children bring from their homes and communities—"Discourses" are ways of knowing, acting, thinking, and doing that involve literate practice (Gee, 2000). For example, Heath found that the middle-class parents who frequently asked questions that elicited elaborated responses from children were similar to those asked by the teachers in school. These children did well in school. In contrast, the White working-class families of "Roadville" and the Black working-class familes of "Trackton" used language and print in ways that were out of sync with teachers' expectations and practices. The children in these communities were at a disadvantage when it came to providing elaborated responses to texts in school, not because they lacked the intellectual capacity, but because they were unfamiliar with the types of questions they were being asked in school. When teachers later became aware of these different ways of using language, they were able to adjust their questioning and become more transparent about their use of questions.

Similarly, Au (1980) found that when Hawaiian children used a culturally familiar discourse style known as "talk-story" to discuss the stories they read, they were able to comprehend them at a higher level than when they engaged in more traditional turn-taking story discussions. In Hawaiian communities, talk-story is a communicative event where several participants talk together to produce an idea or story. In most mainstream school contexts, such overlapping talk about texts would be perceived as disorganized, unmanageable or ineffective. Yet these participation structures were what students needed to maximize their text comprehension.

This research indicates that literacy achievement is more likely to happen when school–home literacy and language practices are aligned. By comparing our own teaching practices to students' ways of using language and print across multiple contexts, we can identify and bridge gaps between home–school discourses.

FUNDS OF KNOWLEDGE

Closely aligned with recognizing literacy as a set of cultural practices is the idea that children come to school with *funds of knowledge* (Moll & Gonzalez, 1994) that can be used to create meaningful classroom instruction. Teachers learn about children's linguistic competence and cultural practices and make instructional and curricula changes to accommodate this knowledge. The funds of knowledge project involves gathering family stories to better understand how families and communities use knowledge and skills to participate in a range of practices that help them sustain their households, earn a living, and maintain relationships. Gonzalez, Moll, and Amanti (2004) describe a teacher who learned from families that many of the children in her class sold candy. She then created a literacy-based "candy-making and selling" unit that addressed school standards in the areas of mathematics, health, science, and consumer economics.

While successful teachers draw upon students' funds of knowledge to create learning experiences that will motivate and engage their students, some worry about how to do this without straying too far away from official curriculums. Teaching in the "third space" (Gutiérrez, 2008) intentionally connects children's existing knowledge to the official curriculum. Practices such as cultural modeling (Lee, 2007) reflect third-space, or hybrid, school practices. In cultural modeling, Lee focuses on helping students identify the complex reasoning skills needed to generate and interpret culturally familiar literacies like hip-hop lyrics and how these same conceptual tools can be tapped to understand the literary features and messages contained in school-based texts.

DIVERSE CONSTRUCTIVIST VIEW

Au (1998) established the diverse constructivist orientation, based on Cummins' (1986) theoretical framework for empowering culturally diverse children. This framework considers "the links between events in the school and conditions in the larger society, the centrality of the teacher's role in mediating learning, the inseparability of affective or motivational factors and academic achievement, and the connections between schooled knowledge and personal experience." Au (1998) proposed that teachers could successfully serve children who are culturally different from themselves if they

1. establish students' ownership of literacy as the overarching goal;
2. recognize the importance of students' home languages and come to see biliteracy as an attainable and desirable outcome;

3. use materials that present diverse cultures in an authentic manner, especially through the works of authors from diverse backgrounds;

4. become culturally responsive in their management of classrooms and interactions with students;

5. make stronger links to the community;

6. provide students with both authentic literacy activities and a considerable amount of instruction in specific literacy skills needed for full participation in the culture of power; and

7. use forms of assessment that eliminate or reduce sources of bias (such as prior knowledge, language, and question type) and more accurately reflect students' literacy achievement. (p. 304)

Each of these practices is supported by a considerable body of research. For example, underlying the position on language diversity (item 2) is the notion that language and identity are inexorably fused, and that children will be more motivated to acquire more standard forms of English if their own ways of using language are validated in the classroom (Delpit, 2002; Charity-Hudley & Mallinson, 2011). African American Language (AAL) is often a language form that is stigmatized as "sloppy English"; it is none-theless logical, rule-governed, and legitimate (Labov, 1972; Smitherman, 1995), and it is important for us to understand the history and structure of the language. Spanglish is a mixture of English and Spanish and is developing as a new American dialect (Stavans, 2003). Children's acqui-sition of more standard forms of English require that teachers recognize the beauty and legitimacy of students' first languages and that they select literacy events, like some forms of writing and formal speaking, that al-low students time to reflect on their language choices (Delpit & Dowdy, 2002). Helping English language learners become biliterate requires that teachers must also scrutinize the language demands of the classroom; understand differences between conversational and academic language proficiency; scaffold just beyond students' language abilities; provide au-thentic communicative opportunities; help students draw from the skills and strategies they know in their primary language to learn a second lan-guage; and reduce the level of anxiety associated with performing in a second language (Lucas, 2011).

In addition, Au writes that multicultural literature "can be used to promote critical analysis of social and historical issues and to empower students to work on the resolution of social problems" (1998, p. 311). This aligns with notions about the transformative nature of CR teaching, which are exemplified by the critical literacy movement.

CRITICAL LITERACY

Critical literacy encourages teachers to help students understand the existence of oppression and develop solutions to confront it (Freire, 1970). This view aligns with Banks' (1999) notion of transformation and social action approaches to teaching that help students identify and confront social issues from various perspectives (Christensen, 2000, 2009; Heffernan & Lewison, 2005; McDaniel, 2006).

Much of the focus of critical literacy is on helping children interpret literature in critical ways, which includes interrogating the viewpoints and motivations of authors and illustrators, evaluating elements of cultural authenticity and accuracy in books, and discussing the serious and often controversial messages that are contained in texts. Oftentimes I have found that teachers tend to avoid or gloss over topics like language prejudice, ethnic stereotyping, and structural racism—topics that often surface in literature that reflects the heritage and experiences of children in nondominant groups. This resistance stems from insecurities about not knowing enough about the history and experiences of particular cultural groups, not being able to facilitate the emotionally charged conversations that can emerge in these literature discussions, or believing that children, especially young children, need to be protected from having to deal with these serious issues in school.

Transformative teachers, however, position their students as activists who can create a more socially equitable world. This means helping them understand the social inequities that currently exist. An example of this kind of teaching is found in Mary Cowhey's book *Black Ants and Buddhists: Thinking Critically and Teaching Differently in the Primary Grades* (2006). Cowhey's "peace classroom" serves culturally diverse 1st- and 2nd-graders who are positioned as activists. Their school literacy practices are often entwined with solving social problems, such as participating in voter registration drives and recycling campaigns and helping those who are less fortunate. Cowhey confronts serious issues like racism and colonialism by reading books like *From Slave Ship to Freedom Road* (Lester, 1998) and *Harriet and the Promised Land* (Lawrence, 1997). Her students are taught to question texts, generate their own research questions, and write pieces that inform others about the history of marginalized people. Cowhey's classroom is an example of teaching that helps to develop students who can both understand and critique the existing social order (Ladson-Billings, 1995).

The ability to teach in ways that are consistent with a critical, social equity orientation to literacy teaching are dependent on teachers understanding of power relationships in society, a topic I will explore next.

SOCIAL EQUITY VIEW OF TEACHING

Teachers who operate from a social equity perspective see the big picture. In other words, they see literacy learning and teaching within a social context—and power is a major variable within this context. They understand that it is necessary to empower learners because they recognize we live in a socially, economically, and racially stratified society and that many of the culturally and linguistically diverse students they serve are among the most marginalized.

Within the ecological landscape, we need to recognize how race and class converge to shape children's access to the literacies valued in school (Villegas & Lucas, 2002). We need to know that poverty is a primary factor that undermines children's academic achievement and also understand how racism has worked to undermine life opportunities for children of color, in terms of their family's access to employment, housing, education, and health care. If we look closely at schools that serve children in high poverty communities, many examples of structural racism surface. These schools often do not have libraries, art or music teachers, or adequate support professionals such as reading specialists and counselors. When teachers compare these conditions with their own advantages in accessing texts and education, they realize that the playing field is uneven for children.

While it is often easy for us to see how poverty impacts educational opportunity, it is much harder for us to acknowledge the impact of racism because we live in a society that tends to hide, deny, downplay, and gloss over its impact.

CRITICAL RACE THEORY

Critical race theory helps us see and confront racism as it is manifested in society, schools, and even classrooms, especially as it affects students' access to academic excellence (Ladson-Billings, 1998). The first tenet of critical race theory is that racism is normalized in society, embedded in the policies and practices of institutions. The tendency to place students of color in the lower academic tracks or adopting reading anthologies written by White, mainstream authors are examples of institutional racism in schools. Oftentimes, we have to look closely to root out schooling practices and policies that deny students opportunities to realize their fullest academic potential. The goal is to scrutinize what seems "ordinary" or "natural" in order to unmask race-based inequalities.

The second tenet of critical race theory is that we can only really understand racism best from the perspectives of those who are subjugated by it. Narratives of people of color provide valid experiential knowledge that communicates the significance of race in one's life. Awareness of racism is dependent on reading and listening to these stories and using them as evidence to press for racial equality.

The third tenet takes issue with liberalism, or the sublime belief that ours is a country of freedom and equality for all. According to critical race theory, liberal thought has been too ineffectual to address the problems of structural racism that exist today. Overcoming racism requires radical changes in societal structures. For instance, the Civil Rights Act of 1964 made racial segregation of public schools illegal, yet de facto racial segregation continues to exist. So-called apartheid schools serve primarily and often exclusively students of color and these schools tend to have lower expectations of students, less experienced teachers, fewer resources, and limited opportunities for academic excellence (Kozol, 2005). Critical race theory contends that liberalism, and the idea that justice can be served through legislation and the legal system, is a naïve position.

Lastly, critical race theory supports the view that Whites will work for the cause of racial justice primarily when it benefits them. This is also described as "interest convergence"—that the interests of Blacks will be served when they complement the interests of Whites. The *Brown v. Board of Education* decision to end racial segregation of public schools is used as an example of interest convergence. Many Whites understood the economic and political benefits of integration and how their status in the world would be elevated if they supported the *Brown* decision. According to Derrick Bell (2004), this decision helped to get third-world countries to side with America in its struggle with communist countries.

Using critical race theory to confront racial inequalities in education can involve examining curricula to see if it mirrors the experiences and heritages of children of color, scrutinizing tracking and special education placement patterns in a school, and interrogating our own beliefs about the literate potential of students of color. These practices are consistent with culturally responsive teaching.

All of these principles converge to support culturally responsive teaching. As a researcher who has spent a professional career studying this topic, visiting schools, educating teachers, and publishing research, I am still learning about how CR teaching is applied across different classroom contexts and what impact it has on student development. Each of us is on a distinct path toward developing this knowledge. In the next section, I explore some of the research that has been done in this area.

PERSPECTIVES ON TEACHER GROWTH

A body of research has been devoted to understanding how teachers come to know the principles and practices associated with CR teaching (Castro, 2010; Sleeter, 2007). Studies have found that teachers' understandings about culture in relation to literacy teaching can evolve in the course of much study, reflection, self-interrogation, and work with children of nondominant groups (Kidd, Sanchez, & Thorp, 2008; Lazar, 2004, 2007; Milner, 2009; Ruggiano Schmidt, 1998, 2001; Willis, 2003).

This work involves examining the complexities of culture (Nieto, 1999), because this concept is often presented superficially in schools through a focus on "holidays and heroes" (Banks, 1999). It is also the case that many Whites do not believe they have a culture and that others who "have it" deviate from "the norm." Movement beyond these narrow conceptions is necessary for recognizing who we are in relation to the children we teach and for making important cultural connections with students. Culture includes the learned values, beliefs, and practices shared by social communities and are shaped by various sociohistorical factors. These values, beliefs, and practices shift as we move in and out of social communities across space and time. Understanding this is key to recognizing the funds of knowledge and the various forms of cultural capital that students bring from their home communities to school (Compton-Lilly, 2007a, 2007b).

For the last 20 years Patricia's (Ruggiano Schmidt, 1998, 2001) work has focused on complicated teachers' notions of culture through the ABC model, a project that will be discussed in Chapter 15. She has determined that when preservice and practicing teachers write about their own cultural histories, interview people who are culturally different from themselves, and examine these differences through several analytic lenses, they can begin to understand the ways that race, class, experiences, beliefs, and values have an impact on our choices and opportunities. Teachers involved in this work begin to understand the complexities of culture and cultural difference, but they also discover the ways they connect with culturally different others. It is through this process that teachers come to see themselves and others through the lens of culture.

Part of moving forward involves exploring how race, poverty, gender, and language impact academic achievement. Generally, this work is focused on becoming aware of our own positions of dominance and subordination relative to others, especially to the children we serve. This often means exploring the impact of racist discourses on how we see our students and ourselves. We need to do this because we are bombarded by racist messages every day, but, as I explained earlier, most of us tend not to notice these messages because they are so normalized in society. The process of unpacking these messages and understanding how they have influenced us is an important part of racial identity growth (Cross, 1987; Helms, 1990; Howard, 1999). This allows us to move away from a color-blind state to one that acknowledges how race impacts students' access to education.

Using Howard's (1999) White Identity Orientations framework, I (Lazar, 2004) traced how preservice teachers moved from fundamentalist orientations of race (lack of acknowledgment and responsibility regarding racial inequities) to integrationist orientations (acknowledging inequities but not knowing what to do about it) to transformative orientations (acknowledging and taking responsibility for racial inequality through continued learning and self-scrutiny). Growth required long-term exposure to studying issues of race, and this involved reflecting on life experiences and engaging in multiple university-based engagements with these issues and working directly with children in schools. One goal of this work is to question the idea that achievement in this country functions as a *meritocracy*, the system of equal opportunity that depends only on one's innate ability and hard work.

It is also necessary to recognize the social capital that all children and families possess, and we can do this by reading ethnographic accounts of children, families, and communities (Compton-Lilly, 2007a, 2007b; Taylor & Dorsey-Gaines, 1988); studying the popular literacies that engage children's lives and imaginations (Dyson, 2003); and becoming aware of the ways that families actively contest the conditions that negatively impact them (Li, 2007). Most importantly, our growth depends upon working directly with children and families, especially in spaces that are not encumbered by the limitations of curriculum and standardized testing, such as churches (McMillon & Edwards, 2004) or community centers (Rogers, Marshall, & Tyson, 2006).

The ultimate goal is to be "generative" teachers (Ball, 2009). Generative teachers can flexibly combine their own personal and professional knowledge with knowledge of their students, and the convergence of these two sources drives their instruction. Whether they are motivated by anger or a strong moral obligation to do what is right, generative teachers monitor and scrutinize their teaching behaviors and draw from these reflections to consider possible solutions or new approaches to teaching. Teachers operate as advocates and activists, challenging the policies and practices that undermine students' learning. As cultural mediators, these teachers try to know their students well and go out of their way to reach out to families. Generative teachers understand that to give children the best education possible, they must learn from students, families, and communities. They must also learn about the theories and practices of others and systematically study their own teaching practices (Cochran-Smith & Lytle, 1998). This kind of learning can happen when teachers are committed to social equity and when they are provided the resources and support they need to grow professionally.

CONCLUSION

All teachers can acquire the mindset and skills necessary to serve a growing population of students from culturally nondominant communities. Culturally responsive teaching is a significant and research-based ideology of teaching practice aimed toward student empowerment and achievement. I have provided an overview of CR teaching to help you interpret the beliefs and actions of teachers who are guided by this pedagogy. You will read about how they structure their classrooms, interact with their students, set high expectations, connect with families, appreciate students' home languages while helping them acquire standardized forms of English, use literature that celebrates students' heritages and experiences, teach in the third space, and advocate for students in the context of mandated school policies and practices. The thoughtful teachers featured in this book do amazing things in their classrooms, but most of us never get to see them work or hear about how they make it possible to advance the literacy development of the children in their classrooms. It is now time to share their stories. It is my hope that these chapters will help you see the possibilities of serving the literacy needs of children in culturally and linguistically nondominant groups.

REFERENCES

Au, K. (1998). Social constructivism and the school literacy learning of students of diverse cultural backgrounds. *Journal of Literacy Research, 30*(2), 297–319.

Au, K., & Jordan, C. (1981). Teaching reading to Hawaiian children: Finding a culturally appropriate solution. In H. T. Trueba, G. P. Guthrie, & K. Au (Eds.), *Culture and the bilingual classroom: Studies in classroom ethnography* (pp. 139–152). Rowley, MA: Newbury.

Ball, A. F. (2009). Toward a theory of generative change in culturally and linguistically complex classrooms. *American Educational Research Journal, 46*(1), 45–72.

Banks, J. A. (1999). *An introduction to multicultural education* (2nd ed.). Boston: Allyn and Bacon.

Bell, D. (2004). *Silent covenants: Brown v. Board of Education and the unfulfilled hopes for racial reform.* New York: Oxford University Press.

Castro, A. J. (2010). Themes in the research on preservice teachers' views of cultural diversity: Implications for researching millennial preservice teachers. *Educational Researcher, 39*(3), 198–210.

Cazden, C., & Leggett, E. (1981). Culturally responsive education: Recommendations for achieving Lau remedies II. In H. T. Trueba, G. P. Guthrie, & K. Au (Eds.), *Culture and the bilingual classroom: Studies in classroom ethnography* (pp. 69–86). Rowley, MA: Newbury.

Charity-Hudley, A. H., & Mallinson, C. (2011). *Understanding English language variation in U.S. schools.* New York: Teachers College Press.

Christensen, L. (2000). *Reading, writing, and rising up: Teaching about social justice and the power of the written word.* Milwaukee, WI: Rethinking Schools.

Christensen, L. (2009). *Teaching for joy and justice: Re-imagining the language arts classroom.* Milwaukee, WI: Rethinking Schools.

Cochran-Smith, M., & Lytle, S. (1998). Teacher research: The question that persists. *International Journal of Leadership in Education: Theory and Practice, 1*(1), 19–36.

Compton-Lilly, C. (2007a). *Rereading families: The literate lives of urban children, the intermediate years.* New York: Teachers College Press.

Compton-Lilly, C. (2007b). Exploring reading capital in two Puerto Rican families. *Reading Research Quarterly, 42*(1), 72–98.

Corak, M. (2005). Principles and practicalities for measuring child poverty in rich countries. UNICEF Discussion Paper No. 1579. Retrieved October 10, 2010, from www.unicef.org/socialpolicy/files/Principles_and_Practicalities.pdf

Cowhey, M. (2006). *Black ants and Buddhists: Thinking critically and teaching differently in the primary grades.* Portland, ME: Stenhouse.

Cross, W. E. (1987). A two-factor theory of Black identity: Implications for the study of identity development in minority children. In J. S. Phinney & M. J. Rotheram (Eds.), *Children's ethnic socialization: Pluralism and development.* (pp. 117–133). Newbury Park, CA: Sage.

Cummins, J. (1986). Empowering minority *students:* A framework for intervention. *Harvard Educational Review, 56,* 18–36.

Cummins, J. (2000). *Language, power, and pedagogy: Bilingual children in the crossfire.* New York: Multilingual Matters.

Darling-Hammond, L., & Bransford, J. (2005). *Preparing teachers for a changing world.* San Francisco: Jossey-Bass.

Delpit, L. (2002). No kinda sense. In L. Delpit & J. K. Dowdy (Eds.). *The skin that we speak: Thoughts and language and culture in the classroom.* New York: New Press.

Delpit, L., & Dowdy, J. K. (2002). *The skin that we speak: Thoughts and language and culture in the classroom.* New York: New Press.

Dyson, A. H. (2003). *The brothers and sisters learn to write: Popular literacies in childhood and school cultures.* New York: Teachers College Press.

Fitzgerald, J., & Noblit, G. W. (1999). About hopes aspirations and uncertainty: First grade English language learners' emergent reading. *Journal of Literacy Research, 31*(2),133–182.

Freire, P. (1970). *Pedagogy of the oppressed.* New York: Herder and Herder.

Gay, G. (2000). *Culturally responsive teaching: Theory, research, & practice.* New York: Teachers College Press.

Gee, J. (2000). The New Literacy Studies and the social turn. In D. Barton, M. Hamilton, & R. Ivanic (Eds.), *Situated literacies: Reading and writing in context* (pp. 180–196) London: Routledge.

González, N., Moll, L., & Amanti, C. (Eds.). (2004). *Funds of knowledge: Theorizing practices in households, communities, and classrooms.* Mahwah, NJ: Erlbaum.

Gunderson, L. (2007). *English-only instruction and immigrant children in secondary schools: A critical examination.* Mahwah, NJ: Erlbaum.

Gunderson, L. (2009, February). *Where are the English language learners?* Paper presented at English Language Learner Institute at the annual convention of the International Reading Association, Phoenix, AZ.

Gutiérrez, K. (2008). Developing a sociocritical literacy in the third space. *Reading Research Quarterly, 43*(2), 148–164.

Heath, S. B. (1983). *Ways with words: Language, life, work in communities and classrooms.* Cambridge, UK: Cambridge University Press.

Heffernan, L., & Lewison, M. (2005). What's lunch got to do with it'? Critical literacy and the discourse of the lunchroom. *Language Arts, 83*(2), 107–117.

Helms, J. (1990). Toward a model of White racial identity development. In J. Helms (Ed.), *Black and White racial identity: Theory, research, and practice* (pp. 49–66). Westport, CT: Greenwood.

Howard, G. R. (1999). *We can't teach what we don't know: White teachers, multiracial schools.* New York: Teachers College Press.

Kidd, J. K., Sanchez, S. Y., & Thorp, E. K. (2008). Defining moments: Developing culturally responsive dispositions and teaching practices in early childhood preservice teachers. *Teaching and Teacher Education: An International Journal of Research and Studies, 24*(2), 316–329.

Kozol, J. (2005). *The shame of the nation: The restoration of apartheid schooling in America.* New York: Three Rivers Press.

Labov, W. (1972). *Language in the inner city: Studies in the Black English vernacular.* Philadelphia: University of Pennsylvania Press.

Ladson-Billings, G. (1992). Reading between the lines and beyond the pages: A culturally relevant approach to literacy teaching. *Theory into Practice, 31*(4), 312–320.

Ladson-Billings, G. (1994). *The dreamkeepers.* San Francisco: Jossey-Bass.

Ladson-Billings, G. (1995). Toward a theory of culturally relevant pedagogy. *American Educational Research Journal, 32*(3), 465–491.

Ladson-Billings, G. (1998). Just what is critical race theory and what's it doing in a nice field like education? *International Journal of Qualitative Studies in Education, 11*(1), 7–24.

Lawrence, J. (1997). *Harriet in the promised land.* New York: Simon & Schuster.

Lazar, A. (2004). *Learning to be literacy teachers in urban schools: Stories of growth and change.* Newark, DE: International Reading Association.

Lazar, A. (2007). It's not just about teaching kids to read: Helping preservice teachers acquire a mindset for teaching children in urban communities. *Journal of Literacy Research, 39*(4), 411–443.

Lee, C. D. (2007). *Culture, literacy, and learning: Taking bloom in the midst of the whirlwind.* New York: Teachers College Press.

Lester, J. (1998). *From slave ship to Freedom Road.* New York: Dial Books.

Li, G. (2007). *Culturally contested literacies: America's "rainbow underclass" and urban schools.* New York: Routledge.

Lucas, T. (2011). *Teacher preparation for linguistically diverse classrooms: A resource for teacher educators.* New York: Routledge.

McDaniel, C. A. (2006). *Critical literacy: A way of thinking, a way of life,* New York: Peter Lang.

McMillon, G. M. T., & Edwards, P. A. (2004). The African American church: A beacon of light on the pathway to literacy for African American children. In E. Gregory, S. Long, & D. Volk, (Eds.), *Many pathways to literacy* (pp. 182–194). London: Routledge Falmer.

Milner, H. R. (Ed.). (2009). *Diversity and education: Teachers, teaching, and teacher education.* Springfield, IL: Charles C. Thomas.

Mohatt, G., & Erickson, F. (1981). Cultural differences in teaching styles in an Odawa school: A sociolinguistic approach. In H. T. Trueba, G. P. Guthrie, & K. Au (Eds.), *Culture and the bilingual classroom: Studies in classroom ethnography* (pp. 105–119). Rowley, MA: Newbury.

Moll, L., Amanti, C., Neff, D., & Gonzalez, N. (1992). Funds of knowledge for teaching using a qualitative approach to connect homes and classrooms. *Theory into Practice, 31*(2), 132–141.

Moll, L., & González, N. (1994). Lessons from research with language minority children. *Journal of Reading Behavior, 26*(4), 439–456.

Morrow, L. M., Rueda, R., & Lapp, D. (Eds.). (2009). *Handbook of research on literacy and diversity.* New York: Guilford Press.

National Poverty Center. (2006). *Poverty in the United States: Frequently asked questions.* Retrieved May 5, 2010, from http://www.npc.umich.edu/poverty

Nieto, S. (1999). *The light in their eyes: Creating multicultural learning communities.* New York: Teachers College Press.

Rogers, T., Marshall, E., & Tyson, C. A. (2006, April/May/June). Dialogic narratives of literacy, teaching, and schooling: Preparing literacy teachers for diverse settings. *Reading Research Quarterly, 41*(2), 202–224.

Rogoff, B. (1990). *Apprenticeship in thinking: Cognitive development in social context.* Oxford, UK: Oxford University Press.

Ruggiano Schmidt, P. R. (1998). The ABCs of cultural understanding and communication. *Equity and Excellence in Education, 31*(2), 28–38.

Ruggiano Schmidt, P. R. (2001). The power to empower. In P. R. Ruggiano Schmidt & P. B. Mosenthal (Eds.), *Reconceptualizing literacy in the new age of multiculturalism and pluralism.* Greenwich, CT: Information Age.

Ruggiano Schmidt, P. R. (2002). *Cultural conflict and struggle: Literacy learning in a kindergarten program.* New York: Peter Lang.

Ruggiano Schmidt, P. R., & Ma, W. (2006). *50 literacy strategies for culturally responsive teaching, K–8.* Thousand Oaks, CA: Corwin Press.

Scribner, S., & Cole, M. (1981). *The psychology of literacy.* Cambridge, MA: Harvard University Press.

Sleeter, C. E. (2007). Preparing teachers for multiracial and historically underserved schools. In G. Orfield & E. Frankenburg (Eds.), *Lessons in integration: Realizing the promise of racial diversity in America's schools* (pp. 171–198). Charlottesville, VA: University of Virginia Press.

Smitherman, G. (1995). Students' right to their own language: A retrospective. *The English Journal, 84*(1), 2–27.

Stavans, I. (2004). *Spanglish: The making of a new American language.* New York: Rayo.

Street, B. (1995). *Social literacies. Critical approaches to literacy in development, ethnography and education.* New York: Longman.

Taylor, D., & Dorsey-Gaines, C. (1988). *Growing up literate: Learning from inner-city families.* Portsmouth, NH: Heinemann.

U.S. Department of Health and Human Services. (2008). The 2008 HHS poverty guidelines: One version of the [U.S.] federal poverty measure. Retrieved January 16, 2010, from http://aspe.hhs.gov/poverty/08Poverty.shtml

U.S. Department of Education, National Center for Educational Statistics. (2008). *Language minority school-age children.* Retrieved March 17, 2010, from http://nces.ed.gov/programs/coe/2009/section1/indicator08.asp

Villegas, A. M., & Lucas, T. (2002). Preparing culturally responsive teachers: Rethinking the curriculum. *Journal of Teacher Education, 53*(1), 20–32.

Vygotsky, L. S. (1978). *Mind in society.* New York: Cambridge University Press.

Willis, A. I. (2003). Parallax: Addressing race in preservice literacy education. In S. Greene & D. Abt-Perkins (Eds.), *Making race visible: Literacy research for cultural understanding.* New York: Teachers College Press.

Part II

CENTERING STUDENTS IN THE CURRICULUM

When our children feel empowered to learn, they take control of and responsibility for their own education (Cummins, 2000). When they feel disempowered, they frequently act in socially inappropriate ways or adopt the invisibility of the disenfranchised (Rist, 1978). All too often, students from underrepresented groups experience feelings of disempowerment. If they live in poverty, speak languages other than English, or possess cultures different from the dominant European-American cultures promoted in school curricula, they experience exclusion. Much of the school curriculum seems foreign and unrelated to their lives. Many of them drop out as a result, which excludes them from any further social and economic progress.

Unfortunately, the teachers of the disempowered may not understand the contributions that these students can make in the classroom and school. Many of these students from differing backgrounds bring an international element into the education system, an element that might better prepare all children for the global society. Children who learn to appreciate diverse languages and cultures may, in the future, promote collaboration that benefits the entire world.

One significant way culturally responsive teachers center students in the curriculum is through literature. The literature of a culture reflects its values and offers a window into understanding its perspectives (Bishop, 2003; Loh, 2006). Students who read literature that reflects their own cultures take pride in their backgrounds and origins. They also see the teacher as someone who respects their families and communities. As a result, students more readily participate when they understand relevancy and make connections between the known and the new (Ruggiano Schmidt, 2001). As one kindergarten child from Sudan explained, "I read the book. The boy looks like me!"

Furthermore, when students are centered in the curriculum, they learn about each other's cultures, they begin to recognize worlds outside of their own, giving them more opportunities to appreciate similarities and differences among people. Developing such cosmopolitan views at an early age would seem beneficial when considering our shrinking world.

For example, graphic novels as well as picture books with significant themes related to particular content areas promote reading, writing, listening, speaking, and viewing (Kinney, 2007). Furthermore, the esthetic values related to beautiful illustrations foster an appreciation for artistic endeavors around the world (Rosenblatt, 1982). Another important feature of picture books is visual cues, since they support the learning and understanding of English language arts. Too often we forget to use illustrated literature in the upper grades, fearing that such reading may be childish. But the powerful themes found in many of these books provide students with opportunities for discussion and inquiry (Ruggiano Schmidt & Pailliotet, 2001).

Finally, young adult novels also deal with cultural differences and the struggles that ensue, and using these novels in the classroom offers a chance for students to see themselves in the stories and connect with main characters. These novels also relate to many curriculum content areas and provide language that is more easily understood than that found in text books (Florio-Ruane, 2001).

Therefore, in this section the authors believe that teachers can enliven their own classrooms by connecting students' backgrounds and experiences to the curriculum through numerous literacy strategies and practices. They are able to center their students in the curriculum simply because they have the power to imagine and demonstrate to students what can be accomplished when they are empowered with culturally responsive literacy teaching and learning in elementary and secondary schools. They share Maxine Greene's beliefs (1995), "We want our classrooms to be just and caring, full of various conceptions of good. We want them to be articulate, with dialogue involving as many persons as possible, opening to one another, opening to the world (pp. 167)."

The culturally responsive teachers in this section connect literature and culture in unique and joyous ways.

REFERENCES

Bishop, R. S. (2003). Reframing the debate about cultural authenticity. In D. L. Fox & K. G. Short (Eds.), *Stories matter: The complexity of cultural authenticity in children's literature* (pp. 25–34). Urbana, IL: National Council of Teachers of English.

Cummins, J. (2000). *Language, power, and pedagogy: Bilingual children in the crossfire.* New York: Multilingual Matters.

Florio-Ruane, S. (2001). *Teacher education and the cultural imagination: Autobiography, conversation, and narrative.* Mahwah, NJ: Erlbaum.

Greene, M. (1995). *Releasing the imagination.* San Francisco: Jossey-Bass.

Kinney, J. (2007). *The diary of a whimpy kid.* New York: Abrams.

Loh, V. (2006). Quantity and quality: The need for culturally authentic trade books in Asian American young adult literature. *The ALAN Review, 34*(1), 36–53.

Rist, R. (1978). *The invisible children.* Cambridge, MA: Harvard University Press.

Rosenblatt, R. (1982). The literacy transaction: Evocation and response. *Theory into Practice, 21*, 268–277.

Ruggiano Schmidt, P. R. (2001). *Cultural conflict and struggle: Literacy learning in a kindergarten program.* New York: Peter Lang.

Ruggiano Schmidt, P. R., & Pailliotet, A. W. (2001). *Exploring values through literature, multimedia, and literacy events: Making connections.* Newark, DE: International Reading Association.

CHAPTER 2

From *Nightjohn* to *Sundiata*

A Heritage-Based Approach to Engaging Students in Literacy

Tara Ranzy

I am an African American woman who teaches 5th grade for a charter school in a major mid-Atlantic city. My students are primarily African American and they live in mostly working-class urban neighborhoods. Many of my students come to me far behind in their literacy skills and have much catching up to do. I have no doubt about their ability to do this, but there's no time to waste. Unfortunately, too many children in my classroom associate scholarship with *Whiteness*—and reading with *being a nerd*. I work hard to encourage students to embrace literacy achievement as part of *their own* legacy by exposing them to both the classics and the literary genius that exists within their own communities. This approach stems from my own experience of having little cultural affirmation in school but then learning about the significance of my heritage when I became an adult. Now I am determined to help my students realize their own literacy potential, and I do so by drawing upon what I know about my students' heritage to advance literacy learning.

DISCOVERING MY OWN HERITAGE

Most people who grow up in poverty attend low quality schools. I was no different. As I recall my middle and high school years, I have more memories about the jokes we played on teachers and the overall chaos of our daily environment, than I do any rich or inspiring literacy experiences. In fact, the only time I reference my K–12 literacy experience is when I'm comparing it to how much more I learned in college. Though I was capable of so much more as a scholar—very little was expected of me. It was not difficult to make merit or honor roll in my high school; all you needed to do was to show effort—academic success had nothing to do with mastering the skill. It wasn't until college that I realized how low my literacy skills actually were. As a freshman, I was placed in remedial reading, writing, and math classes. During my Composition 101 class, I was embarrassed to learn that I didn't even know how to use a comma.

While most of my peers were partying, dropping out of school, getting high or pregnant, I was being encouraged to do something different. Fortunately, I had many positive experiences outside of the classroom: Mentors, coaches, and guest speakers (some who looked like me, some who did not) moved me to want to *stay in school*. I saw what an education had done for them, and I hoped it would do the same for me. School became my knight in shining armor, but how I made it to college on a horse with no legs is a miracle.

For years I went through a system that ignored my reality—as an African American and as a woman. As a result, I was not culturally centered, that is, I did not know who I was, where I came from, or where I was going. I had plenty of hope and an undying belief that I could do anything, but there was nothing tangible that confirmed my dreams—no classic tales of heroes in texts, no affirming images of *beautiful* women who looked like me on television, and no reflections of *my* story in the daily lessons at school. Like a leaf with no stem, I floated through many worlds never feeling quite at home.

In 1993, I landed at the University of Rochester where I received my first lessons in African-centered history. After 12 years of schooling, I was finally learning about African American history—and, more importantly, about myself. I developed a *real* passion for learning; this passion was not based on my grades, survival, or elevating my social status: This was what it felt like—to be *fully* present in a literacy experience. It was the first time in my educational career that I felt visible. I began to understand my own literacy potential. I was now grounded in the reforming power of a culturally relevant education.

From the bookshelves of African American professors Leon and Michelle Dockery, I discovered a literary utopia. My appetite for more stories (stories about *people who looked like me*) was insatiable. Through these readings, I became connected with my ancestors. I gained a profound respect for them; their persistence, courage, and intelligence made me feel that I could do anything. Malcolm X, in particular, became an especially meaningful role model. Though most people tend to focus on Malcolm's "rage stage" (the period of time he spent rallying for Black separatism), I learned to appreciate *all* of his changes. For instance, I learned that during his later years he became a strong supporter of women's rights, and he developed a global perspective on the Muslim experience; he also began to emerge to see Whites as potential allies. I learned a great deal from Malcolm's life experience, and, eventually, I would mirror a similar life's path.

In 1995, I transferred to the Department of African American Studies at Temple University to satisfy my craving for a culturally relevant education. I felt that Temple University, and the city of Philadelphia, would provide the historical, cultural, and academic foundation that I desired as a part of my college experience. The African American Studies department helped me to articulate the questions that, as a younger student, I did not know how to ask:

Why are so many people who look like me going to prison?
Why don't I see positive images of people who look like me in magazines, television, and school books?
Why are people who look like me so negatively depicted in the media?
Why are our only heroes comedians, entertainers, and athletes?
Why do so many people who look like me drop out of school?
Why am I seen as the exception to the rule? What is the rule?

These unanswered questions led to more questions that eventually led to anger and rage.

Despite my invisibility within the K–12 curriculum, it was as a college student that I began to discriminate as a person of a particular race and culture; for it was in college that I felt for the first time the arduous weight of racial alienation. As a young student, I was unconscious of the forces of institutionalized racism and was just now beginning to realize the impact that these forces had on my reality. The recovery of *my* history, in my mind, had brought to light these forces. Having been deprived of my truth for far too long, I identified Whites as the enemy. I did not see America as my home. My interest in history peaked, and I spiraled from literary emptiness to literary fullness to a historically hollow shell. Consequently, I spent the remainder of my college career buried in everything *Black*.

By graduate school, I was forced to reevaluate my position on race relations when my humanity was tested: I was assigned a case working with a White, 15-year-old mentally challenged girl living in foster care. My job was to help her adjust both socially and emotionally to the high school environment. I had to choose between race pride and helping a child in need. Though I chose to help the child, I made an erroneous cultural assumption about her ability to follow the lead of a person of color and about the limitations of her disability. Surprisingly, my student attended a majority African American school and was being raised by African American parents. This student embraced me wholly, and I was often overwhelmed by her affections. She was interested in what I had to say, and she followed my direction.

Inspired by Herbert Kohl's *Growing Minds on Becoming a Teacher*, I recognized that to be a good teacher, I had to acknowledge her reality. I asked myself, *How does she see the world? What is important to her?* Finally, I structured a program that reflected her center. Her center was her strength (very important). I knew this better than anyone. Working with a child with a disability brought me back to *my* center. It also helped me to grow with regard to my racial identity and to recognize that children need to be in a school that validates who they are and where they come from culturally.

My experiences have brought me to a place where I now recognize children's agency and the need to build curriculum around *their* experiences. I am committed to empowering my students by providing a literacy program that is centered on their culture and heritage. In this chapter, I provide vignettes of how I have done this for my fifth graders through the writer's workshop and a "Liberation Arts" class that I teach to 7th-grade students in my school.

WRITER'S WORKSHOP

Fifth-grade writing is a literature-based course designed to help students expand the writing concepts, skills, and strategies learned in earlier grades. Using Lucy Calkins' Writer's Workshop model (1994), my students work to deepen their understanding of the writing process. Students study a variety of literary genres including fiction, nonfiction, drama, and poetry in an effort to compare and to implement different techniques in their own writing. In addition to studying the writing process, students have the opportunity to review basic writing skills, including grammar and punctuation, cursive writing, and sentence and paragraph development. Students also work to improve communication skills, for example, oratory and deep listening.

Step 1: Getting Students Engaged

After drafting a course overview that reflects both the standards for writing and the needs of my students, I must decide on a hook to capture their interest in writing. I chose *Nightjohn* by Gary Paulsen. *Nightjohn* is a powerful story about an American slave in the 1850s who teaches other slaves to read and write despite the constant threat of being beaten. This story resonates with my students because (1) it connects them with their own African American heritage, and (2) it communicates the significance of learning to write. *Writing is a privilege that some of our ancestors had to earn, fight for, and even die for.* I want to inspire students to want to write because *it is* a tool for liberation, *it is* a privilege, and *it is* a valuable skill.

In front of my room is a large sheet of chart paper with a T-chart labeled *Privileges We Have Today* on one side and *Privileges During Slavery* on the other. After each chapter, students will add to both sides of the T-chart. By the end of the book, we will have a long list of privileges that we enjoy today. The list on the other side, of course, will not be as long. I will say to my kids, "Here are the ancestors, and here we are today with all these privileges. What are *you* going to do with them?" Throughout the rest of the year, *Nightjohn* will sit leaning on the board in the front of the class for all of us to see. I will reference *Nightjohn* whenever a student does something well: *Nightjohn would be proud of the way you did that.* I reference him when a student does something disappointing: *Nightjohn would be sad because he worked so hard to give us this privilege.* He becomes a living literary figure in my classroom. I want students to remember and to be motivated by their ancestors' sacrifices.

Step 2: Identifying as Writers

During the first few lessons, I try to convince my students that everyone in the room is already a writer. I say, "When you were a small child, your folks gave you a pen and a piece of paper. At that very moment when the pen in your hand hit that piece of paper, you became a writer! How many of you have scribbled words on a piece of paper? You are a writer. The goal of this class is to make you a great writer!!!"

The next step is to create the writer's notebook. First, I show students my notebook: It is decorated with photos and empowering words that reflect my values and the things that are important to me. Then, I give one composition book to each student, and, as instructed by Calkins, I make the writer's notebook a very big deal. I tell them that their notebooks are sacred. I exaggerate when I pick them up, holding them gently as if they were gold. We spend a week or so personalizing these notebooks; students are told to bring special photos of family members, favorite stickers, sayings, and other images. Keep in mind that it's been a few weeks, and they still haven't written in them. The idea is to *tease, tease, tease* them so they are practically begging to write. Though we have not begun the writing process, the class is reading *Nightjohn* and receiving formal instruction to develop their basic skills. Given that 90% or more of our students come to us missing basic writing skills, including the ability to write in cursive—I make teaching these skills a top priority. I will spend the entire year teaching and re-teaching these skills.

Neither reading *Nightjohn* nor teaching basic skills is a compromise to teaching the standards: Giving students these skills now will actually help build their confidence and will help to improve their writing. Teaching *all* students the basics, even those who "don't need it" helps to remove the "this is baby work" stigma. I am very transparent with students about why we revisit cursive writing as well as the other basics. To my surprise, most of them are grateful. The stronger students become my tutors, and as an incentive for both struggling and mastery level students, I attach an award system to my weekly assessment. For every student who earns a 10 out of 10 on his or her quiz, the class earns a point. The first class to earn 100 points wins a pizza party. Again, teaching basic skills does not neglect the standards. Eventually, basic skills instruction will be limited to 20 minutes once we launch Writer's Workshop (when I expand their writing time to at least 30 to 40 minutes per day).

After the notebooks are completed, the next step is to introduce Writer's Workshop. I say, "Can you keep a secret? This message is for writers only, so if you're not a writer, please cover your ears. Today, you will learn the sacred structures and rituals of Writer's Workshop. Writers, if we work as a team to use this formula, we will all become great writers." Once students have their notebooks, and they are clear about the expectations of Writer's Workshop, it is time to set students up for success. Before they can begin writing, we must tell them that they have plenty of important things to say. We have to convince our students that they have stories worth writing about. I say, "Good writers know that their stories are worth writing about. Who you are and where you came from is important, and your stories are interesting because you are interesting."

By now, students are asking when are we going to write? They are practically begging to write in their notebooks. But not yet! We must show them a few strategies that good writers use to get ideas. This is an important reference point for students who get stuck.

By now, it is time to say good-bye to *Nightjohn*. I always hear their sighs and "awhs" as we finish the book. Kids love this story. During the read-aloud, they are on the edges of their seats. I always finish the book no matter how long it takes. After revisiting the T-chart, I have students write a letter thanking *Nightjohn* for the sacrifices he made to teach children to read and write. They also note in this letter how they plan to continue *Nightjohn's* legacy. This assignment is drafted outside of the notebook. I also have given them the option of reading the letters aloud to the class. I thank them for all the effort and heart they put into the letter. In fact, *every time* they publish a finished product I make a big deal of it.

Now that students have a few strategies under their belts, it's time to give them the okay. I start the day by saying, "Today is a big day! It's time to use the writers' notebooks." First, we will share our covers. Second, we will brainstorm what kind of writing should go into our notebooks. Lastly, we will *write* in our notebooks for the *first* time. Students can hardly wait at this point. There will be one or two students who need my support, but the majority of the class is pouring their ideas out onto the pages. At first I do not criticize their writing at all: Everyone is giving a great effort and has so many interesting ideas. It is important to continue to build students' confidence before I help them with writing conventions.

My students learn to write using techniques from multiple genres, including personal narratives, fiction, realistic fiction, persuasive and literary essays, and poetry. Through these pieces, we address the conventions of writing, including sentence formation, paragraphing, punctuation, and spelling. To inspire and model the writing across multiple genres, I use several mentor texts, and it is important to me that these texts are culturally relevant and reflect students' lives. To teach personal narratives, I use Common's *I Like You but I Love Me* and *The Mirror and Me*; to teach onomatopoeia and suspense, I use *Shortcut* by Donald Crews; to teach story elements (e.g., opening, buildup, problem/dilemma, resolution, ending), I use *Peter's Chair* by Ezra Jack Keats; and for writing stories with emotional weight, I use *Coming on Home Soon* by Jacqueline Woodson and E. B. Lewis—to name a few.

Celebrating Writing and Public Speaking

In my classroom there is a short table draped with a turquoise cloth. On top of this table is a vase full of fresh, bright, colorful flowers. In the back of the classroom, there are red and white curtains. There is a tall lamp standing next to a microphone, a speaker, and a little orange stool centered just in front of a sign that says *VIP*. Today is Author's Chair. Every other Friday, students have the opportunity to share either published works or works in progress during Author's Chair. These works can include poetry, music, short stories, or any form of written work that the students themselves have created. Students will not receive feedback during this activity, for this time is dedicated to nurturing the student as both writer and public speaker. Students will be encouraged to ask their peers for feedback during peer conferencing *only*. I have almost 90% participation during Author's Chair. It is evident, that this is something that my students look forward to.

Another public speaking opportunity entitled Debate Fridays happens bi-weekly in writing class as well. Students will practice making arguments with supporting details and examples. I label one side of the room *pros* and the other side of the room *cons*. One student reads a student-centered topic aloud. Students must get up out of their seats to choose a side. The teacher gives the entire room a minute to discuss that topic. After 1 minute, I pull two names out of a hat. These students must engage in a healthy debate in front of the classroom. There are two chairs also labeled *pros* and *cons*. Students must sit in the seat that matches their initial choice. Each student will have 1 minute to convince the audience to take their side. They will have 1 additional minute to face their opponents. The entire group will debrief afterwards. Students will be able to choose two students to give them feedback on the *things they did well* and two students to give them feedback on the *things they can do better next time*.

Listening to beautifully written books, engaging in daily writing experiences, and having opportunities to express themselves orally are the kinds of literacy experiences that contribute to my students' literacy growth. Meeting students where they are and pushing them forward has been the key to advancing literacy learning in writing class this year. I take the time to re-teach the basics; I use mentor texts that reflect my students' stories; and I honor the state's standards. As a result, I have seen a tremendous amount of growth: So far, 92% of my students passed the 2nd trimester midterm. Eighty-eight percent have mastered basic writing skills, and almost 90% know how to write 5-paragraph, thesis-driven essays. I have seen how far my students have come in literacy, and I know that they will perform well on state tests. Bring it on!

LIBERATION ARTS CLASS

I believe that if children are reading literature that reflects their story, they are going to want to read it, and if they read, their writing will improve. One of the best ways to get my students to read is through the Liberation Arts course that I created. Liberation Arts is a literature-based course designed to bridge the gap between America's historically represented and underrepresented groups. Students are introduced to a variety of worldviews intended to provide a foundation for thinking about the question of race, ethnic identity, and minority status as it relates to American society. Students study U.S. history with a special emphasis on race, class, power, and social justice, because the best window for viewing the world is through a critical understanding of power—who has it, and how it is used. The following tenets are emphasized in the Liberation Arts curriculum:

1. Respect your elders.
2. Take responsibility for yourself and your community.
3. Never construct your identity around what you are compared to— mainstream culture.
4. Value collectivism instead of individualism. The universe is interconnected and interdependent; so are the people in it. Relationships are the basis of human existence.
5. Learn from the past. Knowledge is just information if it is not applied.

When I launched this course, our population was approximately 83% African American, 15% Puerto Rican, and 2% Mexican. The initial plan was to develop an African American history curriculum. I did not want to leave anyone out, so I adjusted the curriculum to also meet the needs of children who call themselves Puerto Rican or Mexican-American. I spent many weeks throughout the summer planning and researching for this course. I wanted to make sure that I could give my students a culturally relevant education; I wanted to give them *everything* that I did not get in middle and high school. At the same time, I knew that I had to be careful, critical, and confident about these *new* stories—out of respect for those whose stories I would tell, and for a student population who may not want to buy the side of history that I wanted to sell. Again, my intention was to present a more holistic interpretation of our national history as well as give a voice to the historically invisible.

Inspired by Ronald Takaki's *Iron Cages* and James W. Loewen's *Lies My Teacher Told Me*, I decided to use the traditional American history textbook as a skeleton for the course outline. Students used primary and secondary texts including novels and textbooks to study critical events, issues, individuals, and groups in American history from the colonial period to the 21st century. Specifically, students learned about traditional Native-American (aboriginal) and African societies, European colonialism, indentured servitude and slavery both in the United States and in the Caribbean, pre- and post-colonial Puerto Rico, westward expansion, migration, the Civil War, reconstruction, and the Civil Rights movement. My unit summaries are as follows:

Units one (The Aborigine) and two (Native Americans and Enslavement) examine the historical and contemporary experiences of a few Native-American groups. Students learn about Native Americans' lives before and after Europe's conquest. In units three (Ancient African Civilizations) and four (Africans and Enslavement), students explore the historical and contemporary experiences of the children of West Africa. Students study West Africans' lives before and after the transatlantic slave trade. Unit five (Westward Expansion) serves as a catalyst for unit six (Puerto Rico), which describes how the United States annexed Puerto Rico. Students evaluate how this arranged marriage transpired and where it stands today. In unit seven (Civics), students have the opportunity to take a closer look at America's governing documents, for example, the U.S. Constitution, the Bill of Rights, and the Declaration of Independence. Students consider the haunting contradiction between these documents and the day-to-day lives of some of America's citizens—how these contradictions led to civil war and eventually to slavery's end. Unit eight (Reconstruction and Jim Crow Laws) highlights the events and personal experiences that led to unit nine (The Civil Rights Movement). The last unit (Empowerment) includes a series of seminars, debates, and discussions designed to encourage students to take action and to apply the information they learned during class to their daily lives.

Because most American history texts present a unilateral view of history, I incorporate novels, newspaper articles, documentaries, firsthand accounts, and even college texts into the curriculum to make it culturally relevant. Though many of the resources used for Liberation Arts are above my students' reading levels, I expose them to this type of literature anyway. Advanced readers love the challenge of the more sophisticated texts, but for students who are struggling readers, I offer them lots of support in conveying the content. For these occasions, I split the class into small reading groups. Students who are able to work independently become the lead teachers within their reading groups. I work personally with the students who need my help the most. For these students, I read the text aloud; I invite them to take notes and to ask questions as needed.

I make copies of most of our readings so that my students can interact with the texts. I teach them how to skim, underline key words, highlight major themes, write comments, and so on. These exercises help them acquire the kinds of reading and study strategies they will use in high school and college. I encourage students to ask questions both during the process of learning new information and when they encounter intimidating texts. I find that a lot of literacy development happens when students ask questions. Consequently, establishing healthy boundaries and setting a tone of respect is essential for making this class successful as Liberation Arts students are challenged to become better readers and writers.

My formula for teaching this course is simple. I begin and end each unit in the same way. First, I assess students' stereotypes and prior knowledge at the beginning of each unit. Since our kids have been exposed to so much political correctness in the media, they tend not to stereotype people so much in history. However, I do find that they tend to stereotype certain groups of people, like Native Americans, Whites, and Africans. Assessing students' stereotypes and prior knowledge at the onset helps me to determine the level of instruction needed for that unit. It is also an opportunity for us to both identify and evaluate how these misconceptions impact our interpretations of a group's history.

Second, I am careful to present each group's traditional way of life, that is, what their lives were like before colonialism and enslavement. I never begin with slavery. You cannot start talking to kids about their history by starting with where they are losing. They need to know what life was like beforehand. We begin by discussing how their ancestors lived in ancient civilizations. The intention here is not to romanticize the way it once was or produce fossilized notions of a particular people living in the past but to show students that there was a life before the African slave trade. It is crucial that they be exposed to well-established civilizations whose systems of government, education, and way of life were led and defined by *people of color* (people who look like the students). They need to see that people who look like them have controlled their own destinies for centuries.

When I teach the traditional way of life, I begin well before America's colonial period. For example, we read *Sundiata: An Epic of Old Mali* by D. T. Niane for our discussion on ancient African civilizations. This book tells of Sundiata, founder of the Mali Empire, celebrated as a hero of the Malinke people of West Africa. The kids really relate to this story because Sundiata was just an average person who rose to the top to unite an entire nation. I like novels that depict the rise of the downtrodden and the resilience of human nature because many of my students can relate to these struggles.

After reading *Sundiata*, students usually discover that Africa has cities, wealth, conflicts and struggles, and heroes and villains. They realize that Africa is a *continent, not a country;* and that it is worthy of historical research and study. Africa, for a lot of my students, becomes real.

Third, I discuss in graphic detail the process of enslavement. In our studies, I make sure my students know that Africans were not the only group enslaved in the American South. African Americans are unique among American immigrants because they are the only group who did not come to this land by choice, but it is essential that students know that at one time Native Americans, Whites, and Africans worked side by side on American plantations. We study the process and the institutionalization of slavery as well as the slaves' responses to their condition using select chapters from *The Making of Black America* by Ira Berlin. This book speaks to the foundation of race and class and the decision to make slavery a *Black* thing. It is a dense text for students, but it is a great read for teachers who want to learn more about their nations' untold stories.

On the first day, I introduce students to this topic using powerful images. The classroom is dark, and the PowerPoint slides are on automatic. The only sound you hear is Sweet Honey in the Rock's *Jordan River* and *Ella's Song*. The first slides reveal images of ancient Africa: Egyptian pyramids, then colorful images of Africa and its people. Then the slides change abruptly to images of the Middle Passage. These include photos of African children, men and women squeezed tightly in the cargo holds of the slave ships and human beings being scrubbed down on the decks and eating from pig troughs. When I show this, I can tell that my kids are profoundly affected. I see some students begin to tear up; I see others begin to frown. I see a myriad of emotions.

When teaching about African enslavement, I deliberately resist the "official" curriculum that often emphasizes the victimization of African slaves. Instead, I emphasize the innovation, resistance, creativity, and survival skills that our African American ancestors possessed. Yes, we talk about the ways in which they were mistreated, but I want to emphasize the strategies they used to deal with the challenges they faced. To me, that's the real essence of a people. I want my kids to be encouraged to tap into their own inner strength and capacity when they read the stories of the ancestors who were able to empower themselves in a powerless situation.

Finally, it is important to connect the past to the present and to examine the experiences of different cultural groups from the perspectives of subjugation and liberation. At the end of each unit, we gather the groups' contemporary stories (films, short stories, whatever we can find). We study these stories to gain a clear picture of the groups' present-day experience. We consider a series of questions including: What is the current condition of this community? What lessons has this community learned? What lessons still need to be learned? We consider the groups' current struggles, and we check ourselves. We ask: How are we contributing to this group's suffering, for example, through perpetuating stereotypes, ignorance about their history, and so on? How are we contributing to this group's progress? In this way, we are holding the group and ourselves accountable; we are looking the group members as individuals. The story becomes more real— more intimate and less detached; we see the humanity in their stories and therefore we see the humanity in ours. Human beings make history. Human beings are connected. *Your* story is *my* story.

This approach to history helps students realize the impact that history has on modern times as well as the impact that *we* have on one another. For example, after watching the film *The Whale Rider* (a story about a Maori family's struggle to preserve the integrity of their cultural traditions in modern society), my students said:

This movie showed me that the elders should respect kids and kids
   should respect elders.
Be who you are and not what someone else wants you to be.
It makes me appreciate who I really am and to not want to be somebody
   else.
This film makes you feel happy that you were born.
Not all cultures are the same [and that's okay].
It makes me think about how disrespectful we've been to our race,
   culture, and families.
It keeps you in check to keep your culture going and [not] stop [the
   positive things about] your culture.
This film makes you have courage if someone tells you to [give up], not in
   a disrespectful way, but never give up.
The movie is not just entertainment—it opens your eyes that something
   is really wrong with us—that what we're doing in this society and in
   this world is wrong.

CONCLUSION

Placing my students at the center of the curriculum has been necessary for advancing their literacy growth. I have found that the writer's workshop and the Liberation Arts class offer excellent literacy-based opportunities for centering students in the curriculum. By helping my students recognize their rich heritage and the struggles of those who have sacrificed so much to become literate and liberated, my students no longer see literacy achievement as belonging to others. They understand that literacy achievement is consistent with their own cultural past, and because of this, they have grown to see themselves as students who are supposed to achieve in school and in life.

MAKE THIS HAPPEN IN YOUR CLASSROOM

Organizing for Writing Instruction:

- Consider what your students need. Based on the school's testing data and/or your previous year's lessons, what are your students' greatest needs? Do students need to develop their basic writing skills or do they need more enrichment?
- Design your long-term plan. What standards will I teach? What are my learning goals? In what order will I teach these standards? What is the title of each unit?
- Take an inventory of your resources. What resources do I have available? Are my resources culturally relevant? What culturally relevant texts can I apply to each unit?
- Decide on a hook for each unit. What are my students' interests? How can I make each unit relevant to my students' interests? How can I make each unit relevant to my students' everyday lives? What student-centered theme will I use for each unit?
- Know your center. Think about what's important to you and bring it to your instruction. What lessons do I bring to the table? What lessons have I learned from past and present educational experiences, and how can I use these lessons to inform my instruction? What are my instructional strengths, and what are the areas that I need to develop?
- Create a comfortable classroom atmosphere. Decorating your classroom is one of the few areas within your control. It is your space too, so make it a space that you look forward to teaching in. How will I use esthetics to create comfort in my classroom? What images will I use? How will I incorporate images of my children and the people that they find important? How will I incorporate images of myself and the scholars that I admire? Will I use plants and/or flowers? Will I have a carpeted area for Writer's Workshop?

- Teach the basics, but also use writing as meaningful communication. Instill in students a sense of being authors by inviting them to select their own topics for their own purposes, writing for real purposes.

Organizing for a Liberation Arts Class:

- Make students present in the history of the lesson. If it is a lesson on the American Revolution, for example, consider the role your students' group may have played during that time period: What were Native Americans, Puerto Ricans, or African Americans doing during this war? Whenever possible, include examples of books that reflect their stories to guide the lesson; and be knowledgeable about their walk through American society.
- Recognize that racism still matters. It is wrong to teach children of color without some knowledge of the role that racism has played in their daily existence. This is a great start to developing a culturally relevant and instructionally enticing curriculum.
- Read great books to strengthen your teaching. Here are some books that have have had a major impact on my teaching:

Berlin, I. (2010). *The making of African America: The four great migrations.* New York: Viking Adult.

Codell, E. R. (1999). *Educating Esme: Diary of a teacher's first year.* New York: Algonquin Books of Chapel Hill.

Covey, S. (2008). *The leader in me: How schools and parents around the world are inspiring greatness, one child at a time.* New York: Free Press.

Covey, S. (2004). *The 7 habits of highly effective people.* New York: Free Press.

Freire, P., & Ramos, M. B. (2000). *Pedagogy of the oppressed.* New York: Continuum.

Kindlon, D., & Thompson, M. (2000). *Raising Cain: Protecting the emotional life of boys.* New York: Ballantine.

Kohl, H. (1984). *Growing minds on becoming a teacher.* New York: HarperCollins.

Levine, D., Lowe, R., Peterson, B., & Tenerio, R. (1995). *Rethinking schools: An agenda for change.* New York: Free Press.

Loewen, J. (1996). *Lies my teacher told me.* Austin, TX: Touchstone.

Noffke, S. E., & Stevenson, R. B. (1995). *Educational action research: Becoming practically critical.* New York: Teachers College Press.

Noll, J. W. (1995). *Taking sides: Clashing views on controversial educational issues.* Guilford, CT: Dushkin.

Patterson, K., Grenny, J., McMillan, R., Switzler, A., & Covey, S. R. (2002). *Crucial conversations: Tools for talking when stakes are high.* New York: McGraw-Hill.

Suskind, R. (1998). *A hope in the unseen: An American odyssey from the inner city to the ivy league.* New York: Broadway Books.

Takaki, R. (1979). *Iron cages: Race and culture in 19th-century America.* New York: Oxford University Press.

Tatum, B. D. (1997). *Why are all the Black kids sitting together in the cafeteria?* New York: Basic Books.

- Find great books and materials to supplement your curriculum. Here are some books and materials that I have used:

Barnett, J. (Producer), & Caro, N. (Director). (2001). *The Whale Rider* [Motion picture]. New Zealand: South Pacific Pictures.

Berlin, I. (2010). *The making of African America : The four great migrations.* New York: Viking Adult.

Common. (2006). *I like you but I love me.* Chicago, IL: Hip Hop School House.

Common. (2005). *The mirror and me.* Chicago, IL: Hip Hop School House.

Crews, D. (1996). *Shortcut.* New York: Mulberry.

Keats, E. J. (1998). *Peter's chair.* New York: Viking.

Niane, T. (2006). *Sundiata: An epic of old Mali.* New York: Longman.

Paulson, G. (1993). *Nightjohn.* New York: Bantam Doubleday Dell.

Woodson, J. (2004). *Coming on home soon.* New York: Putnam.

REFERENCE

Calkins, L. (1994). *The art of teaching writing.* Portsmouth, NH: Heinemann.

CHAPTER 3

Driving in Both Lanes

Practicing Culturally Responsive Literacy Teaching While Addressing Standards and Accountability

Amelia Coleman-Brown

My mother always said I was her most simple child. Not simple meaning, foolish or plain. Just simple. I was the easy-going kid, not too complex—uncomplicated. I was the type of child that would select the box of Duncan Hines cake mix over the experience of gathering all the needed ingredients and making a cake from scratch. I remember thinking as a kid, "Wow, someone figured out how to fit all that 'stuff' in a little box so that we wouldn't have to waste time at the Shop & Bag buying all the cake parts." I was truly in awe! I was always fascinated by those geniuses that figured out how to make the process easier, but still made sure the ending was great. I was the kid always looking for ways to make a situation less complex. And I grew up believing that was a good thing. My mother thought I was good at that; she would often say, "Melia, you are always using your smarts, figuring out how to do things well and with time to spare."

I came from humble beginnings. No, actually, I came from complex times. I was raised in a community where drugs were abundant and gangs were on the rise. We were poor. Money and space was always tight; but so was our family unit. We were a close-knit group. My childhood was filled with love. I loved my family and I loved learning. My mother made learning the priority in our home. She filled the house with books, encyclopedias, and all types of learning games. My sisters would tease me endlessly of my obsession with becoming a teacher. Every opportunity I had to emulate one of my Catholic school educators, I took it.

I guess it came as no surprise to my mother or my six sisters when I decided to pursue a degree in education. Or even when I decided to work in communities very similar to the North Philadelphia neighborhood in which we were raised. Honestly, I sometimes think I was born to do what I do. I was born to figure out how to utilize resources and make learning fun and meaningful for my students, in spite of what may be going on in their lives, in their communities. It is my job to make the outside world less complex and learning the priority. I wish the task were simple, but it is not. The reality is that I am expected to teach well. Perhaps more noteworthy is the fact that my students are often expected to learn well amidst very complex circumstances.

Nonetheless, I realize that the more I am able to understand my life experiences and past circumstances, the more competent I become in my role as educator. In an attempt to communicate learning best with my students, I take steps to learn about their cultural and individual life experiences well. I work to help my students realize their potential. I work to ensure that students achieve at a high level, develop a positive sense of self, and acquire a commitment to change the world for good. *This, I believe, would be called culturally responsive literacy teaching. This is the teaching that connects with my students' lives and makes learning a meaningful experience.* At the same time, I also have to meet the standards that are established in the core curriculum for our district. So now I'm the one who has to figure out how to put all these "ingredients in the box." In this chapter, I describe the ways I take the complexities that are handed to me—the standards and the core curriculum, my students' different literacy needs, and the culturally diverse out-of-school lives they lead—and how I attend to these things in order to inspire and nurture my students' literacy growth.

I serve a diverse population in a large urban school district. Many of our parents are members of the working-class community. Some of our parents hold jobs at the neighboring university and a few are small business owners. A majority of my students are African Americans but some are native Africans who have recently arrived from the continent of Africa, and approximately 5% of my students come from Southeast Asia, primarily from Cambodia.

Like many districts across the country ours is looking to ensure that every child is pulled forward and that *no child be left behind*. As a result, we adopted a standards-based curriculum to be used at every grade level for all major and tested subjects: math, reading, writing, and science. A planning and scheduling timeline is provided to approximate how much teaching and learning time should be allotted to individual lessons. And many administrators and teachers work endlessly to find ways to implement a clear understanding of what constitutes proficiency. Fortunately for my students and me, our school principal and I share a common belief that literacy is one of the most effective vehicles for change. To that end, he affords me the space to foster and nurture a community of learners.

BUILDING COMMUNITY AND CONNECTING WITH THE EXISTING CULTURE OF MY STUDENTS

Providing my students with an authentic literacy experience allows me the opportunity to better understand the culture of my students and their families, while teaching with and beyond the mandated curriculum. One of my favorite teaching experiences is based on the poem "Mother to Son" by Langston Hughes. The primary goal of this week-long unit is to address the literacy standard of "identifying the author's purpose and type." "Mother to Son" has proven to be an ideal text for many reasons. It provides many windows or entry points into the mind of the author. It provides teachers an opportunity to scaffold learning effectively. In addition, most people can appreciate the relationship between a mother and her son.

When we begin this unit, the students are told, "This week we will spend a little bit of every day unpacking the poem, 'Mother to Son' by Langston Hughes. The learning experience challenge is to be able to identify the author's purpose for writing and to support your response with examples from the text." We begin the whole group lesson by honing in on the second line of the poem, "Life for me ain't been no crystal stair." Students are asked to take a minute to jot down all the words that come to mind when they think of the characteristics of a crystal stair. After 1 minute I chart the responses of the students: "shiny," "fancy," "smooth," and "beautiful." I recognize my students' contributions with a response: "Wow, how about that? This author sends home a strong statement as early as the second line of this poem." I then prompt them to further consider Hughes' words: "What is the mother saying to her son?"

Students concede that life for the mother has been "hard," "rough," and "not easy at all." It has had "tacks in it, Ouch"! But all the time she never gave up. At this point, I invite students to think about Hughes' writing style: "Langston Hughes really knows how to use figurative language to make writing more beautiful and interesting. And you guys really did a great job unpacking that poem so far. How about we go a bit deeper and allow this piece to inspire. Let us start with preparing to write a strong metaphorical statement."

I then ask students to relate Hughes' poem to themselves and invite them to jot down characteristics of their lives. In most instances I would model for students what the process of brainstorming for this writing experience would look and feel like for me. What type of life did I have at the age of 10? What words would I use to describe my background? I write, "definitely not expensive, but not all the way rough." For homework they are required to brainstorm further with family members and to think of an object that may embody similar characteristics. My students think deeply about how to best connect an object to their life story, really wanting the metaphorical statement to be a true depiction of their lives.

One tenacious student, Keith, wrote of his life in the future, comparing it to a sleek racing car, expensive, fast, and always starting up on time. My always-pleasant-and-serious student, Amayah, wrote of her amusement park life. She wrote of emotional rollercoaster rides, and the butterflies that fluttered in her tummy as she hoped and prayed her best prayers that her father would become more involved in her life. But mostly she wrote of a fun life, filled with great surprises. She wrote of the sweet cotton candy life her beautiful and hard-working mother provided. Amayah's closing stanza read: "Not all amusement park trips are perfect, but most are fun and all of them are worth remembering. My life is an amusement park, mostly fun but not always perfect." Another student borrowed Hughes' style and wrote the following poem:

Win or Lose

Life for me is a game of basketball
Sometimes I win and sometimes I lose
Dribble fast, Dribble slow
My mom and I are always on the go
Rebounds, fouls, and 52 fake outs
Money comes and goes
But I don't pout and shout about
Because in the end I have to choose
I plan to not give up every time I lose
Practice hard, work it out
Sometime I win and sometime I lose
Life for me is a game of basketball

We completed this learning experience 3 days later than planned because the students were so engaged in it. The time spent on this learning experience was "academically purposeful" for several reasons. Many of the students met the desired goal of identifying the author's purpose and type. Not only were many of them able to identify the purpose and type of writing, (as a result of this and similar types of learning experiences) they learned to write with a purpose and audience in mind. My students were beginning to better understand how to utilize language to make their own writing more beautiful and interesting. They were beginning to see themselves as writers and skillful readers. Equally as important, our classroom community was growing closer and stronger.

Just about everything that happens in our class is deliberate and comprehensive. It's important to me that my students see themselves as a positive part of the larger society. The works of authors like Langston Hughes often serve as a dual resource. First, I work to select literature that affords my students the opportunity to see a manifestation of their life experiences, which is a key principle in culturally responsive teaching. The work of the noted educator Lisa Delpit reminds me to utilize familiar metaphors and experiences from the world of my students. As a result, my students are motivated to listen more closely and learn more deeply because they feel personally connected to the learning experience. Second, I look for ways to cover content more deeply. Typically, I look to utilize a variety of texts as models of writings to help students "write like readers" and, ultimately, "read like writers."

FINDING TOUCHSTONE TEXTS

Helping students "write like readers" and "read like writers" involves the selection of mentor or touchstone texts. Before I search for these, however, I make certain what my academic goals will be. In the beginning of the school year I review what has to be accomplished according to the various frameworks and standards. Then I look at what I can do to meet those goals in ways that will best reach a majority of students—in ways that will help them connect to the work and retain new understandings. It's important to me that they learn how to apply their knowledge to different situations in the world, not just to be able to answer questions on the state assessment. One of the noted differences between those students who are successful and those who are not is their ability to apply what they've learned in different situations and contexts. So, as I look to best utilize my resources and ensure that my students achieve at a high level, develop a positive sense of self, and acquire a commitment to change the world for good, I turn to a good book.

The novelist E. L. Doctorow says, "Any book you pick up, if it's good, is a printed circuit for your own life to flow through so when you read a book, you are engaged in the events of the mind of the writer. You are bringing your own creative faculties into sync. You're imagining the words, the sounds of words, and you are thinking of the various characters in terms of people you've known, not in terms of the writer's experience, but your own" (quoted in Harvey & Goudvis, 2000, p. 5). In some classrooms, these purposefully selected books are referred to as mentor or touchstone texts. In my classroom we refer to the authors of our book studies as the "experts we can't afford to pay to visit our classrooms." So we work to squeeze everything we can out of a "good book" to help us become better readers, writers, and ultimately great learners. And we borrow from the minds of many different authors, across various genres, however, many of the touchstone texts I have used more frequently are written by the following authors: Eve Bunting, Faith Ringgold, Lucille Clifton, Sandra Cisneros, Walter Dean Myers, and Patricia Polacco. These authors provide windows of opportunity for my students to connect, and grow deeply and widely.

For example, I like to use the book *Thank You Mr. Falker* by Patricia Polacco at the start of a new school year. In the story, Polacco honors a 5th-grade teacher who took the time to notice her as a learner and to identify her as a student with several reading disabilities that impeded her ability to thrive as a reader for many years. I use the story, *Thank You Mr. Falker*, to help frame the work of our classroom community and to share my expectations for teaching and learning. After reading the book aloud, I share with my students that much like the character Mr. Falker, I will use various ways to notice and support the needs of all students in our learning community.

I say to my students, "My hope is that you will allow the story of the young and resilient Patricia Polacco and the knowledge of the great writer she became to encourage you to work hard and never give up. We will not give up, in spite of anything that has happened in your past or is happening now. Together we will make this 5th-grade year, a year to celebrate." Usually I end the discussion by humbly stating, "One day I hope one of you will write a book in my honor, entitled *Thank You Mrs. Brown.*"

SATISFYING THE STANDARDS

In my 5th-grade classroom, I am responsible for ensuring that my students master grade-level standards in literacy. At times the structure and the accompanying demands of the core curriculum may feel insurmountable.

We understand that particular content and strategies need to be covered at predetermined times and my colleagues and I are expected to adhere to the core curriculum with fidelity. I often find myself at a crossroads, searching for ways to meet the demands of the timelines and the needs of my students. I often find myself negotiating the turn: Should I slow down to ensure that more of my students acquire an adequate amount of understanding? Or do I continue driving forward, confident that the scheduling timeline will provide another opportunity to build understanding for those who did not get it the first time around? Mostly, I find myself cautiously driving in both lanes, in search of ways to ensure that most of my students reach the desired destination and with hope for time to spare to support those who did not.

Students learn in different ways and are motivated in different ways. More often than not, I find that curriculum materials are not frequently adapted to meet the varying needs of our students. Often, I find ways to effectively modify instruction to best meet the needs of all students. "Figurative-language week" is one example of how I work to meet the diverse needs of my students while ensuring they master grade-level content and skills in a timely fashion. During figurative-language week I work to address a number of core standards. However, the primary goal of this week is to address the following literacy standard: Evaluate how the author uses literary devices to convey meaning (Figurative Language: personification, simile, metaphor, hyperbole). During figurative-language week, we work to study intensely the work of one author. Several pieces of text by the selected author are identified as touchstone texts to accompany the learning experiences. And I work, using literature, to connect what students know well already to what I want them to know and understand more deeply.

In this example, I used the work of Lucille Clifton to help students better understand how the author uses simile to convey meaning. We study the poem "My Mama Moved Among the Days" by Lucille Clifton; we begin the learning experience using the technique of Readers Theater. I begin by saying to my students, "What I believe is that we really know how to identify simile in poetry. However, what we should be able to do, by the end of 5th grade, is to explain how an author uses this literary device to convey meaning." I instruct all my students to stand up and prepare to bring to life the lines of Clifton's poem. We start with the first line, "My Mama moved among the days." Okay! I say to my students, "Let's see you begin to move among the days like the 'Mama' Lucille Clifton writes about in the poem." Students follow my lead and begin to walk around the room at varying speeds, some briskly, others very slowly. All of them, happily, laughing and giggling. I say to the students, "I see some of you are zooming through the days of the week, others are taking their time getting through Monday, Tuesday . . . Okay, freeze. I have a question." Was that first line an example of the author using simile?" The students respond almost in unison, "No." I praise them, "Smart cookies you are!" I ask them to close their eyes as they listen closely to the second line of the poem, because it may help them imitate Mama's movement the second time around. I read the next line, "like a dream walker in a field." I begin to ask probing questions. "Can you see Mama walking in the field like a dream walker?" Some of the students respond, "Yes!" Then I ask, "Do you see her walking fast?" My students respond, "No!" I ask, "How is she walking through the days?" And my students begin to respond. "Slowly!" some shout out. One student says, "She was walking blindly, with her eyes closed shut." Another student states, "Because she is asleep. She is probably dreaming." I ask the question, "Is the author using simile now?" The students respond in unison, "Yes!" "How do we know?" I ask. Someone says, "She uses the words *like* or *as* to compare."

I affirm their responses: "Great, but I knew you guys had it, and you're getting close to meeting our focused goal. Let's see if you will work to imitate Mama differently now. This time listen as I read the entire first stanza." I read aloud the first stanza and my students begin to travel around the room in a daze, eyes half shut, and very much in the fashion of a "dream walker." The learning experience continues until the very end of the poem. And we unpack the experience in a grand conversation (Eeds & Wells, 1989). Students note that one way for a reader to evaluate how an author uses figurative language to convey meaning is to "try to see the words in your mind." Yes, I affirm my students thinking, it helps to just close your eyes and bring the words to life. Mandated curriculum or not, adapting materials and method to the individual needs of our students is essential to meeting academic success in a high-level learning community.

Also similar to many districts, teachers are required to put into practice frequent assessments regulated by a district-wide schedule. Frequent assessment requires mastery of content and skills not always familiar to students. While many students demonstrate mastery of standards frequently, too many students continue to fall short of the desired goal—and for various reasons. It is no secret that past professional practices have fallen short in assisting students in meeting grade-level standards, and now these students and teachers are playing catch-up. My students come from varying social economic situations and cultural backgrounds; they learn differently and at varying rates. In my classroom alone, at least 13 of the 33 students in my 5th-grade class are reading and writing two grade levels below where they should; this is close to one-third of my student population. In addition, approximately 20% of my students are nonnative English speakers. By the end of the 5th-grade year the state will expect all of these students to show proficiency on its grade-level assessment. For those students, I have to figure out how to best utilize time and the available resources to pull them up to grade level while pulling them forward, in hopes of leaving NO child behind. Sometimes the structure and ideas of the core curriculum serve me well in that regard, but always the needs of my students motivate me to use my professional knowledge and to craft ways to respond to their diverse learning needs.

ASSESSMENTS THAT INFORM INSTRUCTION: TARGETING INFERENTIAL READING

To ensure quality education for all, assessment of learning is essential. However, there should be a balance between standardized tests and various purposeful classroom assessments. Assessment results should literally drive instruction, and they should always be continuous and meaningful. Also, assessments should build confidence, not a sense of hopelessness.

The assessments I use help me understand what my students are learning, how they are learning, and they help me to think of ways to teach differently—to teach better. Students often need different approaches to the curriculum they are responsible for learning. A bridging of the curriculum with assessments is often required. To that end, continual and purposeful talk about assessment is a daily ritual of my classroom practice. Making sure students understand what they will be assessed on and why is key to moving forward.

One example of using assessment to inform instruction is in the area of teaching inferential thinking. Research shows that many of our students have difficulties with the level of inferential thinking that is required to access the implicit meanings embedded in written text, including many of the passages that appear on state assessments. The breakdown of inferential thinking comes, most often, from two things: lack of adequate background knowledge and overlooking clues implied by the author. As a result, I look for ways to help my students recognize when they are engaged in inferential thinking.

In the following lesson, adapted from the book *Strategies at Work* (Harvey & Goudvis, 2000), I describe how I use writing and a great book to help build on my students' strengths and to work to take them further:

I begin by saying "Good morning, friends. Today I would like to start this morning's learning experience with a read-aloud. Grab your reading response journals, a pencil, and come comfortably close. Now, I want you to listen closely because today I want you to listen for two purposes. The first purpose is easy—I just want you to listen and learn about one of America's great heroes. That's a skill we are all good at, reading books and learning. The second purpose is the true challenge of today. I challenge you to practice the skill of inferring. Now, I know you are really good at figuring out how to read facial expressions, and body language, and things like that. You are really good at reading the world. Remember the time we spent the morning helping each other figure out how to use inferential thinking to read the moods of our parents? That was fun. Now I need to see how well you are applying that skill to the reading of words. Does that make sense?"

They respond with an enthusiastic *yes!*

I continue, "Good! So, I know I will not get to read the entire book today, but I will read the book in its entirety by the end of tomorrow because I really want you to learn about this great American hero. Okay. Expect me to pause every now to ask a question and to give you time to respond in your journal. Don't worry about feeling rushed; I have the questions written on the chart paper. I planned to have us practice only three times today. So do your best, I know what you are capable of. Does that seem fair?"

Again, they respond, Yes! Great!

I return to the lesson: "Now remember this assessment is about you showing how much you are learning, and no matter where you are, my job is to help you connect new learning to your existing knowledge to take you to the next level of understanding. Okay, are you ready to open your journals and show us what you got?"

They shout yes!

"Great. Today's story is entitled *Teammates*, by Peter Golenbock. It is a story about the challenging life of Jackie Robinson and how he was able to break into an all-White major league. It is about the racial inequalities he faced; but this story is also very much about the strong friendship he formed with fellow teammate Pee Wee Reese. In your journals I would like for you to create a T-chart. In one column I want you to write down all you know about racial inequalities, the feelings associated with those times, even the two words separately—what ever comes to mind. So let's engage in a quick write for the next 3 minutes. Don't worry about spelling, just record your thoughts on paper."

My students and I brainstorm for 3 minutes, writing down all that we can think of about racial inequalities; we follow up doing much of the same for the topic of friendship. Once the quick write is completed, we compare notes. On the large T-chart I created I begin to record some of the thoughts of the class. Under the theme of racial inequality, I record the following thoughts: sadness, anger, unfair, separate, and segregation. Under the theme of friendship, I recorded the following related words: forever, happy, good, respect, love.

I say to my students: "Great, we are halfway there. We are working to use what we know to build stronger background knowledge, and we are working to make sure we catch the author's clues. This is what good readers do when they work to figure out the deep meaning of a story."

I begin to read the story *Teammates*. I stop midway through the story and ask my students to answer the following three questions in their journals:

Why do you think the author names the book *Teammates*?
Why do you think Branch Rickey, the owner of the Brooklyn Dodgers,
    was looking for someone who possessed self-control?
How do you think the author feels about racial inequality?

I collect the journals and use them to inform my teaching over the next few days. Their written responses to these questions helps me to determine how well they are reading between the lines to figure out the implied meaning of text. Lessons like these help my students master the skills and strategies that will afford them the chance to access implicit meanings to text, not only on the state assessment, but also across the curriculum, and ultimately for the rest of their lives.

I believe this work has been instrumental in raising my students' literacy performance. In the 2 years that I have implemented culturally responsive teaching techniques, my students' literacy achievement has increased substantially. The percentage of students in the "proficient" category of performance on state literacy tests has increased (from 16.4% to 32%) and the percentage of students in the advanced category also increased, by almost 4% (from 3.6% to 7%). Additionally, the students in the "below basic" category decreased by 25% (from 57.4% to 32%). This performance is consistent with more informal measurements of literacy growth. Last year, all of my students made between one and two grade levels of growth in reading, based on their performance on the Qualitative Reading Inventory (Leslie & Caldwell, 2005). Targeting instruction to my students' literacy abilities and cultural lives was key to making these gains.

CONCLUSION

I have described my ways of making standards, assessment, instruction, and culture fit together. The core curriculum provides a blueprint for what is to be taught. I must build upon this blueprint by observing my students and listening to them. I need to use this information to make the core curriculum relevant to my students' literacy needs and cultural lives. A central idea in my teaching is that it is important that students see a manifestation of their life experiences in the classroom. One of my Writing Project colleagues reminds me to provide "mirror" and "window" learning experiences for my students. Using the "mirror" metaphor, students frequently need to see a reflection of themselves in things that are great. In addition, we have to expose them to "windows" of opportunity to gain knowledge of the unfamiliar. We have to do both things simultaneously, so that students are invested in learning and are able to make critical connections and contributions to the larger society.

MAKE THIS HAPPEN IN YOUR CLASSROOM

- Be clear about what you expect students to know, understand, and be able to do as a result of the learning experiences you create. Work to satisfy the standards, but remember to push students to become critical readers, thinkers, and problem solvers.
- Be committed to students' learning. Build a classroom community that is conducive to high-level teaching and learning. Students learn at high levels in any educational setting that is committed to meeting their needs.
- Utilize your students' culture as an important source of their education. Culture is a means to improve the students' education—especially those students whose cultures and backgrounds have been omitted in schools. Every student has experiences, knowledge, opinions, or emotions to draw upon. It serves our purpose well to remember that our responsibility is to make sure that students are given the opportunity to utilize their prior knowledge and experiences to better understand and connect new knowledge.
- Emphasize meaning. Learning has to be meaningful and it has to make sense if we expect students to be motivated to learn at high levels, whether the subject be literacy, math, or science.
- Identify touchtone texts to be used for multiple purposes. Select literature that connects students' lives and experiences to the reading and writing curriculum.

- Establish a language-rich classroom. Engage students through dialogue and plan for purposeful talk. This ensures that student talk occurs often and that all students are included in the conversation. Provide opportunities to include students' views, judgments, and rationales using text evidence and other substantive support. Remember, sometimes we have to build in various ways to hear student voices. I often provide an opportunity for students to write before sharing. If my students are provided the opportunity to see their thoughts on paper they are more comfortable sharing with the entire group. For those students who prefer not to share, I am able to hear their voices through their writing.
- Listen carefully to assess levels of students' understanding and assist students' learning throughout the conversation by questioning, restating, praising, and encouraging.
- Recognize students' strengths and talents. Contrary to the adage, "sticks and stones may break your bones, but names will never hurt you," words are powerful; they can beat our students down as fast as they can build them up. Throughout the learning day I make a conscious effort to utilize language to empower my students.
- Lastly, establish an ideology for learning and life. Work to learn, respect, and believe in the people you serve in order to serve them well. Students are not only a part of our culture; they are a part of our future and we are a part of theirs. I share the following words with my school community: "Watch your thoughts, for they become words. Watch your words, for they become actions. Watch your actions, for they become habits. Watch your habits, for they become character. Watch your character, for it becomes your destiny."

REFERENCES

Clifton, L. (1973). My Mama moved along in days. In A. Adolf & G. Brooks (Eds), *The poetry of Black America: Anthology of the twentieth century.* New York: Harper-Teen.

Eeds, M., & Wells, D. (1989). Grand conversations: An exploration of meaning construction in literature study groups. Research in the Teaching of English, 23(1), 4–29.

Goldenbock, P. (1990). *Teammates.* Boston, MA: Harcourt Children's Books.

Harvey, S., & Goudvis, A. (2000). *Strategies that work: Teaching comprehension to enhance understanding.* York, ME: Stenhouse.

Leslie, L., & Caldwell, J. S. (2005). *Qualitative reading inventory* (4th ed.). Boston: Allyn & Bacon.

Polacco, P. (1998). *Thank you Mr. Falker.* New York: Philomel Books.

CHAPTER 4

It All Came Down to This: "Know Thyself, Understand Others"

A First-Year Teacher's Journey Through a New World

Jamie Gartner

Today, new teachers know how hard it is to find that perfect job—or even just a job teaching. When I finally received that offer, the usual congratulations, high fives and excitement ensued—until they asked the question "Where?" Then the quips became familiar: They would recommend different types of "heat" I should pack, warn me not to forget the Kevlar vest, and give me that concerned/bewildered look asking if I was sure I wanted to teach at that place.

Foreman High School is a city school with a bad reputation in one of the highest poverty areas in the Northeast. To be exact, it is the zip code area with the third highest poverty rate in New York State and twelfth highest in the United States. While I was nervous upon entering this new reality with my primarily White middle-class suburban/rural background, I never could have guessed where this job would take me.

In this chapter, I reflect on my first year of teaching at Foreman and on the realities that come with working in a high-poverty city school district. I will share some of my experiences and the methods I used during my first year to connect with my students and their various cultures and describe how an appreciation of cultural diversity through representative literature and themes of social justice enhanced teaching and learning in my classroom. Using literature that reflected my students' cultures and histories opened them up to a recognition that academia related to them, rather than excluded them. By making these constant connections in the classroom to their worlds, learning began to make a strong appearance in my students' realities.

MY REALITY

My students live in the "now." When they write in my class on the first day of the school year, many express one goal for the future: to live to be 21. Merely surviving is their way of life. Understanding this mindset in the terms of Maslow's hierarchy helped me as a teacher to understand why my students often had difficulty focusing on the higher levels and concepts of self-actualization and an appreciation of and desire for learning. It inspired me to reach beyond the prescribed curriculum to find new places of accessibility in the classroom for students who were preoccupied with concerns about their own mortality.

In that first year, my students learned more about themselves and the world around them through what we accomplished in the classroom—which was much more than grammar and essay writing. I learned that I had a long way to go to be the teacher I hoped to become. I learned from my students as they shared their lives and world. And I learned about myself—as a teacher, and as a person. This was what culturally responsive teaching of the English language arts was for me. I recalled a line from one of my favorite teacher preparation courses, "Know thyself; understand others." In this first year, I concluded that culturally responsive teaching is more than just a technique or a method of pedagogy: It is a lifestyle choice.

June 25, 2009, was the last day of the school year: the culmination of my first full year of teaching. It had been a long year, but one for which I could never accurately describe how much I had changed and grown as a teacher, and as a person. That last day, I took one last look at my room—what had been my shelter for the past 180-plus days. There were no windows; only a select few classrooms in the building actually had access to the world outside. The splotchy walls with big holes and spots of peeled paint were bare. The students' artwork and poems had been taken home or recycled, and the posters and reminders were stored away in my towering black cabinet—ready to be brought back out in September to hide the dilapidated walls once more. (The walls aren't really even walls—just some dividers thrown up to create another classroom.) My desk, with its broken leg, sat unoccupied at the front corner of the classroom and my mismatched collection of bookshelves were empty in preparation for the summer program that would be held in all the classrooms. There was a large hole in the door, and another in the wall—evidence of students who had lost their tempers for one reason or another. Those same holes were there when I stepped into this classroom at the beginning of the year; they were there when my colleague had taught in the same room the year before. I turned off the lights and walked away, but the memories would hold me through the summer, until September when the battle would begin again.

I say "battle," and some people might think that the word fits. They might think it's associated with the idea that I work in an inner city school with kids who come from high-poverty backgrounds; the idea that those kids have kids; and the idea that the word *home* is rarely associated with the ideas of comfort, support, and love. They might believe there must be gangs and drugs and sex all over that school. Many people might think that it must be a battle every day to stop students from fighting and to force them to listen, to be respectful, maybe even learn something.

It is all true.

There are more than 20 different languages spoken in my school, and 45% of the students are identified as ELL or learning disabled. At least 74 teenage girls, out of our school of 1,200, were pregnant last year, some for the 2nd or 3rd time. Down the street are gangs; boarded up, decrepit old buildings; single-parent and broken households; 40% unemployment; physical and substance abuse; and a whole lot of fear, sadness, and despair.

I have students that have been arrested, are in gangs, and have seen more drug deals, deaths, and fights than anyone, much less teenagers, should ever have to see. Many of my students come to school every day exhausted from a night spent tossing and turning, listening to shouting or shooting or parties in the street keeping them up all night. They come to school late, because they have to put their little brothers and sisters on the buses. Sometimes they don't come at all because they have to translate for their parents at the doctor's or the bank, or they're moving once again—to another broken down rental property down the street. These are some of the struggles my students and many students in high-poverty areas deal with every day.

When I asked a retired police officer, who was a friend of mine, about the reality of gangs, he gave me new insight that I had not considered before. He listed a few blocks and streets in the city and told me that if you lived on these streets and you did not belong to a gang, you were dead. "As simple as that." These are the realities of their lives.

But in truth—my "battle" is not with the students' attitudes or lack of respect. The biggest battle I have with them is to get them to believe in themselves, to see a greater future, to understand that what we are teaching *is* relevant for them, because they *can* go to college—not just someday, but in only a couple of years. My battle is with the media, who for too long portray my students as criminals and who rarely find the room to publish the positive things that are happening in the city schools. My battle is with cell phones and video games, drug dealers and gang bangers— all of which are competing to deter my students from this dream of a life that is, actually, life. My battle is with the apathy that accompanies the loss of identity and the absence of horizons filled with dreams. My battle is with the place that all this leads to: the place of despair from which students give up and drop out.

According to the National Center for Education Statistics (2006), children from the lowest income quarter are more than six times as likely to drop out of high school as kids from the highest quarter. Kathleen Kingsbury (2008) confirms this information, suggesting, "It's a staggering statistic: one in four American teenagers drops out of school before graduation, a rate that rises to one in three among Black and Hispanic students." This frightening reality confronts teachers every day.

Putting that information aside, my students have some of the most endearing and infectious personalities. They are strong and tough kids, but when they dare to love and to trust . . . there is nothing you can find that is more genuine. They inspire and encourage me every single day, but they live in a frightening world—a world completely incomprehensible to the White middle-class population of teachers who serve them. But my students and my colleagues have taught me that we must stop pointing fingers. It is time to understand these students, not just as victims of poverty, but as people and individuals who actively contest the challenges they face every day. I have found that it is possible to lead them to hope and new realities. Many of our students will be first-generation high school graduates; those who attend college will likely be first-generation college students. But, I tell you—not only will they be first-generation college students— they will be first-generation college graduates!

I learned very quickly through experience and from supportive colleagues that culturally responsive teaching is critical to success when working with students who are all too often misunderstood and overlooked. This approach to teaching allowed me to connect with students and understand their lives. Without understanding where our students come from, we cannot effectively teach them, nor bring them to higher levels of understanding and compassion. Being a teacher of ELA also helped me to make these connections to my students' lives in the content area that I teach.

As I progressed through my first year of teaching, my students frequently laughed at me when I would ask them to stay after school to finish their projects: "Miss—you know any time we stay after for you we just talk! We don't ever get any work done!" But these were the times during which their lives, their fears, their dreams, and their nightmares were laid bare. I gave them my time. I listened to them. I did not judge. I only showed them that I cared and wanted the best for them. Through these constant efforts and extra energies consistently put forth, I would always remind myself that we do *not* teach content areas; we do not teach thesis writing and parts of speech and long division or physics . . . we teach students. It is a matter not of *what* we teach, but *who* we teach, because if we do not know our "whos," then the whats will never matter.

THE CULTURALLY RESPONSIVE CLASSROOM AND SOCIETAL CHANGES

Every child deserves to be respected and appreciated for who and what they are. If they are Asian, Hispanic, Black, White, Middle Eastern, Native American; if they are of whatever religion, culture, family structure, socioeconomic status, or sexual orientation—no matter what it is that defines them—children, as students, should be accepted and represented in the classroom. Without this acceptance, understanding, and representation, our students are susceptible either to losing their own identity (cultural or otherwise) or to attaching to their identity a negative perception leading to feelings of guilt and shame. Landt (2006) reinforces this idea of the need for representation in the English language arts classroom by emphasizing the importance of students being able to see themselves in the classroom: "Not seeing one's self, or representation of one's culture in literature can activate feelings of marginalization and cause students to question their place within society" (Landt, 2006). To deny students—White, Black, Hispanic, Asian, and so on—the validation of their cultural identities within the curriculum is doing an enormous disservice to their future achievement and success as men and women in the "real world." (Callins, 2006).

However, today we find that the experiences and heritage of diverse groups of people are often marginalized in school curricula. The social studies curriculum and textbooks primarily represent European-American historical contexts, with little additions regarding slavery, segregation, and the fight for equal rights (Zinn, 2002). The same examples are found in language arts. We are now revising the canon of dead White men to include people of color and women authors. This change, however, can have the effect of overrepresenting literature that reinforces negative messages about specific groups of people.

For example, books that position African Americans as victims of slavery are introduced and emphasized over books that represent their talents, contributions, and acts of resistance. Many do not show African Americans as successful men and women in today's world and their continuing efforts to access equal rights in the areas of housing, employment, health care, and education. Furthermore, Middle Eastern, Native-American and Asian cultures are barely represented in the curricula at all.

The media, too, skews our students' perceptions. African Americans and Hispanics are seen primarily as successful in the arena of sports or entertainment. The children do not often enough see their culture represented by intellectuals or people who have found success through hard work. If this is the only way our students see themselves they will not be able to envision a different future for themselves—a future equal in opportunity and possibility to that of their European-American peers. Educational theorists constantly tell us that students must be able to make connections to and have prior knowledge of what they are learning, and how it impacts them, or the concepts taught will be lost (Ruggiano Schmidt, 2005). When they are not represented, students find it difficult to make connections and see a different reality for themselves.

CULTURALLY RESPONSIVE LITERATURE

My students like to read about real things that have happened, things relevant to them and their lives and lifestyles. The Bluford High Series, published by Townsend Press, includes some of the most popular books in my classroom library. These books feature teenagers of a variety of ethnicities as the protagonists dealing with many viable situations, which the students face every day. Though these books are not on our curriculum list, they offer a way for our students to engage with text, because the experiences found in the books are ones the students can connect to. The reading becomes personal.

My Independent Reading Project seeks to enforce this idea of personal connection and allows me to move beyond the limited selection of books listed on our curriculum lists. There are many books available that may encourage growth through personal connections, but they are unrecognized in many of our curricula. Teachers in my school district have been trying to make our curriculum more equitable by introducing texts such as *Monster* by Walter Dean Myers and *Farewell to Manzanar* by Jeanne Wakatsuki Houston and James Houston. These are the connections that will bring the concepts they are learning to the students' relevant here and now in which they live, fostering new appreciation for learning and reading through recognition.

We must continue our efforts to reform our school curricula so they are as current and pluralistic as the society in which we live. The two major literacy organizations, International Reading Association (IRA) and the National Council of Teachers of English (NCTE), have produced lists of standards concerning the English language arts classroom. Both include a mandate that "students should read works that reflect the diversity of the United States' population in terms of gender, age, social class, religion, and ethnicity and that teachers should consider students' interests carefully when choosing works for inclusion in the curriculum" (in Stallworth, Gibbons, & Fauber, 2006, p. 28). In her article, "I Want to Read," Feger (2006) tells how bringing in these representations to her ELL classroom changed her whole style of teaching and made a vast difference in her students' performance levels: "Culturally relevant literature and nonfiction texts transformed the level of engagement in reading for the English language learners in my class. I could never have dreamed of a better affirmation than the appeal 'I want to read!'" Feger's article alone suggests that when students can connect with books and find their own identity through this literature, they will rise to meet higher expectations.

CROSSING CULTURAL BORDERS THROUGH MEMOIRS

There are a few different projects and policies I have brought into my classroom that have been successful in building a classroom community and in recognizing and appreciating various cultures including those represented in the classroom and throughout the world. "Crossing cultural borders involves understanding the similarities among cultures, while also appreciating the differences. It is this second point that is crucial to interrupting the inner boundary of prejudice and misunderstanding" (Landt, 2006; Ruggiano Schmidt, 1999). Instrumental in encouraging this crossing of cultural borders in the classroom was a memoir project I did with some of my 9th-graders. As we completed this unit, I saw these students brought to a new awareness of themselves and the world in which they live.

The project was loosely based on the *ABCs of Cultural Understanding and Communication* (Ruggiano Schmidt, 1998). I developed a unit around the book *A Long Way Gone: Memoirs of a Boy Soldier*, by Ishmael Beah, who was scheduled to speak in our city. To start off the unit, students learned about the Civil War conflict in Sierra Leone that began in 1991. They researched and studied the conflict through a Wikispace WebQuest that I had created in which they were directed to various sites for familiarizing themselves with the conflict, the usage of children as soldiers, and what was done to these children, as well as with other related topics—genocide, political standpoints of countries and the UN, and connections to other similar instances of warfare using child soldiers and involving genocide.

While researching relevant Web sites through the WebQuest and synthesizing the facts they brought together into a reflection paper, students were also required to contribute to an online discussion through the same Wikispace that held the WebQuest. In this online discussion, students responded to prompts and each other's thoughts regarding the research they uncovered. My intention was that they would debate and then make further connections to their own lives in this discussion board. Here, we learned the idea that child soldiers were not just used halfway around the world, but that the United States itself is teeming with our own versions of child soldiers in the form of gangs. This issue in itself was of prime interest to my students as many of them had had personal experiences with either being in gangs themselves or knowing someone in a gang or someone who had died as a result of gangs. Furthermore, we came to realize how relevant these themes were to many of the students in the class.

In the academic year 2009–2010, Foreman High School enrolled more than 200 student refugees from many different countries. We have students in our school who have lived through civil war and been in refugee camps, and some who may have even been child soldiers themselves. Researching these realities and reading this book allowed my students to connect even to the very peers they go to class with every day, to understand what some of the students in our very large ESL population have actually experienced. One of these students even talked to the class about her own experiences of being a refugee in her own country and having to flee with her whole family. The class learned how lucky these students feel to be able to be in America and away from the violence and fear that they lived through in their homelands. The research, the book—all of it—became real and present in the students' here and now.

After participating in this online project, we moved on to reading Ishmael Beah's memoir, making personal text-to-self connections and reading analytically throughout to understand the implications and underlying themes of survival, identity, and political influence. When we finished reading and reflecting on the book and the societal situations of child soldiers still prevalent today in warring countries, as well as on our own streets through gangs and child prostitutes, the students were then given the opportunity to hear Ishmael Beah speak at a local university. This was one of the most moving experiences in the lives of many of the students. His talk was right in line with what he'd written about in his memoir, but the more personal elements that he added, and being able to see him speaking directly to them—a man who'd lived through unimaginable atrocities—

allowed these students to feel a powerful connection. The central message in his speech that resonated with them was that no matter where you come from, what you've done or lived through, you are capable of rising above it and regaining humanity and the ability to trust and hope.

After internalizing his message and bringing all this information together, the students together created a banner for our hallway, calling for an end to the usage of child soldiers around the world and in our own city. They created posters to inform others about what is really happening right now in the world we are living in. They spoke out and spread the message to their families and to their friends. Many in the school were remarking on the information and bigger concepts these students were highlighting. History, social justice, and global connections were coming alive; these ideas became real and tangible as we moved through the unit.

To be able to read something real, and fairly recent, that someone their age had experienced, survived, and grown from, was an experience none soon forgot. Even as my students return this year, they still make connections back to last year's project. Education is designed to prepare our students for the bigger world; therefore, we must begin to include them in it. They need to be educated about other languages and cultures from around the world to see how their decisions and actions affect others and to see how others, even others their own age, have made an immense impact on society by simply standing up for the right thing. This is part of what they experienced through reading this book. But the venture did not end there.

The *ABCs of Cultural Understanding and Communication* (1998) calls for a third element of autobiographical connection: to understand oneself and how one's own place in the world truly is meaningful and significant (just as Beah's has been). The unit culminated with students writing their own memoir about an event that had taken place in their lives that changed who they were and made them stronger. Some of the memoirs were intensely powerful and made direct connections to what they had experienced in the readings. While it proved to be a fairly difficult assignment for some as they were still so young, most of the students moved to a level of introspection I had not seen in them before. They opened and revealed a piece of themselves in these memoirs, which was very moving and truly inspiring. Though they hadn't all been refugees or child soldiers, each had had their own experiences and struggles dealing with life through which they did feel a connection, and very often a cultural connection, to Ishmael Beah and his experiences.

The overall unit was very effective in crossing cultural borders, making connections and enhancing understanding within the school and my classroom, and motivating the students to feel connected to the bigger world they often forget resides beyond their street corners. They were reminded to see beyond the city blocks and take a prominent place in the local, state, and national societies. Not everything went smoothly in this unit, however. I would change some aspects by bringing in some letters and editorial writing and by incorporating more mini lessons, especially in the use of technology. I would also add modeling more effective ways to respond to Internet discussion boards, a skill they had not yet learned, to guide the students' work more proficiently.

THE CULTURAL SHIFT IN OUR SCHOOL

Besides our incorporation of culturally responsive teaching within each of our classrooms, my school also goes to great lengths to support and strengthen the recognition of the diversity in our school. It is something we promote as an attribute of which to be fiercely proud. Each morning, announcements are given in English, Spanish, and Arabic to promote cultural acceptance and inclusion in the school community. Art projects and posters all over the building give evidence to the many nations that are found all together in one student body at our high school. Every year we have two highlighted cultural events that everyone always looks forward to: our multicultural luncheon in the fall, in which our ESL students prepare their favorite cultural foods for everyone to sample, and our multicultural festival in the spring. At the festival, the students prepare cultural dances, songs, and food to share with the rest of the student body. We have guitar songs from Burma/Myanmar, Vietnamese fan dances, sweetened plantains from Liberia, songs from Ghana and Saudi Arabia, and so much more. The students love to see the performances, fill up on great food, and support their fellow students in appreciating the diversity that is so celebrated in our school.

Researcher Dr. Lasisi Ajayi reports on this idea of multiculturalism through experiences with some of her own Hispanic ESL students. She comments that "in their biographical essays, the students rejected assimilation practices and, instead, indicated a preference for recognition as learners with their own histories, languages, cultures and desires. . . . The students in this study seemed to expect their schools to prepare them for a multicultural and multilingual life—where their Hispanic heritage and American culture coexisted without one necessarily dominating the other" (Ajayi, 2006). This is what I believe our school is constantly striving for. Our multicultural festivals bring to light and celebrate the richness of each culture. Our classrooms consistently explore the histories and traditions of various cultures.

I have seen in just 1½ years of teaching at this high school the many ways in which Foreman High School's students, teachers, and staff are always striving to find new ways to celebrate culture, while also discovering unity within our diversity. Students are appreciated for the unique perspectives they do bring to the table. The teachers are always trying to learn about the backgrounds of our students. Very often this is the key to seeing the truth in a student's successes and difficulties. When one realizes how some students come from high schools in Puerto Rico, where every day they see shooting and gang violence in their schools (Delgado, 2006), one can understand more holistically a student's defense mechanisms. It is all brought back to the place of seeing past a student's behaviors—positive and negative—and looking toward the root of it all. Only then can we work with a student to encourage their successes.

CONCLUSION

My students are still striving for success. The first Saturday after I left my classroom for the summer, we had our high school graduation. That first graduation that I attended is one I will never forget. That day the city and the government saw an extremely low graduation rate, but we also saw something very different. We saw five homeless students walk across the stage to receive their diplomas. We saw a young woman who could have settled for a local diploma drive to earn the college entrance diploma. We saw students who were teenage mothers and fathers, and despite all odds and obstacles—graduated. We heard a young woman belt out the most beautiful rendition of the "Star Spangled Banner" we'd ever heard and a hard-working valedictorian move an entire audience to tears with a speech imbued with the hope, integrity, and inspiration that he was never handed, that he hadn't started with, but that he worked for, with his teachers and family members beside him. That day we saw 127 students, 127 success stories, 127 changed lives walk across that stage.

I tell you all this, because many will tell you about the hardships, the obstacles, the frustrations and disappointments of working in a city school. They will show you statistics of poor graduation rates and politicians trying to close schools instead of supporting the children and teachers, and they will show you every reason why you should not work in a city school. But that graduation day—at the end of a long, exhausting, frustrating, and intensely moving first year—I would never trade for the world. To work in a city school is the most rewarding and meaningful life choice you can make. As President Obama said in his first State of the Union Address on January 27, 2010, "The best anti-poverty program around is a world-class education." It will take time. There will be successes and failures, frustration, heartache and exhilarations, but in the end, one day, this will be a battle that we will win. We will win because we fight, because we are strong, and because our children are worth fighting for—every moment of every day.

MAKE THIS HAPPEN IN YOUR CLASSROOM

- Develop relationships with your *students:* Talk to them outside your class, go to the special events and games they invite you to, be ready to listen whenever they need you. People would often remind me my first year of teaching that sometimes I might be the only person to smile at or even acknowledge that student that day.
- Bring culturally responsive literature into your classroom. Incorporate cultural diversity and identity formation concepts into as much of your curriculum as possible. Remember that cultural diversity extends to all nationalities, even ones not represented in your school or classroom, and to age, gender, sexual orientation, and more.
- Educate yourself on students' cultures and backgrounds, especially be aware of cultural norms when it comes to body language and behaviors. They may not be being disrespectful when they don't look into your eyes when talking to you; many cultures view it as a gesture of respect to avoid eye contact. Learn these details through your own research, through ESL teachers, and by asking the students. Often they are very proud of their culture and love to talk about their cultural traditions.
- Don't forget that being a teacher is not a solo career. Older teachers have experience, wisdom, and great ideas. They are a great support that should be utilized. Younger teachers are fresh out of school and often have all the newest education theories, technologies, and methods fresh in their minds. Teaching is not a static profession; it is always changing, growing, and maturing, as should we.
- Work with your whole school to create a school environment that appreciates and celebrates diversity through posters, flags, multilingual announcements, incorporation of different cultures in the yearbook, and multicultural festivals.

- Foster communication about diversity and unity whenever you can. Web 2.0 technologies of Wikispaces, blogs, and WebQuests allow for real honest discussion with anyone who cares to join the conversation, and these technologies are meaningful to this generation of students. Action doesn't take place until problems are seen, discussed, and understood.
- Remind yourself every day why you work as a teacher and why you chose your school. Even amidst those frustrating days, remember the successes and triumphs, learn from the mistakes, and always keep going. Sometimes, you may be the most important and most stable figure in a student's life.

REFERENCES

Ajayi, L. (2006). Multiple voices, multiple realities: Self-defined images of self among adolescent Hispanic English language learners. *Education, 126*(3), 468–480.

Callins, T. (2006). Culturally responsive literacy instruction. *Teaching Exceptional Children, 39*(2), 62–65.

Delgado, B. (2006). Violencia en las escuelas. Retrieved March 6, 2010, from http://www.tendenciaspr.com/Educacion/Tablas/04Incidencias_registradas_en_las_escuelas.htm

Feger, M. (2006). "I want to read": How culturally relevant texts increase student engagement in reading. *Multicultural Education, 13*(3), 18–19.

Landt, S. (2006). Multicultural literature and young adolescents: A kaleidoscope of opportunity. *Journal of Adolescent & Adult Literacy, 49*(8), 690–697.

Kingsbury, K (November 6, 2008). Should kids be able to graduate after the 10th grade? *Time Magazine.* Retrieved February 16, 2010, from http://www.time.com/time/nation/article/0,8599,1857336,00.html

National Center for Educational Statistics. (2006). Retrieved from February 20, 2010, http://nces.ed.gov/

President Barack Obama's Inaugural Address (January 28, 2009). Retrieved February 21, 2010, from http://www.whitehouse.gov/blog/inaugural-address/

Ruggiano Schmidt, P. (1998). ABCs of cultural understanding and communication. *Equity and Excellence in Education, 31*(2), 28–38.

Ruggiano Schmidt, P. (1999). Focus on research: Know thyself and understand others. *Language Arts, 76*(4), 332–340.

Ruggiano Schmidt, P. (2005). Culturally responsive instruction: Promoting literacy in secondary content areas. Adolescent Literacy. Naperville, IL: Learning Point Associates. Retrieved February 21, 2010, from http://.www.learningpt.org

Stallworth, B., Gibbons, L., & Fauber, L. (2006). It's not on the list: An exploration of teachers' perspectives on using multicultural literature. *Journal of Adolescent & Adult Literacy, 49*(6), 478–489.

Zinn, H. (2002). *A peoples history of the United States.* New York: Harpercollins.

CHAPTER 5

Taking Risks

Building Bridges with Students in an Alternative School

Crystal Ponto and Tanja Cosentino

When we were still preservice teachers in college, we did not think we would be teaching in the alternative education classrooms that we now command. *Command* may not be the right word. Often we wonder just who exactly is in charge of the ship! As English teachers, we realized early on that it was our subject area that students struggled with the most. With reading and writing across the curriculum as the focal point of alternative education, we desperately needed to make this vessel stay afloat, but we also yearned for our passengers to not abandon ship. A strong and engaging literacy program was the best way to anchor the ship and encourage our students.

We knew something was working when one day the bus garage called and the caller asked, "These alternative ed kids are reading on the bus. That's just not normal. Are they reading something appropriate?"

We smiled and replied, "Of course they are! We should know. We're their English teachers!"

Like any stereotype, the assumptions that accompany alternative education students are ugly. People often believe that our students underachieve and behave poorly because they simply do not care. If our students exhibit these characteristics, it is because they have acquired them out of frustration and neglect.

It doesn't have to be this way. We have been able to tap our students' love of literature and help them be part of a classroom community in which their opinions are valued. We do this by inviting our students to have a voice in what we read. We scaffold this by sharing new books that we ourselves are reading, telling kids to explore online for new books they'd like to see in our classroom library and encouraging them to make a wish list of books they want to read. When we first began doing this, students asked for biographies on TuPac Shakur, Eminem, and other famous rappers and movie stars. They could not believe that we were willing to bring these books into the classroom. But doing so provided rich rewards. It allowed them to begin reading what they loved and then trusting us when we encouraged them to try something new. This step in the learning process is integral to alternative education. It allows students to feel that they can have a major role in making decisions about what they are reading and learning.

ALTERNATIVE EDUCATION

For more than a decade, school districts have adopted a variety of strict discipline policies, including zero-tolerance, that have led to the increased number of alternative education programs (NCSL, 2005). Students who are considered at risk for dropping out are corralled and sent to programs that target specific needs with the hope of helping students adjust successfully to the traditional school setting. For the more than 20,000 alternative schools across the country, many have focused on reducing truancy, improving students' attitudes toward school, accumulating high school credits, and reducing behavior problems (The Principals' Partnership, 2005). In conjunction with meeting these needs of alternative education students, culturally responsive teaching also is integral. Literature can be empowering and liberating and allow students to connect with each other on many levels. In order to accomplish this, the literature of the classroom must reflect a variety of genres, cultures, and perspectives and must follow up with projects and discussions that are just as varied (Gay, 2000; Ruggiano Schmidt & Ma, 2006).

Our alternative education program was designed for similar reasons. Our students have not been successful in the typical school setting. For some of our students this may result from poor attendance, lack of motivation, grade retention, or simply the inability to connect with fellow students or teachers. Our school is located in an urban setting in the mid-Atlantic and northeastern region of the United States, but because we are a regional education center, we serve surrounding school districts that are considered both suburban and rural. Some of our students come from the nearby city while others are bused from rural farming communities 30 minutes away. We serve many culturally diverse groups including those who affiliate as European Americans and as African Americans. Diversity in our program comes not only from the color of our students' skin, but from the depth and breadth of their various life experiences and socioeconomic challenges. We may have students as young as 11 and as old as 17, with varying degrees of ability and aptitude. Many of our students have faced severe academic challenges and often struggle with core knowledge and skills. It often comes down to finding the right teaching tools and learning community to connect with these students who have not experienced success in the schools where they reside. Fortunately, they often find it with us! What we have uncovered are strategies that will help teachers add more tools to their teaching toolbox.

One of the key components of our program is having a full-time social worker who meets with students regularly—both individually and in a group environment. We choose literature that will engage students quickly. To do so, we choose topics that are important to our students. Such topics include teen pregnancy, domestic violence, drug and alcohol abuse, and mental health issues. Teachers and social workers often collaborate in choosing the literature so that individual and group discussions sometimes carry over from the English classroom to counseling sessions. Due to the sensitive nature of the topics addressed, these books are often read aloud in a small group setting with ample time for group discussion.

There is certainly enough merit to reading these books even if a social worker is not a part of the structure of your school or program. We see a strong connection with student achievement when students are reading literature they feel reflects their life experiences. As facilitators, we allow them to explore and express their connections through differentiated instruction. Traditional assignments such as journaling and written responses certainly pertain, but our students are most empowered by instruction and assessment that allows them to think outside the box.

Counseling literature drives communication between teachers and students. We choose literature that reflects the struggles our students are facing at school, at home, and within their communities. Diversity takes on so many definitions and levels that it does not just pertain to color and heritage but experiences and life choices.

GETTING STARTED

Because we often have students from multiple grade levels in a classroom with a wide variety of reading and writing abilities, self-esteem and a strong classroom community is established before we tackle any sensitive subject. As we begin the school year, establishing the community is our first order of business. We do this through several project-based assignments that allow us to get to know our students, allow our students to get to know each other, and ultimately assess their reading and comprehension abilities.

One way we do this is through creating a classroom quilt. Each student is given a fabric square and fabric markers. We ask them to design a symbol that represents something about their family or someone important to them. One student drew a lion in a fighting pose and colored it red, white, and blue. When the student presented his crest to the class, he explained the lion represented his family because they tend to fight a lot but they were strong and the colors were of the flag of the Dominican Republic, where his parents were born. He also added that he considered himself American, so he was glad the colors were the same! When the classroom quilt was sewn together and hanging in our hallway, a school administrator was gazing at the quilt and asked who drew the lion. We explained the story behind the crest and the administrator acted surprised. "Wow. I never knew that about him. Very interesting!" This principal had worked with this particular student for 3 years. Taking the time to ask the right questions and develop a connection speaks volumes.

We also create an Assets Board. The students are asked to draw pictures of themselves doing something they are good at or have accomplished. Such a simple task is sometimes difficult for students who lack resiliency and self-esteem. We post their pictures on the Assets Board, and once or twice during the semester, we ask the other students to add an asset to each other's picture. Students who would not normally converse with each other or have any contact with each other in the community have said positive things like "Gino always remembers his social studies homework and that's cool." Teachers add assets as well. By the end of the year, students are amazed at all the positive attributes other people have noticed. We see them checking out the board all the time! An administrator from a component school district once said that our students would seemingly "stand on their heads and spit jelly beans for us" whereas they would "refuse to do the simplest of tasks for somebody else." It all boils down to relationships. Take the time in the beginning to build connections and the results become more meaningful and sustainable.

When parents see the effort that is made to build community and resiliency in our classrooms, they begin to realize that this classroom may not be like all the others. When our first several phone calls home are positive, parents are genuinely surprised and appreciative. This invests a lot of good will in the emotional banks of our families. Parents or guardians are more open to communicating with us and begin to see that our conversations with them about their children are aimed at opening their horizons and providing them with options, not at making them feel inadequate about their child's apparent lack of success. For us, their child's future academic and social performance begins at our doorway.

OPENING DOORWAYS WITH LITERATURE

Once we have established this community, counseling literature is a way to generate some serious personal discussions about deeply personal topics. This being said, we still need to follow curriculum, assess abilities, and build skills.

We have included a number of activities that we use to help us get students involved, keep them interested, and leave them asking for more! The great thing about these projects is that they can be modified to use with any number of novels at a variety of grade levels. We have also included a section of this chapter with examples for connecting and communicating with parents. This is sometimes the toughest part of alternative education. Parental involvement is sometimes difficult to initiate and maintain, so it is important that it is authentic. Parents must see that they are making a difference in their children's school lives. Of the many, we have attempted, some have been much more successful than others. The following examples were positive for both parents and *students:*

We asked the student to write a "needs poem" based on the poem "Needs" by A. R. Ammons (1979). Our discussions revolve around the differences between needs and wants, and we encouraged students to write their own "Needs" poems, similar to what Ammons wrote:

I want something suited to my special needs ...
...I want to mow while riding.

The essence of the poem discusses the narrator's wish to own a riding lawn mower. The author's choice of words always spurs an interesting conversation. A student example shows a heartbreaking interpretation of a "need" and a "want":

I want something suited to my special needs.
I want hugs and soft punches with
Laughs and football tosses.
…and even if I just wish for it
I want a dad.

Or the more lighthearted and certainly honest interpretation:

I want something suited to my special needs.
I want similar tastes in clothes
I want to be invited in, not kicked out
I want to be asked my opinion not told to shut up
…I want a sister who isn't crazy!

Initially this assignment also prompted responses like "I need a new car" or "I need a cute boyfriend," but as we continue to ask the students to write and rewrite, we eventually get responses like Amanda's:

I want something suited to my special needs.
I want to look like my father and not like my mother.
I want a cool name like my cousins. I want to be Black.

This type of honesty and raw emotion allows us to have in-depth conversations about how we identify with others and what acceptance means to each of us. For those students who identify themselves as European American, they were surprised at Amanda's response. But Robbie, who identifies himself as a "White African American" replied, "I hear ya. I know that, too."

An additional assignment includes asking parents to write a needs poem as well. We ask the students to encourage their parents to complete this assignment with the incentive that the student will earn extra credit. Our students are often surprised after reading about their parents' needs and wants. With parental permission, we create a bulletin board showcasing everyone's hard work. Even parents get a kick out of seeing their own work on display. One parent wrote:

I want something suited to my special needs. I want peace and quiet. I want a clean house and sparkling windows . . . I want a son who does housework!

CONNECTING WITH LITERATURE

More often than not, students feel a great connection and a sense of success from the counseling literature presented to them at the beginning of the year. Such literature deals with teen issues, family problems and national concerns that may plague the adolescent mind. Meaningful connections with this literature often segue into the world of classical literature. Students are often quite intimidated by some of the titles, but with guided reading and the right instructional strategies, these classics may become favorites. Many books deemed "classics" still carry that feeling of counseling literature.

Introducing children's literature into the middle and high school curriculum is one way to connect different genres of literature while focusing on differentiated instruction. For many students who struggle to keep up with grade-level reading, children's literature is a way to make them feel comfortable, as vocabulary presents less of a problem, making it possible to focus more on drawing inferences. Children's books such as *Terrible Things* by Eve Bunting may be used in conjunction with the many different young adult novels about the Holocaust. These books allow students to study voice and perspective without feeling hindered by the reading level.

While preparing our students for a field trip to the Jewish Community Center to listen to a Holocaust survivor, our students read excerpts from a survivor's account of her liberation from Bergen-Belsen as well as *Terrible Things*. The account of the liberation was stirring, horrific, and heart wrenching, while the children's book talked about animals of the forest and how because they did not stand together, they ultimately stood alone. When we asked the students to compare the two works and discuss their feelings, one student wrote:

> The Holocaust was really bad. What's worse is that we have to explain this to our kids in a way that they won't make the same mistakes we did.

Using children's books allows our students to safely connect with sensitive and sometimes uncomfortable events. Many of our students become detached and unaffected by atrocities that do not directly affect them. By using the younger literature, in this case, an allegory, students can experience empathy that they may not have had if our readings were purely textual.

Struggling readers need much support to read many of the classics that we teach in English class. A traditional literature circle plan through which students are assigned roles such as text question leader, wordsmith, and quote analyzer may be helpful with these novels. Since many of our students struggle with the complexity of these novels, we have asked students to choose four words per chapter, or section, that they are unfamiliar with and to create a dictionary designed for elementary-level readers. Students were asked to illustrate each entry as well. With its completion, the dictionary was bound and donated to our local library.

Shakespeare is always challenging for students who struggle with reading. Giving alternative education students a positive "Shakesperience" is a challenge, but we have found that packaging is key.

Students can modernize Shakespearean plays by putting certain scenes or soliloquies into their own vernacular. They become highly engaged in this experience because they enjoy the higher-level thinking that is required to translate Shakespeare's words into their own, and they see their own language being valued in the classroom. Here's an example of Robin's interpretation of the balcony scene from *Romeo and Juliet:*

> O Romeo, Romeo! Wherefore art thou Romeo?
> Deny thy father and refuse thy name;
> Or, if thou wilt not, be but sworn my love,
> And I'll no longer be a Capulet.

> "Aw Romero, where you at?
> Who cares about your last name? Tell your pops you don't care . . . or
> if you can't I swear I'll tell mine that I don't want his name no more
> either!"

Students have also designed sets and worn costumes even in the classroom. Students become more connected to a task when they recognize the hard work and effort they put into making the project come to fruition. All it takes is for one student to don the black Hamlet cape or wear Juliet's pink tiara. The rest follow suit. Cody said, "I can't believe you makin' me wear this. I wouldn't do it for anyone but your guys." The laughter is often quite contagious.

Movies in general provide a medium for students to connect the complicated language of Shakespeare to a modern display of sights and sounds. Show the Leonardo DiCaprio version of Shakespeare in which the language is Elizabethan but the look is Baz Luhrmann. Instead of *Hamlet,* show *Renaissance Man* with Danny Devito. In this film Devito is hired by the army to educate a group of soldiers who are struggling to complete basic training. They learn to accept themselves and others by reading *Hamlet* together and finding out that they are capable of anything. *Ten Things I Hate About You* is a modern day twist on *The Taming of the Shrew.* Students are amazed to find Shakespearean links throughout the movie, such as Kat and Bianca attending Padua High School and that their last name is Stratford. Many Shakespearean lines are said throughout the movie. This becomes a game with many of our students to see how many references they can find. Movies, even bad ones, add such depth and breadth to any literary exploration. They provide a catalyst for discussion and will often lead to some very animated conversations during which "the book was WAY better than the movie" will often be heard!

LITERACY AND TECHNOLOGY

Trying to keep pace with our ever-changing technological world is always a challenge. For this project, we ask students to design a paper model of a typical social networking site such as MySpace or Facebook. They take on the role of the character creating an "account" for that character. Students are given a list of questions and descriptors and they create a profile page using poster board, markers, and so on. This project encourages inferential thinking because the student must demonstrate an in-depth understanding of how the character looks and feels, what he or she thinks and sees the world. Stacey made a very interesting MySpace account using Novalee Nation from Billie Letts' novel *Where the Heart Is.* She included such details as these:

> Novalee's favorite meal is a grilled chicken salad from McDonald's . . . because she is always watching her weight and Novalee's favorite song on her iPod is Patsy Cline's "Crazy" because she's going crazy without Forney Hull in her life.

We think even the author would be proud of that level of characterization.

Another project that links technology to the classroom and in this case, classical literature, is our Textually Active project. We ask students to rewrite scenes as if the characters were texting each other. What would

Romeo text Juliet in the balcony scene? What would Hamlet say to Oph-
elia? This allows students to be creative and demonstrate their inferential
thinking skills. Here is Eric's version of the balcony scene in *Romeo and
Juliet*, written as a text message:

Juliet: ? u at, R? Tell ur dad 2 bk off. If u cant I wil. Luv J

For our more visual learners and artistically inclined students, this project has classmates working together to script and design an original movie
trailer as a way to highlight their understanding of key events from a novel.
Students choose five main scenes that they must condense and rewrite in a
way that highlights their understanding of the book. Students use Windows
Media Player or digital recorders to design and peer edit their movie trailers.

We invited students to design a musical score that will accompany the
book. Given a blank CD case, they are required to design a front cover as
well as a track list of eight to ten songs. Each song must be accompanied
by a description of what section of the book this song represents and why
the student chose that particular song. One of the songs Christi-Ann chose
for her musical score after she read *Al Capone Does My Shirts*, by Geni-
fer Choldenko, was Paul Simon's "You Can Call Me Al." Her liner notes
explained that the song was perfect for one of the final scenes in the book
when Moose, the main character, gets a personal note from Al Capone, an
inmate at Alcatraz. "This was a perfect song, especially the line 'There were
incidents and accidents, there were hints and allegations.' I know this song
is, like, really old, but I thought it was perfect!" We think she was right!

Reminiscent of a film festival, students invited parents and home
school personnel to view and vote on their movie trailers and soundtracks.
We used decorations from a local party warehouse and asked everyone to
wear black and white to the event. We decorated the classroom so that it
represented an opening to a major motion picture, and students were introduced while walking the red carpet. We gave awards for best trailer, best
soundtrack, best editing, on so on. We made it so that every student walked
away with at least one award for the evening. When the curtain finally
closed, it had been a very successful event!

READING AND WRITING CONNECTIONS

Essay writing is a frustrating endeavor for many of our students, but the
importance of being able to write a strong essay is imperative to any future

success, whether one is working toward a high school diploma or a General Education Diploma. We took on the critical lens essay with 7th-graders by including an artistic piece that allowed concrete thinkers to get the hang of what a critical lens essay really entailed. After purchasing giant sunglasses from a local store where everything is a dollar, students were each assigned a character from a novel. The students had to decorate the frames of the sunglasses to represent all the different aspects of their assigned character. Then, they had to choose two additional characters who were important to their assigned character. Each additional character was given a "lens" that we asked the students to decorate according to how the assigned character viewed the additional character. For example, Robert was assigned the character of Joey from one of our novels. He decorated his frames with things important to this character: a foam circle representing an ADD medication patch, a miniature plastic dog, an anti-drinking sign, a package of sugar, and so on. One lens was entitled "Mom" and the other lens was entitled "Dad." Robert listed words, like *caring*, *protective*, and *tired*, since that was how Joey viewed his Mom. The "Dad" lens listed words, like *alcoholic*, *unhealthy*, and *talkative*, that reflected Joey's view of his father.

All of the sunglasses, along with their critical lens essays, were displayed on several tri-fold boards throughout the school.

Parade floats put a modern twist on the classic diorama. Students use a shoebox or cereal box to create a parade float in which their favorite scene from the novel is depicted on the top of the box. Students write a short synopsis on one side of the float explaining the plot and major themes of the novel, while the other side explains the scene they have chosen to represent. At the end of the year, we asked students to explain what project they liked best throughout the year. Robert explains:

> I really like the parade float. I got to be creative and create a really cool scene from the book *My Brother Sam Is Dead*. I did the scene where the British soldiers ambush the colonists in a home along a deserted path. When I read I try to picture the scene in my head so this helped me make it come alive.

Many of the novels we choose portray nontraditional families. Novels such as *Willow and Twig* by Jean Little, *The Client* by John Grisham, *Where the Heart Is* by Billie Letts, and *America* by E. R. Frank portray a variety of families and family situations. Students were asked to create a nontraditional-family tree that analyzed their own family connections and dynamics. This tree included obstacles that the family had faced that were visually represented in the form of roots or rocks at the base of the tree. Students were also asked to include important people in their lives that might not necessarily fit in with the traditional family schema. These family trees were often very moving and provoked conversations regarding family and family dynamics. Students have used rocks to represent alcoholism, mental health issues, and divorce as metaphors for what has been difficult for families to deal with or overcome. In creating this type of a family tree, students were able to recognize inherent support systems that they could rely on in times of need.

LITERATURE AND CHARACTER EDUCATION

Many young adult novels focus on moral values and virtues that we find in many character education programs. These programs often disappear as students progress to middle and high school. One way to bring character education back to the upper-level classroom is to discuss the differences between what is tangible and what is intangible. We brainstorm the two vocabulary words with the students and ask for examples of each. We then ask each student to choose an intangible "gift" they would like to give someone they care about. Students decorate a gift box and write a gift tag explaining who and what gift they are giving and why. One student gave the gift of patience to his dad. Another gave the gift of youth to her ailing grandmother. We displayed our gifts under an artificial Christmas tree entitled, "Gifts from the Heart." Our end of the year program included some of our students presenting their loved ones with these gifts.

CONCLUSION

Clearly differentiated instruction benefits all students, but students from diverse backgrounds and socioeconomic settings who have had difficulty succeeding in school often bring different sets of rules and norms to the table. However, it is our job to teach students who do not fit into the traditional academic or social mold. Thinking outside the box and taking calculated risks with the literature we read and the projects we assign has worked to engage students and position them as decision makers.

MAKE THIS HAPPEN IN YOUR CLASSROOM:

- One very successful project that can be employed with any novel uses Bloom's Taxonomy. Dig out those old notes from your education classes and put them to use! Teaching your students the levels of Bloom's Taxonomy helps with many different aspects of differentiated instruction. Ask students to prepare test questions or create rubrics using the various levels. For this project, students were given five choices for each of the six taxonomic levels. Students chose one task from each level, showing the increase of higher-order thinking skills as they progress from the knowledge level to the evaluation level. Tasks range from defining and listing to forming opinions and supporting those opinions with textual evidence. Students are empowered by the choices they are allowed to make and feel as if they have a hand in their own learning process. Have students prepare all of their projects on 8½ x 11 papers and bind their completed work, or ask the students to prepare a presentation of their projects.

Examples of Bloom's Block Project:

Knowledge	Memorize a favorite section of the book and recite it to the class.
Comprehension	Write two paragraphs describing the setting of the story.
Application	Make a list of the problems that the characters had to overcome. Name other characters in the book with similar problems.
Analysis	Plan a fancy dinner menu for the main character. Write the menu out and explain why it would please the main character.
Synthesis	Design a costume one of the characters in the book might have worn.
Evaluation	Compare and contrast a current problem the world is experiencing with one faced in the book.

- Invite parents to an academic fair at the end of every school year. This is a great opportunity for our students to showcase their hard work and creativity. For many, it may be the first positive school event they have been a part of in a very long time. For this particular station, we displayed the students' "Blooms" using a flower theme and handed out seed packets as parting gifts labeled "Thanks for helping us grow." The possibilities are endless!

- Ask students to choose one predominant emotion that connects the reader to a character. Students could then create a papier-mache mask on which that emotion is represented.

REFERENCES

Ammons, A.R. (1979). Needs. In W. Harmon (Ed.), *The Oxford University book of American light verse.* New York: Oxford University Press.

Berk, L., & Winsler, A. (1995). *Scaffolding children's learning: Vygotsky and early childhood learning.* Washington, DC: National Association for Education of Young Children.

Bunting, E. (1993). *Terrible things.* New York: Jewish Publication Society.

Day, J., Spiegel, D. L., McLellan, J., & Brown, V. (2002). *Moving forward with literature circles.* New York: Scholastic.

Gardner, H. (1993). *Multiple intelligences: The theory in practice.* New York: Basic.

Gay, G. (2000). *Culturally responsive teaching: Theory, research, and practice.* New York: Teachers College Press.

National Conference for State Legislators—Alternative Education (2005). Retrieved February 1, 2010, from www. NCSL.org

Prensky, M. (2001, October 5). Digital natives, digital immigrants. *On the Horizon, 9*(5), 1–15.

The Principals' Partnership. Retrieved March 20, 2010, from http://www.principal-spartnership.com

Ruggiano Schmidt, P., & Ma, W. (2006). *50 Literacy Strategies for culturally responsive literacy teaching* (K–8). Thousand Oaks, CA: Corwin Press.

CHAPTER 6

Reading About the Negro Leagues Through the Lens of Critical Literacy

A Springboard to Straight Talk About Race

Kristin R. Luebbert

I have been a teacher for 10 years, mostly serving 7th-graders of color who live in high-poverty and working-class neighborhoods in a large city in the Northeast. The school is situated is a predominantly White neighborhood that is geographically close to several predominantly African American neighborhoods. Most of the immediate (White) neighbors do not send their children to this school. It is not seen as a "desirable" placement. (Whether this has to do with the high number of African American students is an issue that has been hotly debated recently by all stakeholders.) Many use the local Catholic school and others use private schools. However, the school *is* considered to be a desirable school by African American caregivers in the surrounding communities, and many of these families strive to have their children attend this school.

Like many teachers in urban schools, I'm a White woman. I was raised in a suburban community in the 1960s and 1970s. Our town was small but integrated and not far from a historically Black university. The town was not without parochial attitudes and racial tensions, but for the most part groups got along fairly well. My parents raised us with a belief in the equality of all people, and they truly lived that belief.

When I came back to teaching after my children were in school, I was assigned to teach in a school that served primarily African American students. I approached my job with the belief that people of all backgrounds will respond well when treated with respect. Truthfully, this expectation has proven to be correct. As I have continued at my school and taught many members of the same family I do feel that education in this particular community is my calling. I see both the successes and the heartbreaks, and I know that each teacher (no matter his/her race) in my school is important in the lives of the students.

Some may wonder if it is possible for children and parents of color to trust and even bond with a White teacher. What I have found is that most of my students have truly been raised to respect *the position* of teacher. Most children enter school predisposed to trust their teachers (a humbling thought), and as you prove your trustworthiness they respond to that. Parents have much the same attitude. If they can tell by your actions that your primary goal is the success of their child, they will trust you and back you up. I have had wonderful relationships and contentious relationships with parents of all racial backgrounds—many of the problems had nothing to do with race.

As I have come to know my students and their community over the years, I have realized that being raised to believe in the equality of all people does not necessarily equate to being culturally sensitive. It sounds somewhat simplistic, but knowing people of a different culture well is the best way to become culturally sensitive. There are dimensions of my students' African American, southern-based culture (most of them are only one or two generations removed from living below the Mason-Dixon line) that are very different from those of my own European-American, Irish-Italian Catholic background. For example, many of my students are used to a "call and response" participation structure, which manifests itself in students spontaneously responding aloud to some of the things that I say. It took a while for me to get used to, but over the years I have come to understand and appreciate it. Talking to my students (and African American colleagues) and learning about them has enabled me to appreciate and understand their culture.

I feel it is important to reveal who I am racially, because it sets me apart from my students who tend to think about race a lot. In order to connect with them, I must go the extra mile and try to understand their experiences and views. This has been a key element in the approach I have taken toward literature with my students. For my students, race can be an explosive and sensitive topic. It affects their daily lives in many ways. Most of them have had the experience of a proprietor following them when they are browsing in a store. They often point out: "They don't follow the White kids." My students are alert to people (like teachers or other school staff) who have low expectations of them. They will sometimes complain to me that another teacher "thinks I'm stupid" or "thinks I'm a troublemaker." They believe that *some* people do not see them as potentially successful simply *because* they are African American. Many of them have had few positive interactions with White people outside of the school environment.

Like many people of color in poor, urban neighborhoods, my students often share negative feelings toward the police. They believe that the police target their neighborhoods to look for trouble and that people they know are often wrongly accused of crimes. Again, this is a deeply held belief that is rooted in racism that they have either experienced or been told of by relatives who had these experiences.

Though race and the complex history of this country regarding race permeates my students' lives, they have not always wanted to discuss these issues frankly in class. I believe this resistance sprang from two sources: political correctness on my part and theirs and their deference toward and loyalty to me as their teacher (their White teacher).

I knew I somehow wanted to find a way to engage them on difficult topics, but I was not quite sure how to do this—or how to connect it to our required reading and literature curriculum.

RACE AND CRITICAL LITERACY

I had found that engaging my middle school students in constructive and relevant discussions about literature was sometimes a challenge. Students called the literature that they were required to read "boring" or "corny." It was a daunting task to find literature that both interested students and contained themes that would engage them enough to advance their higher order thinking. Another complicating factor was the nonchallenging, "politically correct" way that I had approached literature in the past. In an attempt to engage students, I used multicultural literature that reflected their culture and heritage, but did so in a superficial "let's be friends and be nice" manner—usually looking for *similarities* between cultures and emphasizing the "happy-ending" stories. This prevented me from helping my students fully explore the kinds of serious topics that profoundly affected their lives.

Then things changed when I participated in a graduate program that addressed critical literacy. I discovered that I could invite students to read texts from a critical perspective (McDaniel, 2006), and in doing so, I became better at engaging my students in thoughtful discussions about race, power, and equality. Since then, we have had stimulating conversations that have tapped their ability to understand and critically evaluate issues of race in their own worlds. One of these explorations involved using picture books that focused on the Negro Baseball Leagues. My aim in using these books was to enhance my students' ability to speak about issues of race and racism. And frankly, I wanted to give my students the ability to appreciate their own heritage.

SHARING BASEBALL STORIES

The first year I shared literature through a critical literacy perspective, I had 30 students in my homeroom class. Of these students, 28 were African American and two were White; 19 were girls and 11 were boys. The reading levels of the students ranged from a 3rd- to a 10th-grade level.

I introduced critical literacy concepts to my students using two books about sports (baseball). Many studies have been done that show students do well in reading and literacy when they read about what they are interested in. Sports books have been shown to be a high interest topic for both boys and girls (Worthy, Moorman, & Turner, 1999). My students enjoy sports and they know that I am a sports fan—they are familiar with my love of baseball, and many of them play or are interested in that sport. I reasoned that if I were going to try to teach them a new way to look at reading, I would have to read something that they were interested in. The two books I chose were *We Are the Ship: The Story of Negro League Baseball*, written and illustrated by Kadir Nelson, and *Teammates*, written by Peter Golenbock and illustrated by Paul Bacon. Both of these books deal with the intertwined history of baseball and racism in this country. Neither book glosses over the horrible aspects of the rampant, overt racism that was prevalent during the era these books represent.

Teammates by Peter Golenbock, illustrated by Paul Bacon (1990)

This book (for elementary-school-age children) tells the true story of an incident that occurred during the first season that Major League Baseball was integrated (1947). Jackie Robinson was the first African American to play in the majors—he was subject to racist taunts and threats (some by his own teammates) throughout the season. During one particularly vicious game in Cincinnati, Robinson's teammate Pee Wee Reese—seeing that Robinson was particularly dispirited by the taunts of the crowd—walked from his position to Robinson's and put his arm around Robinson's shoulders. (Some people remember this incident as occurring in Boston—but even Reese and Robinson claimed they did not remember if they were in Cincinnati or Boston when the incident occurred.) This does not seem like a large gesture in this day and age, but all reports are that the crowd audibly gasped to see a White man and a Black man that friendly.

Golenbock does a fine job setting up the story, briefly describing segregation, the Negro leagues, and Branch Rickey's (the general manager of the Brooklyn Dodgers) search to find the man who could integrate baseball. He also describes Pee Wee Reese's southern background and his feelings that Robinson should be given a fair shot to make the team. Golenbock does not gloss over the realities of segregation or racism—he discusses the Dodgers players' attempts to have Robinson banned from the team, the threats on Robinson's life, and the fact that he was legally prevented from eating or sleeping in the same places as his teammates.

The illustrator also does a commendable job of conveying the nature of overt racism during this time in history. He combines realistic watercolors with actual photographs of the principal characters and reproductions of newspaper headlines that relate to the Ku Klux Klan's terror tactics. There is a particularly compelling drawing of the crowd in Cincinnati that clearly illustrates the hate on the spectators' faces.

This book was published in 1990, and the reviews at the time were favorable. *Publisher's Weekly* (1990) stated, "Golenbock's bold and lucid style distills this difficult issue." Bacon's illustrations were credited with presenting "a haunting portrait of one man's isolation." The *School Library Journal* (1990) also gave *Teammates* a positive review, calling it a "wonderful and important story." This book is said to be for ages 9 to 12, but it can also work very well as a read-aloud in the younger grades. Since its publication in 1990, *Teammates* has become a common read-aloud in many urban and suburban classrooms.

We Are the Ship: The Story of Negro League Baseball, written and illustrated by Kadir Nelson (2008)

Nelson, an acclaimed artist and illustrator of many children's books (*Moses: When Harriet Tubman Led Her People to Freedom*, by Carole Weatherford, and *Ellington Was Not a Street*, by Ntozake Shange), takes on writing for the first time with this book. Nelson uses the first person voice of an anonymous, fictional Negro League player to tell the fascinating story of the Negro Baseball leagues. This is a lengthy book (78 pages), and it tells the complete story of the Negro leagues—from their beginnings after African Americans were tacitly banned from the majors in 1884 to their inevitable demise after the major leagues were integrated in 1947. Nelson covers all aspects of playing and living the life of a Negro leaguer—

he talks about the low pay, the lack of suitable accommodations and eateries, and the threatening, rough treatment from some Whites the players came in contact with. Nelson also conveys the talent of the players, their popularity among fellow African Americans, and their love of playing ball. The author relates the differences in playing style between the "black" and "White" games, and the mixed feelings many people had when the Negro leagues ceased to exist because the integration of the game had been successful.

In telling this story, Nelson conveys the joy of the game, the interesting stories and personalities of many of the players, and the enterprising and sometimes corrupt nature of some of the owners. Many of the owners were African American businessmen, and while most were honest, some were numbers runners and racketeers. In fact, while Nelson does mention this, some reviewers (Baker, 2008) felt that Nelson glossed over this shady part of some Negro league teams. Baker also stated that Nelson's book is "riveting" and "magnificent" (2008). The illustrations are realistic and beautiful—Nelson paints many types of scenes, from Jackie Robinson stealing home to a sign that says "cabins for coloreds." All in all, I think that Nelson has written and illustrated a culturally and historically important book. He does not gloss over the racist era or the difficult lives of players, but he also manages to relay the commitment and talent in the Negro leagues.

READING AND DISCUSSING THE BOOKS

Before we read these two books, I discussed how we would approach them and how we would question what we were reading. I knew my students were used to looking for answers in the text, and they were used to asking what the author's purpose was. The purpose boiled down, for them, to two choices—to inform or entertain. They were not used to questioning an author's or illustrator's motives. I told my students that we would be looking at the literature with a "critical eye." I explained to them that we would question the author's intentions—did he/she have an "agenda"? Was he/she trying to convince us of a certain point-of-view or belief system? Could we detect any of the author's beliefs coming through in the ways they chose to present information? We would ask the same sorts of questions of the illustrators.

Because I had only one copy of each book we were reading, I read them aloud to my students. Even though they are 7th-graders, they still enjoy being read to and there is a benefit for them in hearing books read fluently and expressively. I asked them to take notes as I read—just to jot down any questions they had or impressions they got about the author's or illustrator's intentions.

We read *Teammates* first because it is shorter and, in many ways, a less demanding book. As I read, I made sure the students had a chance to see all the illustrations. I asked them to think about their reactions and the way the story was told.

The students (keeping in mind that this was their first exposure to critical literacy processes) had some good impressions and questions. I first asked them what they thought the author wanted to communicate—most of them mentioned racism. They believed that the author wanted to communicate that individual people could fight racism.

They also enjoyed the story, simply as a story—most of them enjoy sports and this is a classic sports story. I decided to ask them a question that was a little more controversial: I told them that I liked this book quite a bit and asked them if my being White might have something to do with my liking the book. (I was the only White person in the room that day.) At first, they looked at me strangely and asked me to repeat the question. When I did, several children said that I might like the story as a White person because it shows that all White people were not racist—even during the time of segregation. I agreed with that opinion and told them my belief that most White people who consider themselves unprejudiced would probably like to believe that they would have acted as Pee Wee Reese acted—even if they had lived in a more overtly racist era.

Since this was our first attempt at critical literacy processes, I was pleased with the students' willingness to try to think in a new way. Research notes that many middle-years students—especially African American boys—may drift away from and become uninterested in reading because they perceive many literacy activities to be culturally irrelevant (Hall & Piazza, 2008).

The students listened attentively and responded enthusiastically to the text and illustrations. Even though I teach 7th-graders, they still loved the illustrations in this book. When they saw the painting of the angry ballpark crowd yelling at Jackie Robinson, they said things like "they are really mean." I pushed and questioned them a little, asking them to look at the composition of the crowd (all White). "What are you really saying when you say 'mean'?" I asked. A couple of students finally said that they really meant racist. They also said that because I was White they did not want to offend me. This was an opportunity for me to assure them that I was fully aware that some White people are racist, and it was fine to talk about that. Another aspect of this story that touched them was the friendship angle. In response to the incident when Pee Wee Reese walked over to Jackie Robinson and put his arm around him, one of my male students said, "You never want your friend to be upset." They know from their own experience how important even one understanding friend can be.

Next we read *We Are the Ship*. We had to read this book over several days because it is a much longer text that tells a complex story. Since this text discusses racism and the effects of segregation in detail, I anticipated a lively discussion and many questions. The students really warmed to the topic—I had read the author's note first because I wanted them to hear Kadir Nelson's story of being fascinated by his research into this part of African American history. One of my male students was eager to share his rather extensive background knowledge about the Negro leagues with the class and his peers listened intently to him. Although we weren't quite doing critical literacy, yet, I think this kind of discussion prepared them to think differently and critically about texts.

As we read more of the story, with its descriptions of the Jim Crow south and the struggles of the leagues to survive, the students related incidents in the text to other instances of segregation they knew about. When the narrator mentioned not being able to eat at most restaurants in the towns they played in, several students mentioned a similar scene in a popular movie, *Remember the Titans*. I asked the students what they thought the title of the book meant. The title comes from Rube Foster's quote about the Negro leagues, "We are the ship, all else the sea." When they heard the entire quote, the students had a couple of interesting responses. One of my students said, "It means that we (African Americans) can get through trouble." Another student said, "It means that we are a family—we're all together—like on a ship."

When I asked the students what they thought the author/illustrator had wanted to communicate in writing this story. I asked them to think critically:

Did the author want to win them over to a certain point of view? Did he want to convince them of something? Had he portrayed the people in his book in a certain way?

Most all of them agreed that Nelson, in telling this story, had wanted to take a part of African American and American history and "give it attention," "tell about other great players," and "talk about *our* past."

After we read these books, several of my students had an interesting question for me. They wanted to know if I (their White teacher) had lived "back then" (in the era of segregation) what side I would have been on. Several of my students have asked me this over the years in response to different topics. I tried to be honest and said that, of course, I like to believe that I would have been against segregation, but that there is no way to really know. This led into a discussion of the racist attitudes that parents instill in their children and if and how these attitudes can be overcome. They pointed out that Pee Wee Reese had been raised in the segregated south, but was able to become friends with Jackie Robinson. The more we talked, the more it seemed they could see the possibility that White people, even while immersed in a racist environment, could unlearn racial prejudice. I knew we had arrived at a pivotal moment when students began to grow in their racial understanding.

When discussing Pee Wee Reese's southern background in relation to his defense of Jackie Robinson's right to be on the team, one of my students commented, "He [Pee Wee] liked talent more than he *dis*-liked Blacks." This statement required that my student saw the situation from Reese's perspective. In reflecting on this student's comment later, I realized that I could have nudged students toward a more critical conversation about Reese's motives. On one hand, Reese may have been willing to put aside his racist attitude to have a talented player on his team so that he and other Whites could be the primary beneficiaries of the team's success. In other words, he still may have held racist views. Then again, Reese received so much criticism for having Robinson on the team, that he could be positioned as White ally and a true crusader for racial integration.

My students were also able to question and wonder about the many disparate feelings brought about by the demise of the Negro leagues. While they all agreed that the integration of Major League Baseball was a positive thing, they were able to ask complicated questions such as, "Is it a little sad that the Negro leagues had to die?" and "Were all Blacks happy about integration?" They were also able to have a fairly complicated discussion about the virtues of "having your own stuff" (the Negro leagues) versus "being with other types of people" (joining the major leagues). Being able to look at both sides of an issue is a hallmark of higher-order thinking.

Teaching through the lens of critical literacy perspective gave my students permission to talk about race. At the end of this period, the students asked me if they could talk. I said yes. They asked about the origins of slavery, and as we were having a brief discussion about slavery throughout civilization, one of my quieter students raised her hand. I called on her, and she asked, "Mrs. Luebbert, do we (African Americans) speak *broken* English?" I really was stunned and wondered where she had heard that characterization of African American Language (AAL). We talked for a while about the origins of AAL and the differences between it and more Standardized English. Due to scheduling, this discussion was brief—but the students asked me later if we could continue it. We will.

ANALYZING THE EXPERIENCE

Because I am a White woman and the large majority of my students are African American, I think that the issue of race has always been an undercurrent in my class. Occasionally, a student would ask me what I thought about racism or my opinion about something "White people" do or did (the girls often ask about hair). They also sometimes ask me about my ethnic/racial background. I always tried to answer questions honestly, but I never really had explicit discussions about race or if they thought what they were learning was culturally important. Through this unit, I have formed a closer bond of trust with my students. It now seems as though an invisible cultural fence between us has been lifted and we can now talk frankly about issues of race and racism.

I also noticed a major shift in my students' attention to their studies as a result of this unit. Many of my students who were not always invested in their studies suddenly showed a great interest in these books and discussions. During these readings and discussions, my students were completely attentive. I have to think that it was because this discussion and the material was truly interesting to them. The permission to openly talk about race seemed to be a relief. I think it can be a little exhausting to always act as if race is not noticed or does not matter. Obviously, African American children know from their daily experience that race does matter.

This unit opened the floodgates for talking about race. Shortly after reading the baseball stories, my students began to question things they read about in social studies. While studying the period in American history that led to the Civil War, students who were assigned to write about John Brown were fascinated by the person one boy came to call "the crazy White man." One of my students said, "I know why a Black man would do it (fight against slavery), but why would a White man?" In their presentation, they touched on topics like why a person of one race would give his life for members of another, and how religious belief can influence a person's actions. When they studied other historical figures, such as the "Apostle of Freedom" Richard Allen, they were able to express pride in his amazing life as well as dismay at the fact that his accomplishments are less well known than those of many White abolitionists. They decided it was racism (and they were probably right)—one girl stated, "I guess White people write about White people [in history books]."

The students responded so eagerly to talking openly about race that I can only surmise that it is something they have needed to talk about. Although I think that our school does a better job than many with using a variety of culturally relevant materials, I think that many teachers are still using what Banks (1994) would call the "contributions" or "additive" approach to teaching and curriculum design. The contributions approach celebrates cultural diversity by focusing on foods, holidays, and superficial dimensions of culture and is generally linked to certain holidays. The additive approach "adds" to the curriculum materials that focus on cultural diversity without really changing students' perspectives about people who are culturally different from themselves. Neither approach is critical in terms of helping students become aware of power relationships between groups of people and how to work toward a more socially just society. I believe there is still much room to be transformative in the literacy curriculum, addressing both literacy standards and, in the process, providing students with the analytical tools to critically evaluate texts and society.

This experience has really made me realize that what Freire (1997) says about all literacy being political is absolutely true. I used to think that politics was irrelevant to my work as a teacher. The truth is that what we choose to teach or not teach carries a political message: We can convey that we think a culture is important, worthwhile, or irrelevant by what we choose to teach and discuss. Giving the students permission to discuss difficult, controversial topics actually contributes to them being able to recognize that their social and cultural capital is worthwhile. This type of teaching practice also helps students and teachers value the funds of knowledge that different cultures bring to school.

CONCLUSION

Critical literacy has been key to strengthening my students' motivation to read and their understanding of texts. My students were eager to discuss the controversial ideas and perspectives contained in books that held their interest. Our engaging discussions helped students become more knowledgeable about a pivotal period of time in our nation's history when forced segregation was beginning to be dismantled. These discussions helped all of us, including myself, become more comfortable addressing race and racism in the classroom. In order to justify our critical literacy activities to administrators and districts, as we must do, it is important to explain the significance of critical literacy for motivating students and for developing higher-order thinking skills. The experience of using critical literacy strategies with students can put all teachers on the road to transformative teaching. It is not always simple to openly discuss uncomfortable topics such as racism, but I believe that this process is worthwhile because it can help students feel empowered in school. Most importantly, critical literacy can help students become the knowledgeable and involved citizens they need to be to fully participate in a democratic society.

MAKE THIS HAPPEN IN YOUR CLASSROOM

- Maintain honesty in your classroom. I teach mostly 7th- and 8th-grade students, and when I first started working with this age group I realized several important things: They are precariously placed between the lure of becoming adults and the relative comfort of remaining children. They are looking (albeit unconsciously) at the different ways in which the adults they know live and conduct their lives. Adult lives are of such interest to them because they are beginning to figure out how they might live their lives. They have little tolerance for dishonesty (from adults) in any form. Since students this age are avidly searching for answers and challenging the world's assumptions, I decided that in my classroom I would answer all honest questions honestly. By this I mean if students ask me a question honestly, maturely, and respectfully, I will answer it to the best of my ability. This includes questions about difficult topics like illness (mental and physical), sexually transmitted diseases, and, sometimes, my own personal beliefs. I admit this can be an uncomfortable and treacherous area for many educators, but I believe that it has always served me well. I also believe it paved the way for me to institute the critical literacy process with my students.
- Establish a "safe zone" for talking about controversial topics. Even if you are not comfortable answering questions on all topics, it is important to establish honest, open communication with students in your classroom. They should know that it is acceptable to voice their

opinions on literature and other topics and that you will hear them out. This kind of open, respectful communication sets a great tone for introducing the critical literacy process. The critical literacy process can surprise students at first because it is not about getting the "right" answer—it is about discussing relevant and important topics. Sometimes, students are afraid they "will get in trouble" for their honest opinion on a story or an author's motive. When the teacher is of a different race or ethnic background from the students, some students can also worry about offending him/her. If a climate of open communication has been established in the classroom, the critical literacy process will not seem completely strange to your students. Make sure you let them know that they will not be in trouble for voicing their opinions as long as they are respectful of others. At first, this process can seem awkward. We all (including students) have become very used to being politically correct in our speech and in expressing ideas and feelings. Critical literacy dissolves these barricades. I believe, however, that students of elementary and middle school age are well suited to this process because they are young and not as entrenched in their habits as adults tend to be.

- Choose literature with powerful themes that are of interest to your students. I find that students can relate and ask astute and interesting questions when they feel some kind of connection to the people and events in the story. My students have always responded well to sports stories—this is something that most of them connect with. Other subjects have proved more difficult, but doable with persistence. When my class (largely African American) studied and read about the Japanese-American internment during World War II, they could not seem to connect or find enough in common with this experience to speak critically about it. However, when we looked at and wrote about archival photos of Japanese Americans before and during the internment, my students were particularly struck by their realizations. Looking at pictures of the Japanese-American neighborhoods, students said things like, "They remind me of me and my friends" or "This could be my neighborhood."

REFERENCES

Baker, K. (2008, June 15). A league of their own. *New York Times*.

Banks, J. A. (1994). *Multiethnic education: Theory and practice*. Boston: Allyn and Bacon.

Copenhaver, J. F. (2000). Silence in the classroom: Learning to talk about issues of race. *Dragon Lode, 18*, 8–16.

Freire, P. (1997). *Pedagogy of the oppressed.* New York: Continuum.

Golenbock, P., & Bacon, P. (1990). *Teammates.* New York: Doubleday.

Hall, L. A., & Piazza, S. V. (2008). Critically reading texts: What students can do and how teachers can help. *Reading Teacher, 62*(1), 32–41.

McDaniel, C. (2006). *Critical literacy: A way of thinking, a way of life.* New York: Peter Lang Publishing.

Nelson, K. (2008). *We are the ship: The story of Negro league baseball.* New York: Jump at the Sun/Hyperion.

Publishers Weekly. (1990). Editorial review of *Teammates.* Retrieved November 15, 2008, from www.amazon.com

School Library Journal. (1990). Editorial review of *Teammates.* Retrieved November 15, 2008, from www.amazon.com

Worthy, J., Moorman, M., & Turner, M. (1999). What Johnny likes to read is hard to find in school. *Reading Research Quarterly, 34*(1), 12–27.

Part III

BUILDING RELATIONSHIPS WITH STUDENTS AND CAREGIVERS

Fostering positive relationships with students is the gateway to establishing a climate of trust and mutual respect in the classroom. Such a climate is esstential for helping students see how school-valued literacies and languages are useful and important to their academic success. It is also important to reach out to parents and see them as resources for understanding students and the challenges that families often face. The first chapters in this section focus on how teachers establish these relationships and how doing so matters for raising students' motivation and achievement.

In the 1980s, Dr. Patricia Edwards expounded on the message of home and school collaboration when she designed the *Parents as Partners in Reading* program. When teaching parents to read to their children, she discovered that the parents couldn't read the simplest children's book. In response, she began a community crusade, visiting saloons, churches, food stores, and shops, preaching the importance of reading, writing, and talking. Her efforts produced a ground swell of interest that created a program to teach parents to read as they read to their children. Dr. Edwards interviewed parents to learn about their children and in the process learned about the families and community. As she states, "You want your medical doctor to know your history, so why wouldn't you want your child's teacher to know your child's history? The doctor and the teacher both want to help you, so it just makes sense to have that information."

Culturally responsive teaching begins with the work that Pat prescribes. It then takes the information gained and connects it to the standard school curriculum, giving each child an authentic look at each discipline's content as it relates to family and community.

This blurring of boundaries between home and school and community and school plays into the African proverb "It takes a village to educate a child." When teachers and families form relationships for the education of the children, students are more likely to achieve success in school and in life. Families and communities are the first teachers of children. They have information not found in student files. Often, parents feel intimidated by schools and the highly educated teachers. They may also fear negative comments about their children from teachers—the same comments they heard when they were in school. As a result, they may avoid conferences and curriculum nights or open house events at school (Edwards, 2004; Li, 2009; Ruggiano Schmidt, 2005). Therefore, it is absolutely essential that teachers reach out to parents and attempt to make contact before the school year begins or early in the school year during the first ten weeks. Positive expressions during first conversations set the stage for the year. Asking the parents how to make this the best year ever for "Julie" or "Tyreek" is a good way to start. Similar to teachers in the previous part of this book, teachers in this part also describe their methods for communicating and connecting for culturally responsive literacy teaching.

REFERENCES

Edwards, P. A. (2004). *Children's literacy development*. Boston: Pearson.

Li, G. (2009). *Multicultural families, home literacies, and mainstream schooling.* Charlotte, NC: Information Age.

Ruggiano Schmidt, P. R. (2005). *Preparing educators to communicate and connect with families and communities.* Greenwich, CT: Information Age.

CHAPTER 7

Extending a Lifeline by Extending Oneself

Gurkan Kose

Teaching is a cultural activity. We learn how to teach indirectly, through years of participation in classroom life (Hiebert & Stiggler, 1999). While studying mathematics education at the undergraduate and graduate levels, teaching seemed to be a profession that I could easily manage. I was able to build a good relationship with students during my student teaching, without any need to take their out-of-school lives into consideration. Most of them were from middle- or upper-class families with high expectations.

One of the two milestones in my teaching career was my first year teaching at an urban school in a small city in the Northeast. That first year of full-time teaching taught me more than any other previous learning experience. It was a milestone because I investigated ways to build relationships with students through mostly extracurricular activities. I was able to understand how my students felt about life, school, and other things. The reflections of those activities were very powerful "catalyzers" for my regular teaching hours.

The second milestone was about my perception of teaching and learning of mathematics. When I started the doctoral program in mathematics education at the large university in the city where I taught, my "traditional" view had changed in many different ways. I realized the importance of being sensitive about cultural and academic diversity within the instruction.

THE FIRST MILESTONE

I heard about a teaching position from a friend of mine, who, at the time, was a graduate assistant at the university. It all happened so quickly and I found myself in front of 7th- and 8th-graders, most of whom I thought did not have much interest in learning anything, especially mathematics. It was a public charter school with a population that was 80% African American, 10% Caucasian, and 10% Latino-Hispanic and other ethnicities. About 85% of the students were on the Federal Free or Reduced Lunch Program. The disciplinary problems were the main focus of the school during its second year of operation. In this school, if you were a teacher who could occupy the students in the classroom for 45-minute periods without any trouble, you would be recognized as a "good teacher." Believe me, it was not an easy task! I remember one day, when a group of eight girls started singing in the middle of the class period, I could do nothing to stop this. Sometimes they would start arguments around boyfriend/girlfriend issues or even "less sophisticated" conflicts. Almost all of my students would run out of the classroom when they heard a staff member yelling at a student or a student screaming "Fight! Fight! Fight!" in the hallway. Even very minor incidents like this used to impact the school atmosphere in negative ways. The administrators, teachers, and students would be "down," and would only talk about what happened, leaving academics behind.

My classroom, Room 106, was bare, floor to ceiling, so I began to decorate with lists of rules. First I created a list of behaviors entitled Classroom Values: Take Care of Yourself, Take Care of Others, Take Care of This Place. I was able to refer to the classroom values easily when I was not happy with a student's behavioral or academic status. The second list contained clear instructions called Classroom Procedures. It took me about four class periods to go over each and every procedure. I even asked the students to role-play some of the items like pencil sharpening. I would not let any student use the electric sharpener during class periods. The procedure was as follows: Raise your pencil when you need it sharpened. I give you the message that I am aware of your need by raising my index finger up (meaning I need a minute to help you because I am busy teaching an important concept). Then I take your pencil and give you one from my set of sharpened pencils. At the end of the class we exchange pencils one more time, so nobody gets distracted because of the noise of the sharpener. Unfortunately, none of the methods courses or general education courses taught me such ideas. I had to observe the students who would use that machine as an excuse to stand up, walk around, and just make some noise. This procedure prevented arguments and encouraged continuous work.

My daily intensive planning for the next day's lessons took place 2 to 3 hours after school and included not only lesson preparation, but also designing procedures for handling misbehavior. Sometimes I rehearsed speeches during those hours before calling the parents of disruptive students. When it came to talking to a mother about her son, I had to sit down and think carefully. I had to take into consideration that phone calls from teachers or other officials may not be welcomed in this high-poverty community; at least, it was a cultural assumption I had about my students' families. That's why I would always find positive things to start the conversation, so that she would know I cared about her son. Based on the anticipated parent responses, I would filter the records of the student and find ways to prevent potential arguments. I would explain that I would work with her child during the week for extra hours. *I am available on Tuesdays, Wednesdays, and Thursdays after school for extra help. Can you please tell him to sign up on the tutoring sign up on the tutoring sheet in the classroom? Also, I ask that you pick up your child whenever he stays after.* Within a couple days after this conversation I would find one positive thing to add to the child's records and call the parent back for a progress report: *I wanted to thank you for your support, he was very attentive today in class and he did a great job on his homework. You should be very proud of him!* This was encouraging to the parent and the child, thus motivating the fact that we as the adults should work together.

One of the most critical things that helped me build good relationships with students was spending time with them outside of regular school hours. This first started with after-school tutoring sessions. I was sincere about appreciating and praising my students, especially the ones who would try hard during extra hours. I always offered them cookies and candies, even though they were behind with the assignments and completing their back work. The news spread quickly and I started having at least five students three times a week. This growing group from different classes would also help me during regular class hours. I made "buddies" who would quiet down the classroom, pass out worksheets, clean up the board, and support me in cases of misunderstandings with some students and parents.

The second group was my Mathcounts team. Mathcounts can be defined as follows:

> Mathcounts is a national enrichment club and competition program that promotes middle school mathematics achievement through grassroots involvement in every U.S. state and territory. At the beginning of each school year, the Mathcounts Foundation provides a complimentary copy of its *School Handbook* to every middle school across the country. Teachers and volunteers use the handbook and activities to coach student Mathletes®, as part of in-class instruction or as an extracurricular activity. (Mathcounts Foundation, 2010)

I was meeting with a small group of 7th- and 8th-graders every Saturday morning for 3 hours. The mathematical problems we discussed were above their academic level at the time, but they enjoyed talking about engaging contexts; it did not feel like doing math, but just like solving real problems of real people. During those sessions, I found myself making so many jokes and being more *casual* and *informal*. They would talk about those sessions with other students during the week and that group also increased in size.

RAY

Ray became one of the 7th-graders in the Mathcounts group. He was one of the toughest kids in the building, being extremely talkative and hyper. I don't remember one class period that he did not perform at least one of the following: running around the classroom, dropping other students' notebooks and pencils, hitting another student with a straightedge, making strange noises, laughing loudly, or talking back to me without permission. Ray's mom, Candice, was a strong, eventually supportive single parent. She was different from other parents I met that year in a number of ways. My first communication with her was through her "generic e-mail" to all of Ray's teachers in the beginning of the school year. She informed the teachers about the strengths and weaknesses of Ray, and she also suggested some strategies to handle his misbehavior. She also planned to keep the lines of communication open with the school staff to improve Ray's behavior. However, most school staff did not like to communicate with her, because she doggedly pursued in depth details about any negative school occurrence.

A few months after I started teaching Ray, I sent an e-mail to Candice stating my concerns about her son's nonstop classroom disruptions. Her response shocked me: "Can it be because he is getting bored in your class? He says he completes the work ahead of anyone else in class and then he gets bored." This was a message for me to reevaluate and reflect honestly on what I was doing everyday in my classroom. She was right! All I did those days was begin my lesson with timed practice problems, follow with a lecture on a new topic, and then give them exercises that mirrored what I had done on the board. There was no transition between activities at all, because everything was very routine and pre-planned. A friend of mine, who had more experience in teaching math, told me how he was able to engage his students with the "24 Game" cards. In this game, students are expected to make 24 using each of the four numbers given on a card exactly once using four basic operations. From that point on, I started challenging my students like Ray with the 24 Game and a few Mathcounts problems. I think it was the first time I realized differentiation was needed to meet the needs of students with several different backgrounds. Ray liked being challenged and after his first success, he expected advanced problems from me.

That year, the Chapter Competition was a turning point for Ray and my other "Mathletes." As we entered the contest area, I noticed my students whispering anxiously to each other and I heard two of my students say, "Ray, we are the only Black people in this room! It is all Whites and Asians; I don't think we can do well in here today! There is no way we can go to the State Competition . . ."

As they anticipated, we did not rank that year. But, Ray told me he wanted to start preparing for the year after right away! So we continued meeting on Saturdays and I promised a field trip to an amusement park that summer for the students with good attendance and performance. When I announced the trip, the students started saving money and even created a fundraiser.

That summer I rented three rooms near an amusement park and hit the highway with two girls, four boys, and the mother of one of the girls. We worked on Mathcounts problems for 4 days, starting at 9:00 in the morning until 3:00 in the afternoon. Then, we would go to the amusement park and be back to the hotel by 8:00 in the evening. We would watch a movie and evaluate the day before going to bed. By listening to their daily conversations I found out about their lives at home, the issues that drove them crazy, and things they liked and disliked. Even though it was a program with a small group of students, I was able to apply most of my learning on that trip to a broader audience during the following years.

At the end of our trip, I assigned each student packages with 200 problems to be completed over the summer, and most completed the assignment. In short, that trip helped students realize that it was a good thing to be excited about mathematics. They started talking about doing better than the "Whites and Asians."

During my second year at the school, I felt more confident. Simple strategies like showing the entire class pictures from the trip during the last 5 minutes of the period, or just assigning one of the pictures as my desktop background would trigger conversations around how much fun we had during the trip. Those kinds of things helped me get more and more students to believe in the idea that "Math is fun!" That year, my relationship with Ray evolved as well. He would look me in the eye and understand I was not going to be happy with what he was about to do. Then, he would change his mind and act appropriately.

On the morning of Mathcounts Competition day, my students were excited. They felt prepared, and Ray was running and jumping all around the contest area. At the end of the written competition, while we were waiting for the scores, Ray stepped into the room, smiling, holding his hand on his mouth to keep himself calm. He approached me and said, "Mr. Kose, we made it! We've got the second place as a team, we are going to the State Finals!" I told him to calm down, because we had to watch the Countdown Round, and we had to act professional until the award ceremony. After the third place team was announced, it was time for us to yell, scream, and jump! "The Second Place Team this year is the team from City Academy of Science! Congratulations!"

"Hard Work Adds Up to Success" was the headline in the local newspaper after we gave them an interview at school. A week later, we were at the evening news of a local TV channel.

When we went to the state finals, we placed 36th out of 52 top schools. This helped the students realize that they still had a lot of work to do. About a month after the state finals, I challenged them to come on Saturdays to study for the Math A High School Exam, even though they were only 8th-graders. Twenty-two students attended that program and at the end of six weeks, ten took the exam, passed it with good scores, and earned high school credit for mathematics. That small group of Saturday students grew rapidly. By the junior year, they were preparing for the SATs and visiting colleges.

Ray was one of the students who skipped Algebra 1, the regular 9th-grade course, and started high school math with Geometry. My relationship with him and his mother turned into mutual friendship with my wife and me. My communication with Candice was always around mutual trust and understanding. One day she said, "My husband decided not to be a father for my son. His older brother is 32 and lives far away from us . . . so you are the *only male role model for him*. He respects you so much."

ACADEMIC FIELD TRIPS

Having an academic-oriented trip at the end of each school year became a custom for me. One year we went to Boston, studied for college entrance exams, and visited Yale, Harvard, and MIT. I arranged a trip to Cornell University's Department of Architecture for Ray and two more students who were interested in architecture.

Another trip was a 2-week-long trip to the Netherlands, Belgium, France, and Turkey. Not only myself, but also the students learned through spending time together. They had chances to appreciate diversity through their engagement in cultural activities in different countries. They also learned how to behave as mature adults during those trips.

Ray was one of the few 11th-graders taking AP Calculus. It was a college-level course, and it required conceptual understanding of the entire school mathematics, from kindergarten to high school. I started problem-solving sessions for my calculus group. Most of them were working after school at part-time jobs and it was hard to arrange. We started meeting every Thursday morning in my class. They would come to school at around 7:45. I would buy donuts, Ray would bring coffee for the group, and we would work on problems until 8:55. Then they would go to their first period classes at 9:00. They felt very special about this, since most of the faculty was not in the building during those sessions. These students were the only students who were allowed to enter the building on Thursday mornings that early.

Our trip to an Ivy League University during spring recess was another success. We stayed at a hotel and studied calculus in high-tech classrooms. I invited a senior math teacher, author of two major textbooks on statistics and calculus, to give my students some tricks before the AP exam. He talked about how the exams were being scored, common mistakes made by students, and test taking tips for raising their scores. All of those students including Ray qualified for college credits on the AP Calculus Exam.

PARENT SUPPORT

One thing I need to state is that parental support came after they believed in my goals and objectives about their children's future. This did not happen in just 1 year. I continuously had to be in contact with them through home visits, phone calls, and e-mails. I tried to attend students' out-of-school activities as much as I could.

Ray now is a senior and waiting to hear from universities like Cornell, Caltech, and UC San Diego. I believe he will continue to be successful for the rest of his life.

THE SECOND MILESTONE:
BEING CULTURALLY SENSITIVE WITHIN THE INSTRUCTION

When I was in college, I found the ideas and theories I was taught very ineffective and inapplicable. Part of the reason for this was my professors' lack of experience in real classrooms. Later on, I started taking graduate courses from a college in the city where I taught. The course named Multicultural Literacy Methods was the first time I really enjoyed an education course. The instructor, Dr. Patricia Ruggiano Schmidt, was very resourceful about culturally responsive instruction. I was a practitioner in the classroom, so my practices were results of experience most of the time. But, when I was introduced to Dr. Ruggiano Schmidt's ABCs of Cultural Understanding and Communication model (Ruggiano Schmidt & Finkbeiner, 2006), everything started making more sense. I realized that what I was trying to do constituted a kind of culturally responsive teaching. Gay (2000) defines culturally responsive teaching:

> . . . using the cultural characteristics, experiences, and perspectives of ethnically diverse students as conduits for teaching them more effectively. It is based on the assumption that when academic knowledge and skills are situated within the lived experiences and frames of reference of students, they are more personally meaningful, have higher interest appeal, and are learned more easily and thoroughly.

As a math teacher in a diverse setting, I found this definition very descriptive and practical. Spending time with the students outside of regular classroom hours helped me to design my instruction around the lived experiences of my students. For instance, I remember listening to my students during a trip while they were arguing about the free-throw averages of famous basketball players. I realized basketball was a very effective tool to engage African American students, especially in rich discussions involving mathematical concepts such as mean, ratio, and proportion. Hence, I decided to write my group activities and homework questions about such sports statistics.

Another idea was to use music as a tool for culturally responsive mathematics teaching. I found a Web-based application (Rensselaer Polytechnic Institute, 2004) that makes use of rhythm wheels to present ratios and proportional reasoning. I used to take my students to the computer lab and give them assignments on rhythm wheels. Using these wheels, students had the chance to choose from different music styles like hip-hop, rock, country, folk, and so on. They would make rhythm wheels of 3 to 4 loops and recognize the least common multiple of the numbers, so that when they played the rhythms, the music ended at the same time the rhythmic loop ended. For instance, having three instruments on a wheel and four on the other one, the loop length had to be twelve so that they could stop at the same time. Through this activity, students were actively involved in a culturally relevant and enjoyable math lesson.

But my first graduate-level course, Mathematical Communication, after I started the doctoral program was an eye-opening experience for me. My professor was always prepared with wonderful ideas and discussions for the course meetings. She had experience in several different math classrooms;

so she knew what would actually work and what would not. The focus of the course was on reading, writing, and oral communication within the mathematics classrooms. I had a chance to read researchers' studies and started applying some of their ideas in my classroom. When I experienced even my low-achieving students succeeding with sophisticated content, like exponential and logarithmic functions, graphical transformations, and trigonometric functions, I was very proud.

One of the most important things that helped me deliver culturally responsive instruction was using language that enabled students to comprehend the concepts better. Unfortunately, my students did not have the academic language background that is valued at school. Students do not automatically use precise mathematical language—teachers need to guide them in doing so (Cobb, Wood, & Yackel, 1994)—neither do they understand when we talk using formal mathematical vocabulary. Therefore, the teacher's role is critical at this point. I started with everyday language that is familiar to the students. I let the students develop an appreciation of the need for precise definitions (National Council of Teachers of Mathematics, 2000). I tried using bridging language, which I created with the students during class discussions (Herbel-Eisenmann, 2002). Examples would be calling the "slope" of a line the "steepness" or naming an exponential function in the context of a bacteria growth problem as "doubling function."

I also realized that it is important to choose *rich tasks* that are worth exploring. For something to be a problem for a student, he or she must (1) see it as a challenge and (2) want to know the answer (Hiebert, 1997). Also, I found that it was critical to give students exercises that they could accomplish successfully; this helped them focus on the mathematics of the problem. By experience, I found out that students shut down easily and would say, "This is so hard and complicated; there is no way I can answer this question." In such a case, there is little you can do to help them. But, if you plan tasks that offer success to *all* students, then with proper scaffolding, you can guide them to success. I found exploratory statements that start with "Tell me what you know about" to be very powerful. Provided with an appropriate entry point, the student finds himself or herself engaged in doing mathematics. And that engagement breeds confidence. Letting my students *wrestle* with good problems for a while before showing them the solution also helped them a lot for building self-confidence.

Creating a discourse-rich classroom environment is another thing that is critical when working with a diverse group of students. If young people are asked to work in silence and they are not asked to offer their own ideas and perspectives, they often feel disempowered and disenfranchised, ultimately choosing to leave mathematics even when they have performed well (Boaler, 2000). It was not easy at the beginning since the students were not ready to share their ideas in front of their peers. They also did not welcome comments or critics. But I tried to model using incomplete and/or incorrect answers as teachable moments, being kind about criticisms and freely sharing ideas with the whole group. Eventually, through many practices, they learned how to discuss things properly.

MAKE THIS HAPPEN IN YOUR CLASSROOM

- Understanding how students feel about life, school, and other things is the most critical item on my list for being culturally responsive in the classroom. This happens if you spend time with the students through academic and nonacademic trips, extra study hours, and by attending their out-of-school activities.
- When working with parents, it is very important to give them the *sincere* message that you don't have any personal issues with their children. Contacting them more for progress reports and less for problems would be a way to achieve that. Home visits, in-person meetings, and at least phone calls and e-mails are the important tools you can use to gain their support.
- When it comes to instructional strategies, one thing that helped me most is the use of *bridging language* (Herbel-Eisenmann, 2002). You cannot disregard the kind of languages that students bring to classroom. That's why it is crucial to make sure you use a language that helps them *own* the big ideas of mathematics, even though they give them different names!
- Being very careful about choosing tasks that engage the kids and create opportunities to be successful is the next thing. We have to make sure *none* of the students shut down before even trying.
- Creating a classroom environment that welcomes the ideas of each and every student helps improve the classroom culture. The best way to achieve this important goal for me was through modeling and practice. You, as the teacher, have to show what you expect from them.

REFERENCES

Boaler, J. (2000). *Multiple perspectives on mathematics teaching and learning.* Westport, CT: Ablex.

Cobb, P., Wood, T., & Yackel, E. (1994). *Discourse, mathematical thinking, and classroom practice*. New York: Oxford University Press.

Gay, G. (2000). *Culturally responsive teaching: Theory, research, and practice*. New York: Teachers College Press.

Herbel-Eisenmann, B. A. (2002). Using student contributions and multiple representations to develop mathematical language. *Mathematics Teaching in the Middle School, 8*(2), 100–105.

Hiebert, J. E. (1997). *Making sense: Teaching and learning mathematics with understanding*. Portsmouth, NH: Heinemann.

Hiebert, J. E., & Stiggler, J. (1999). *The teaching gap: Best ideas from the world's teachers for improving education in the classroom*. New York: Free Press.

Mathcounts Foundation. (2010, April 27). Mathcounts Foundation—About us—How it works. Retrieved April 27, 2010, from https://mathcounts.org/Page.aspx?pid=207

National Council of Teachers of Mathematics. (2000). *Principles and standards for school mathematics*. Reston, VA: NCTM.

Rensselaer Polytechnic Institute, (2004). *Web-based application*. Retrieved April, 2010 from http://rcos.cs.rpi.edu/

Ruggiano Schmidt, P. R., & Finkbeiner, C. (2006). *ABCs of cultural understanding and communication: National and international adaptations*. Greenwich, CT: Information Age.

CHAPTER 8

From Pasta to Poets

Creating a Classroom Community Through Cultural Sharing

Kevin Salamone

In my 7 years of teaching middle school English in an urban classroom, I have come to regard relationship building through connections with the home and community to be paramount in fostering student achievement. I find every phone call I make to the home (I average about 250 a year), every student interview with a parent or community elder (I assign several a year), every meeting I have with a parent, and every open classroom event I sponsor brings me closer to the students both personally and academically. This intimacy helps me to strategize in terms of planning, and it ultimately maximizes student achievement. When I have a deeper academic and social connection with my students, I can find more creative ways to motivate them. From a sheer selfish perspective, I enjoy my students more as individuals and I enjoy my teaching experience more.

I think every middle school teacher looks for ways to focus the energy that every student possesses. We all want well-behaved, motivated students, so we want that control that makes a classroom hum with learning. In my experience, the urban teacher should begin and end the search for such magic by building relationships and involving the home with the learning process. My classroom is not perfect by any means. Just like any other middle school teacher, I struggle for that perfect balance of control, rigor, and student engagement. I think every teacher understands that this is a constant struggle without a perfect solution. I will, however, say my test scores have increased more than 30% in the past 4 years, with most students passing, and my level of culturally responsive teaching appears to be the key to student success.

MY SCHOOL, MY CLASSROOM, MY STUDENTS

I am in my 7th year as a 7th- and 8th-grade English language arts teacher. I work in a small Northeastern urban school in a small city tragically experiencing 40% to 50% unemployment in the school's part of town. I am 47 years old, and this is my second career. My school is typically diverse for an urban school with 59% of all students eligible for either free or reduced-price lunch. Fifty-eight percent of all students in the school are African American, 35% are Caucasian, 4% are Hispanic, 1% are Asian, and 1% are Native American. This school serves pre-kindergarten through 8th grade and is relatively small in terms of student body. Each grade level boasts only three sections. My three sections usually have about 25 students per classroom. About one-third of all students have an Individualized Education Plan.

My classroom practices are shaped by the co-teaching model used in our school. Representatives from Schools of Promise, a program run out of a local university's school of education, entered our school in a consulting role. They looked at the teaching resources and the special education model utilized in our school and determined that our students can be better served by converting to a complete inclusion model where all students with an Individualized Education Plan are included in every classroom with minimal (if any) pull-outs or separate attention. Each classroom has two adults co-teaching every lesson. I am currently sharing my teaching responsibilities with another teacher who is dually certified in English and Special Education. We share all teaching responsibilities, from planning, to classroom instruction, and, even, to grading. Even though my co-teacher is the special education teacher in charge of the IEP goals for all students who have them, I work directly with all of his students in the classroom. Conversely, even though I am the regular education "teacher of record" for these classrooms, you will see my co-teacher delivering an equal amount of general classroom instruction.

The special education efforts in the classroom are, therefore, transparent. Anyone stepping into our classroom would have a hard time telling who was a typical student and who has an IEP. They would also have a hard time telling who was the special education and who was the regular education teacher. Our school is in the second year of this model, and my co-teacher and I enjoy this program on many levels. All aspects of the academic experience—student engagement, inclusion, and achievement—are enhanced by this program. It is also worth mentioning that I am applying the collective "we" to the following discussions, indicating that the efforts mentioned are shared between my co-teacher and myself. I owe him a great deal of credit in these efforts.

WHAT I LEARNED FROM MY GRADUATE PROGRAM OF STUDY

Making connections with my students' families is not just a practice I picked up from recommendations from fellow teachers and administrators, but it is an empirically supported practice I learned in my master's degree program. The first practice I engage in is one-on-one parent communication. I find the many phone calls I make are worth the time spent, since they are a very effective method of communication. My co-teacher and I typically make approximately 250 phone calls per year. I do my best to address all connections in a constructive, strategizing tone with the aim of producing a positive outcome. I try to call every parent, at least once per year, to discuss the student's progress and overall learning strategies. I always try to discuss concrete things such as homework. I prefer focusing on concrete things to help steer the discussions away from any problematic behavior, which any teacher knows can be difficult to discuss on the telephone. I also mention upcoming projects and tests and encourage the parent to come in and visit when they can. These are all very positive and constructive discussions. I find that when I do this, the times I have to report a negative transgression down the road lead to much more productive discussion. The parent will know that I don't "have it in" for the child and that I want what is best for the student. Most importantly, the student will better understand that I am on their side. This practice pays dividends in so many ways.

I had one student, I'll call her Jeanne, who was missing several homework assignments in a row. Jeanne was usually very conscientious and proud of her good grades. After a week of missing work, I brought her into the hall and asked her about the change. She confided in me that her mom's work hours had changed and that she was responsible for the care of younger siblings while her mother was working. Jeanne was also one of my AVID students. AVID is a program designed to help middle-tier students bound for college build organizational, study, and life skills. I teach one section of AVID in addition to my ELA classes.

Part of the AVID program involves the student, teacher, and parents signing a study and homework contract. Part of this contract involves the parent and child working out a suitable time and place for homework. All parties would sign the contract and agree to keep this time and place sacred. I was able to use this contract as a basis for the conversation I had with Jeanne's mother. This was not an easy conversation to have. I wanted to be sensitive to the difficult nature of the mother's work situation, but also to emphasize the needs of my student in her quest to keep her grades up. I knew the contract should, therefore, not be used as leverage, but as a basis for solving a problem. Our conversation worked out very well. Her mom decided to have a trusted neighbor watch the children when Jeanne got home from school, so that she could get her work done. The contracted time for homework was not the same as originally noted, so we had to change the time and sign a new contract. It was a positive outcome that satisfied all of us. Jeanne's grades went back up to the high honor roll level we all were expecting from her.

Again, keeping the conversation on concrete things, the grades and the learning contract, along with expressing concern for the child and sensitivity for the family were key to making this communication successful. Not all communications work out this well, but keeping the elements of concrete examples along with concern and sensitivity usually leads, over time, to success.

I also had one example of a student who was in danger of failing the 7th grade for the second time (he had already been held back once). This student was a constant behavior problem, acting out in class, disrupting, even bullying. I called home to his mom on a regular basis. She would take away privileges and took several other punitive approaches. Nothing seemed to be working.

What I found is that when I spoke to the student directly, it was clear that he truly wanted to do better, but he didn't believe in himself. His grades were very close to failing across all subjects. He believed there was no hope, that no matter what he did he wouldn't pass. He had given up. I got a copy of his report card grades and did the math for him. I showed him that it was close, but that if he decided to concentrate on his studies just a half hour more daily, his grades would improve. He was overjoyed with this information. I then asked his mom if I could bypass talking with her and call him, in particular, on a nightly basis to make sure he had what he needed and that he got his work done. She consented, and I proceeded to call him directly. I would talk to his teachers at the end of each day and find out what he owed. I'd then call him nightly to make sure he understood the work and that he set aside the time to do it. This was not a perfect solution as his classroom behavior improved slightly, but problems still persisted. He, at least, got enough work done to pass the grade. I then looped up to 8th grade with this student and he entered my AVID class (this was a stretch since he was not a perfect fit for the class). His grades are now up to the C level. He should be doing even better, but he is slowly beginning to believe in himself. It's a process.

THE STUDENT/PARENT INTERVIEW

Another strategy I find effective is the student/parent interview. The student is assigned the task of interviewing a family or community member about a certain matter relevant to a classroom project. Most English teachers understand the power of building strong background knowledge before reading a novel or any piece of writing. The background information helps students connect to the piece and therefore dig deeper for meanings and themes. Having the student conduct an interview for such information can make this process more meaningful for the student.

Before we teach *The Outsiders* (Hinton, 1967), we'll send home an interview worksheet where the student is to seek out an elder family or community member who remembers the late 1950s and early 1960s, the time frame in which this book is set. The worksheet asks questions about the culture of the times, music, clothing styles, attitudes, technology, and so on. This approach helps in many ways. Not only does it provide the student with powerful firsthand background information for the novel, it also helps the student and elder connect in ways that they perhaps would not have otherwise, and involves the adult directly in the student's learning. Additionally, students would also have a point of reference when certain period terms, clothing, or other cultural points are discussed in the book. Each year, a number of students report that their parents decided to read the book with them. In some cases, however, parents of my current students are usually too young to remember the time frame, which forces the student to dig a little bit and find age-appropriate extended family or even community members (one student who had a hard time finding interviewees old enough opted to interview his bus driver). This digging and persistence for finding answers is an important research skill for the student to use later in his or her academic career.

I find that the subsequent classroom discussions of their findings are a great deal of fun and very meaningful. On the day of this discussion, we make sure to include plenty of Elvis and Beatles music (both artists are mentioned in the book) as well as Chuck Berry and other more diverse period music. The students love to talk about what their parents were like when they were young—the types of clothes they wore—and there are always discussions about how kids entertained themselves "back in the day." When we are done with this exercise (which is simple and short), the students are generally fired up for the experience of reading this book. They already love the subject before we even begin.

THE OPEN CLASSROOM EVENT

Lastly, I'll discuss what I'll call the open classroom event. This idea can be a lot of work, but it is probably the most important and deepest home/school connection we make all year. Each year we have the National African American Parent Involvement Day (NAAPID) Poetry Buffet. I got the idea for this activity from the book *Teacherman* by Frank McCourt. McCourt essentially said that the way to a student's heart is through the stomach. He brought in food to the classroom and helped to create a community atmosphere. He also made note that recipes look a lot like poetry. I happened to be reading this passage the same weekend I was trying to come up with an engaging poetry unit. I immediately called my wife who was at the grocery store and asked her to pick up the ingredients for Italian sauce. (We sometimes have to spend our own money for the classroom, but I was inspired, and it felt worth it.) I made a batch of my famous Papa Salamone's Italian Sauce. My dad coached me as a child, and my Italian wife helped me raise this recipe to perfection. I put the sauce in a crock-pot that night and the next morning bought some fresh Italian bread from the bakery down the street. I plugged the crock-pot in the back of the classroom, and as the kids walked in they smelled grandma's kitchen. After the usual classroom procedures, I turned student attention to the back of the classroom where the sauce was simmering. I explained how, as a boy, I used to love to sneak behind my Italian dad and peel off an end to the fresh crusty bread and dip it in the sauce for a delicious pre-meal treat. My dad used to snap me with the wooden spoon when he'd catch me. The students liked my personal story about trouble with my dad. I then invited each student up to get a ladle of sauce in a plastic cup and a chunk of bread to enjoy.

At this point, it probably does not seem like an English lesson, but there is a deep academic angle to this whole activity. I devised a worksheet that instructed them to come up with descriptions of the tasting experience using similes, metaphors, personification, and sound devices (e.g., alliteration and rhyme)—all the poetic terms they are responsible for in the 8th grade. To help them, I even had some fresh basil, tomatoes, and garlic available for them to smell, see, and feel. They would have fun eating, smelling, tasting and exchanging descriptions of the experience. I heard the sauce described as being as hot as lava and the basil smelling of a fresh meadow. For the last half hour, the students constructed 10- to 16-line poems about the sauce, using their own figurative language. Below is an example of one student's work. Given that this was an impromptu piece done in a short time, it is far from perfected work, but you can see the student experimenting with figurative language (similes, personification) and the poem has a semblance of a rhyme scheme.

Mr. Sal's Sauce
Sauce, sauce
Red and steamy
Over the bread,
It makes me dreamy
Down the slope
It flows like lava
The taste so dope
It's better than Java
In my mouth it
It dances a beat
Such a little cup
There's more to eat!
Let's stand up and cheer
Get on your feet.
Mr. Sal's sauce
Is hard to beat.

We then celebrated by having a session of Café 303, where we pretend that we are in an old coffee house. Whenever students recite their own poetry in my classroom, we turn the lights down low. I bring out a bongo drum, and we call each other "cats" and snap our fingers in celebration of a poem well performed: "Scoodly-wow!" The students find this whole exercise a great deal of fun. (A typical student comment: "Mr. Salamone, you really liked the 60's . . . you're ooooold!")

We continue the next day with more writing and discussion. The students journal about their own favorite food, traditional feasts, or food experiences. The results of this exercise are as diverse as the student population. One teen talked about the frequent meals they have at a local sports grill. Her family usually goes to this restaurant to watch a popular college basketball game. Her family enjoys hot wings, burgers, and pizza while cheering the hometown team. Many of the African American students speak proudly of the soul food their families cook up on special occasions. The competitive repartee surrounding this subject becomes humorous ("My Mom's mac-n-cheese is the best"). We discuss Irish stews, Greek moussaka, homemade pizza, Creole rice and beans. Our collective mouths water as we get deeper into the subject. We also end up discussing customs and holidays—Christmas, Kwanza, the Fourth of July. Not only do we exchange stories about food, we also hear about culture, customs, clothing, and, most importantly, pride. We even have some students debate the merits of the best local foods—our town boasts several local hot dog makers and pork barbeques. Culture becomes everything, the hook for all the learning.

I must say that the student engagement during these exercises is extraordinary. Hands are in the air, students proudly and enthusiastically discuss their backgrounds and cultures. They write with passion. I sometimes worry, when starting such discussions, that students who have difficult home situations might feel left out of this discussion. For them, I offer my own affinity for the cafeteria food as a lead for anyone to use as their own idea. I find that all students, however, have someone who has brought them to a special meal or has made them a special dish, or they have a favorite food.

NAAPID

The next step is the planning for National African American Parent Involvement Day (NAAPID). NAAPID is a full-day celebration during Black History Month during which parents are encouraged to come to school and get involved with the learning at hand. In our school, all parents, from all races and backgrounds, get involved. We, therefore, celebrate diversity as a theme of the lesson. This day consists of students, parents, and other family members contributing food to a pot-luck dinner held in our Home and Careers room. Parents are invited to share a dish with the class while students take turns reciting their poems. We encourage parents or family members to perform each poem with their child. You may think that such action might push the "cool" envelope for the students, but these barriers quickly break down as the celebrations begin. We teach the parents in attendance that we do not clap for a well-delivered poem. We do, however, snap our fingers and say, in our best gravelly, cool voice, "Scoodly-wow!"

This planning begins with well-developed, polished poems based on favorite foods or meals. We require that the student include at least 14 lines of poetry complete with similes, metaphors, sound devices, and so on.

We walk them through the usual writing process starting with the brainstorming journal mentioned above. They complete a draft and then check it against a rubric before handing it in. After the teacher offers suggestions, students transfer their poems to construction paper with creative decorations added.

I'll never forget two girls from very different backgrounds exchanging long, deep thoughts about their cultural backgrounds while decorating their poems. One African American girl talked about her Christmas celebration with aunts and uncles and how they all join in the cooking of collard greens and macaroni and cheese. She was sharing these thoughts with a girl of Greek heritage, who had recently lost her father to a sudden illness. That teen discussed how her mom still managed to put together some traditional dishes for Greek Easter and planned to contribute moussaka for NAAPID. It was a poignant moment, and to me, it was the true essence of learning.

I've had many memorable poems created throughout the years. I remember specifically a humorous one from a student who didn't like his mom's cooking, so he'd have to sneak in the kitchen and toast up some Hot Pockets on the sly. Others were heartfelt poems about Mom and Grandma putting together a Christmas meal and poems about a secret family dish. All are performed and celebrated while the smell of grits, pizza, and Creole rice fill the air along with the sounds of kind words being exchanged.

The NAAPID project goes a long way to establishing deeper connections to the home and community, but the whole classroom experience plays into the success. Parents come in and see the students and teachers in a comfortable setting where their child's work is being celebrated. Cultural diversity is on display in prideful exchanges. I also think it's important for parents to see teachers taking an interest in the child and their community. The same can be said, of course, for students' deeper connection to school with the parent taking an obvious interest in the school activity. If the child senses this interest, I think they will be more willing to perform in the classroom. Students walk away saying it was the best English class ever. My co-teacher and I, after running three separate meals for the three sections we teach, walk away tired, *stuffed*, and pumping our fists in celebration for a job well done.

CONCLUSION

I think every teacher wrestles with the question of how close they should get to a student. "If I am their friend, how can I remain objective and grade them fairly?" I think all good teachers go back to the idea that a professional distance must be maintained. We are, however, human beings. We can't help but develop a certain level of intimacy with our students. Most of us spend 6 hours a day with these students in our classrooms, in our halls, and in our auditoriums. We make phone calls to parents; we attend after-school activities. This is not to mention the countless chance meetings at the mall and grocery store. Think of it, there is probably no profession more hooked into community affairs than teaching, and the responsibility is profound. So to answer the question, I would say getting close with the student is paramount. You *must* do it or the whole process suffers. Without these relationships, classroom trust cannot be built, students don't take academic risks, and learning ceases. You can, however, build and maintain those relationships and maintain that professional distance. Everything you do must hook back to the learning process and academics. Talk about favorite foods? How does it relate to poetry? Talk about sports? There must be a math lesson in there. Bring the culture into the classroom and enjoy the kids. Break bread with the students, and watch them learn.

MAKE THIS HAPPEN IN YOUR CLASSROOM

- The most important element of this unit or any one like it is actually *trust*. Anyone who has set foot in a middle school classroom knows that kids at this stage of development are intensely aware of others and their perceptions. Standing in front of a class and celebrating yourself is a difficult thing to do. A child must feel like they can trust the classroom culture and take academic and social risks. They must feel that their beliefs, backgrounds, and families will not be ridiculed. This is where the culture of the classroom and relationship building are crucial. Consistent rules and classroom management help this process. If the student is comfortable moving in the classroom and understands routines and rules, it helps them relax and take risks. If the student knows the teachers have a relationship with their parents that is based on constructive discussion and genuine concern (again, those 250 phone calls help here), they will feel more comfortable about taking risks. Having a fun, yet rigorous, atmosphere also helps. The silly yet harmless use of the bongos, the finger snaps, and the "scoodly-wow" also help, and allow students to relax and take some academic and social risks.

- Grading and enforcing any level of academic rigor for this project is difficult. The intense effort I see being put into this project, as well as the close connection to the student as a person, makes it difficult for me to give any student an objective grade. Clear, written expectations and some embedded feedback and assessment help ensure that the students' efforts reach expectations. To those students, who perhaps get a lower grade, they at least understand why. In the end, however, almost all the results are magnificent. My co-teacher and I do a push up for every A earned in our class. We walk away with sore arms when we have to "pay up" after this project.

REFERENCE

Hinton, S. E. (1967). *The outsiders.* New York: Viking.

CHAPTER 9

Communities as Resources

Two Teachers' Reciprocal Learning from Nondominant Cultural Communities

June Estrada, Ernie Estrada, and Guofang Li

Cultural discontinuity between school and home has been cited as one of the major barriers to the achievement of students of nondominant cultural groups. In order to break this barrier, teachers need to become familiar with the expectations and cultural beliefs of parents about their children's education if they differ from their own expectations and beliefs. Such familiarity may help teachers to better understand and assess students' in-class behavior and performance, as well as to better adjust classroom instruction to accommodate the children's specific needs. Li (2006) suggests that teachers and parents can adopt a "culturally reciprocal" stance, whereby both school and family systems acquire new cultural patterns as they develop and mature and each can be endowed with new energy that changes the parent-school relations. This stance will help teachers to enact culturally responsive literacy teaching and incorporate diverse learning styles and traditions in their classrooms.

In the following pages, we describe two high school teachers' engagement in learning about the cultures and beliefs of minority communities such as the Islamic and Hispanic communities and how such reciprocal learning has brought deepened understanding and collaboration between teachers and parents in facilitating the English language learners' learning inside and outside of school. In order to learn more about their Muslim students' culture and faith, for example, the teachers attended an annual open house offered by the local Islamic center. This visit allowed the teachers to acquire a valuable text resource, personal stories and experiences of the community members, and establish a connection with a family from

Egypt, who later came to the teachers' class to show Islamic culture and life experiences as immigrants to their students. In their engagement with the Hispanic community, the teachers met with a community of Spanish-speaking families, listened to their concerns, and exchanged views about expectations for their children and strategies they could use to help their children to be successful. This kind of cultural reciprocity helped build a stronger parent-teacher partnership, which in turn helped these teachers take important action to improve the teaching and learning in their classrooms.

JUNE'S STORY:
RECIPROCAL LEARNING FROM THE ISLAMIC COMMUNITY

Teaching in an urban school with a diverse population can be as much of a blessing as it is a challenge. Every day is a new experience; every student has his or her own story. Finding a way to connect to students' lives and interests is a goal of virtually every educator in America, but in a high school with a population of 1,500 students, where 20% of those students are English language learners, the challenge is overwhelming. My husband Ernie, a math teacher of Hispanic background, and I have had the unique opportunity of sharing these challenges and blessings together for several years now. We have taught side by side in a comprehensive urban high school in the Midwest that serves several cultural communities. These include Nepali, Cuban, Burmese, Iraqi, and many more. Working with a team of two other teachers and approximately 150 high school freshmen a year, the past 14 years presented us with a number of experiences in building community among our students and their parents. As a social studies teacher, it is a goal of mine to always look for ways of bringing cultural learning experiences to my students, and as more of our population becomes English language learners, this priority takes on an even greater degree of importance, especially as we work to build the relationships with our students and their parents.

Coming from a fairly traditional European-American family, and having a parent who was an educator herself, I have always felt a very strong connection to school. Ernie's large Hispanic family, with hard-working immigrant parents who deeply valued the opportunities an education had to offer their children, also made school the center of their lives. Even though we came from very different cultural backgrounds, we both felt a strong sense of community in education and school in our own lives. This has been the case with many of our students today, especially our ELL students. It was rare that we had the chance to meet the parents of these kids, often due to economic factors such as transportation or work schedules. Sometimes because of the language barriers, our ELL parents do not respond to phone calls or attend parent–teacher conferences.

During one of my first years of teaching I was preparing a unit on world religions and realized that I had two Muslim students in my class from different countries, Azerbaijan and Bosnia. Both of these students were recent immigrants with fairly good oral language, but they were very hesitant to participate in class and often struggled with reading and writing activities. Though I knew that embarrassment over their accents or their cultural differences from the majority of the students might be causing their hesitation, I realized that it was important to get to know these kids and their backgrounds better, especially before beginning this particular unit. I spoke to each of them about their faith and culture, and although there were many differences between the two individuals and their backgrounds, I discovered that they both were currently attending the local Islamic center. One of the students mentioned that there was an annual open house scheduled the next month and I immediately decided that this would be an important opportunity for learning and connecting with my students that I couldn't miss.

When it was time for the open house to take place Ernie was not able to attend, so I asked the English teacher from our team if she would like to attend with me and she was excited for the opportunity as well. The open house was held on a Saturday afternoon, and as my colleague and I arrived and entered the center, we were immediately greeted by a young woman who appeared to be of Middle East descent. She politely asked us to remove our shoes and then escorted us into the facility. We found ourselves surrounded by people of all different ethnicities and backgrounds. There were families from Lebanon, Egypt, Indonesia, and India, just to name a few. There were American Muslims and many guests from a variety of religious backgrounds that were there with friends or neighbors or had come alone simply because they were curious about another faith or culture. Many of the individuals that were hosting the event appeared to be wearing traditional Islamic attire, but we quickly realized that there was a variety of different styles. Some women covered their heads and other did not. Some individuals, who appeared to be visitors like us, were dressed in Western attire. We came to realize that they too were members of the center. As the day went on and we had several conversations with people, we realized that many of the differences reflected various national origins, while other differences were simple personal choice.

The center was a very welcoming and open place. We were encouraged to walk around and observe. I had many enlightening conversations that afternoon and learned so much about Islamic ideals and customs. There were specific prayer rooms set up where men and women were separately conducting group prayers. The open house provided us with some useful text materials that we could take back and use in our classes for our world religions unit, but it also allowed us to see many Islamic artifacts and to taste a variety of international foods from the regions of the world represented in the center. However, the personal connections we were able to make that day were by far the most valuable part of this experience.

A woman, who overheard my colleague and me discussing our observations, approached us and began talking with us about the fundamental beliefs of Islam, including the ideals of peace and tolerance that are so often not acknowledged in the media today. She took us to an area where a display of large posters was set up that allowed you to walk through and read about the basis of the faith. The language of the posters was very appropriate for beginners in my class. I told this woman after reading through them myself how helpful and interesting I found them and that I thought this would be very useful information for my students. The woman excused herself for a moment and then returned with a packet of the same information from the posters for myself and the other teacher.

I also saw one of my two students at the event that day and she was able to introduce me to her mother, which was the first time she had met one of her daughter's teachers. Although the mother did not speak English and had to communicate with us through her daughter, she was very kind and seemed to be very appreciative that one of her daughters' teachers had taken the time to attend the events of the day. This brief meeting was going to give me many opportunities for the rest of the school year to ask my student how her family was and to send my well wishes home to them through her.

Another woman who knew the students from our school and had teenage children of her own who attended another local high school was very open to sharing her personal stories with us. She was an immigrant from Egypt and was excited to talk about her own experience being both an English language learner and a Muslim in America. During our conversation she graciously offered to come to our school, speak with our students, and share her culture and stories with my students.

As I left the open house that day I knew that the offer for the guest presentation was an experience that all of my students could gain so much from, but I would soon discover that what it would provide to the Islamic students would truly be a priceless gift. To help our students benefit most from our guest's visit, I began some careful planning and preparations. I spent several lessons comparing the history, tradition, and values of the major world religions. We talked with the students about the historical and ethical values behind dietary limitations, clothing styles, and holiday celebration, which are often stereotypes among several religions such as Judaism, Buddhism, and Islam. This allowed an opportunity for me to use the text materials that I had received at the open house as well as the stories that were shared with my colleague and me. My Islamic ELL students were very excited about the readings and information shared in class and one of them even began assisting the other students with the questions that I had prepared to go with the readings.

Having the benefit of working with a team of teachers from multiple disciplines to prepare for such an event was very helpful. They too were excited to build deeper connections with the ELL students. For example, Ernie, who was working with the same group of students, helped me plan for the day of the scheduled visit. Many phone calls were made to our speaker to discuss the structure and topics of the presentation. We also had the support of the administration for this event. The students were prepared with proper etiquette instructions and a lesson in preparing appropriate questions that they would be taking with them to the presentation. The students were asked to write questions they had, and then we shared them with each other looking for any inappropriate or unclear ideas. We talked as a class about how we feel when we share information about our families and beliefs with others and what questions we may find offensive.

Our guest speaker brought a sister and two friends (all Egyptian) from the center to help her the day of the visit. We held the event in a large meeting room in the school to allow for as many students to participate as possible. That also provided enough room for our guests to set up various displays of clothing, cultural materials, and even a sampling of tasty treats that they brought for the students. Our guests' presentations were a collection of stories about their life in Egypt, what school was like there, how the lives of American teenagers compared to teenagers in Egypt, and the reasons and experience of their move to America. All of the guests wore traditional Islamic attire and the students had many questions about the reasons for it, whether it was comfortable, and other restrictions of their faith. Through the students' questions, students also learned about what their lives were like living a Muslim lifestyle in a predominantly non-Muslim community, where they often felt like outsiders and carried the burden of having to educate others to gain their acceptance.

The learning experience was a huge success and led to so many great questions from our students that we couldn't get them all answered within the time we had. Our two Muslim ELL students showed a great deal of excitement the day of our guest speaker's visit. Having someone that represented a part of their culture and seeing how interested the other students were seemed to mean so much to them. They didn't disappear into the group that day as they so often did during other activities. Both students sat right up front, were very engaged in the presentation, and made a point to personally speak with each of our guests, sometimes in their native Arabic language. This fascinated many of our other students and made the Muslim ELLs the center of positive attention and leaders among their peers that day. They exuded so much joy and pride that day, and as we returned to our class after the presentation they began to open up to their peers about their own background in ways that we had never seen before. One non-ELL student, Katie (all names are pseudonyms), asked one Islamic ELL, Ramla, to show her where her native country was on the class wall map, and another student, Jon, began asking how the other Islamic student, Yousif, celebrated Ramadan with his family. The kids began to reach out to the ELL students and the community of our class grew so much that day.

Our learning did not stop when the visit was over. After the presentations, our students all wrote thank-you letters to our guests and used these letters to continue to ask questions about the practice of Islam, such as what were the traditions of the holidays that were coming up and what were their experiences of immigration. These topics provoked great interest in other ELLs of different cultural backgrounds and were useful in our later units of study as well. These letters kept the learning experience going for much longer than our team had ever anticipated.

ERNIE'S STORY:
RECIPROCAL LEARNING FROM THE HISPANIC COMMUNITY

My parents were first-generation immigrants from Mexico. In the 1960s, they traveled from Mexico to America to look for work and ended up working on the local farms in Michigan. They worked in the onion and potato fields and picked cherries. My father was finally fortunate to find a job for the C & O Railroad Company where he retired as a trackman after 40 years. He became a U.S. citizen at the age of 65. He and my mother had 13 children.

My mom spent most her time making sure her 13 children were well fed and in school getting the best education possible. My mother told my father that if they were going to have children, they were all going to graduate from high school. All of us graduated from the same local high school—a feat my mother is very proud of and continues to brag about at the age of 84. She was even prouder of me when I received a teaching degree, since I was one of the only two of her children who had gone to college. She tells me every time I get a chance to spend time with her how important getting an education was to her. Her philosophy was simple: Teachers are like your parents and we were to do as we were told.

I have been working in the same school district for 30 years and have taught many immigrant students during my career as a teacher. Though I am a high school math teacher, I taught basic reading and writing skills to about 20 Spanish-speaking elementary students one summer while their parents were working on the local farms. I also taught basic reading and writing skills for 2 years to 15 ELL students who spoke mainly Spanish and 5 who spoke Vietnamese. My own Hispanic background, as well as my experiences with these ELLs who come from similar backgrounds as me, made me realize the importance of school and home collaborations.

In spring 2009, June and I were asked by our district's bilingual educational coordinator to attend a meeting with 50 Hispanic parents who wanted to listen to and ask questions about what teachers expected from students who were about to enter our high school. The meeting was a result of two Hispanic parents who, about 6 months ago, decided they wanted to form a group of parents for the purpose of getting to know our local school system. The two parents contacted a school board member to help them hold monthly informational meetings for all Spanish-speaking families. As a result, the counselors, teachers, and also community college provided them with different resources (such as information on how to apply for financial aid).

We were told that these parents were searching for strategies to help their children achieve success and were very motivated to get involved in their children's education. Coming from a strong Mexican family who valued education, I was quite impressed with the parents' proactive approach. As I entered the meeting, I thought about my own parents who only demanded that we listen to our teachers. They separated their role of raising us from that of school, leaving the job of educating their children to the educators. I realized that these parents were doing more than what most parents have done, including my own, who rarely were able to meet with my teachers. These parents not only were concerned about their own children's education, they also were uniting as a community. They were taking it a step further than my parents had by searching for help not only with each other but also with educators from the local school district.

At the meetings, the parents asked about possible strategies that they could use to help their children learn, and June and I exchanged views with the parents and discussed many issues including attendance, nutrition, and being prepared for school. June and I shared with the parents that attending school was the biggest issue for many of our students and that many of our students did not value being on time and many did not even bother to attend class. In addition to the importance of getting the students to school on time, we also discussed the importance of nourishing our students. The majority of our student population is eligible for the free or reduced-price lunches, so we made parents aware of the available financial assistance. As well, we made suggestions for how to help their children come to school organized and prepared. For example, we suggested that the parents make sure their children come to school with the proper supplies for each class, different colored notebooks and folders for every subject. The parents were very interested in learning these simple strategies and were very respectful and appreciative of our time and interest in them. My mother has always spoken about educators with the highest regard and as I stood in front of these parents I felt I had received that same level of respect.

After this experience with a group of parents who shared my cultural background, I would like to help expand parent groups to other nationalities in our community. This parent group could be used as a model for building a community for other parents, forming volunteer groups, inviting parents into our local ELL classrooms, and working as a whole to help our students. Growing up in a bilingual home where education was highly valued, I have always believed that the parents of my ELL students want the same things for their children. The difference that I saw between my own family experience and that of the today's families was the desire to work directly and cooperatively with the schools. These parents seemed willing not only to build a bridge between home and school, but also to take immediate action toward building such a bridge. We educators just need to reach out to respond to their desires and reciprocate their efforts. Only by doing so can we form a partnership to help all of our children to become successful.

CONCLUSION

All kids have needs, and when they come to us we should look for those needs and address them. If a child comes to school hungry we feed them, if they come without a coat we clothe them. When the ELL student comes to us without the target language or knowledge about the target culture, then we teach it to them, but we must remember what they have to give us as well. Teaching and learning is a partnership and our students, all of our students, have so much to give us.

MAKE THIS HAPPEN IN YOUR CLASSROOM

- It is important to provide students with opportunities to share stories about their cultures and to look for ways to connect your lessons with their lives.
- Show your students that you are interested in them by asking them to teach you and their peers about their cultures.
- Include their families by providing translators if needed, transportation, and opportunities for parents, siblings, and other family members to be involved in the students' learning.

REFERENCE

Li, G. (2006). *Culturally contested pedagogy: Battles of literacy and schooling between mainstream teachers and Asian immigrant parents.* Albany: State University of New York Press.

CHAPTER 10

Learning from and with Immigrant and Refugee Families in a Family Literacy Program

Jim Anderson and Fiona Morrison

It is a pleasant autumn morning and we are in the staffroom of Chestnut Grove Elementary School. We are discussing the second session of the PALS in Immigrant Communities family literacy program that we are offering to a group of newly arrived immigrant families from Vietnam. Ashley, the facilitator, comments on the fact that the parents tend to spoon-feed their 4- and 5-year-olds at lunch, a practice that North American families tend to terminate as soon as children become toddlers. A rather heated discussion ensues about cultural differences, parenting, child development, expectations, and so forth.

The purpose of this chapter is to share our experiences working in culturally and linguistically diverse communities in a family literacy program that we developed called PALS or Parents As Literacy Supporters (Anderson & Morrison, 2000). Here, we report on our work with five linguistic groups—Chinese, Farsi, Karen, Punjabi, and Vietnamese—in different communities in the greater Vancouver area of British Columbia. The greater Vancouver area is culturally and linguistically very diverse and in some school districts more than 150 languages are spoken; in some classrooms, children speak more than a dozen different home languages. Most of the families are recent immigrants or refugees, for example, the Karen families lived in refugee camps in Thailand, on the border with their native Myanmar, before recently coming to Canada. Specifically, we focus on the different ways that families support their young children's language and literacy-ways that on the surface may appear to be quite odd to teachers. We first give a very brief background of family literacy and the PALS program. We then share a number of vignettes that we documented as we worked with the families. Fiona, the teacher-facilitator in the program, then responds. We conclude by discussing our experiences and findings, especially in terms of implications for teachers.

PARENTS AS LITERACY SUPPORTERS

Most educators now recognize that the family can be a powerful force for literacy learning. Over the years, educators have shown that this is the case across social and cultural groups (e.g., Gregory, 2005; Mui & Anderson, 2008; Taylor & Dorsey-Gaines, 1988). Family literacy programs reflect Lev Vygotsky's sociohistorical theory in that much learning takes place in social contexts as competent adults and significant others support young children's learning as they engage in meaningful activities in their daily lives. Over the years, family literacy programs have proliferated. One such program is Parents As Literacy Supporters, or PALS (Anderson & Morrison, 2010).

PALS is designed for 3- to 5-year-olds and their parents or other caregivers. The program consists of 10 to 15 2-hour sessions usually held every 2 weeks from October through May. The times and days for the sessions are negotiated with the participants; in some communities, sessions occur in the evening to accommodate parents who work outside the home. Session topics typically include learning the alphabet, early mathematics development, computers/technology and learning, learning to write, environmental print, and reading with children. Sessions begin with the families and facilitators sharing food, after which they spend about half an hour discussing the topic (e.g., early writing) for that session while the children go to their classrooms. Adults are encouraged to share their own experiences with the topic at hand and their observations of their children's engagement in that particular aspect of early literacy. Parents, children, and facilitator then spend an hour in the classroom at a number of literacy and learning centers, where they can observe an activity corresponding to the topic of the day. Sessions conclude with the parents and facilitators discussing what they have observed about the children's learning and possibilities for continuing, expanding, and reinforcing that learning at home and in the community. Families are then presented with a book or other materials/ resources, such as mathematics activities and games. Some sessions are kept open so that topics and issues that parents identify can be addressed. Books; art materials such as crayons, glue, and scissors; and writing materials such as pencils, paper, and markers are provided to the families so that over the course of the program, they accumulate a fairly extensive set of resources.

In many ways, PALS embodies what Pahl and Kelly (2005) conceptualize as a "third space." That is, the literacy activities and practices that occur in the program include practices from home and practices that are more traditional and school-like. For example, in the community where the families are originally from India, the facilitator incorporates texts written in Punjabi, which are imported from India for the program. During the session focusing on language development that we playfully named "Riddles, Raps, and Rhymes," the facilitators working with the Farsi-speaking families incorporated Farsi rhymes, songs, poems, and so forth and culminated the session by recording the families singing and reciting these. They then made CDs of the recordings and distributed them to all of the families. We think practices such as these embody the principles of culturally responsive literacy teaching and learning (e.g., Ruggiano Schmidt & Ma, 2006; Williams Shealy & Callins, 2007).

We also try to tap the "funds of knowledge" (Moll, Amanti, Neff, & Gonzalez, 1992) that families bring to the program. Parents discuss the literacy practices in their homes and communities and share their own literacy experiences in and out of school. We also encourage, promote, and value the literacy activities and practices that families engage in at home and in the community.

As we began to work with increasing numbers of immigrant and refugee families from China, India, Iran, Myanmar, and Vietnam, whose home languages were other than English, we saw it as critically important to support families in maintaining their first language while they learned English. Thus, in the PALS in Immigrant Communities project, the sessions are offered in the first language of the participants. We provide bilingual books and texts for the families. Cognizant that there are cultural differences in conception of early childhood, of literacy teaching and learning, and of parenting, we have been attempting to document and understand the myriad ways that parents from different cultural and linguistic groups mediate and support their young children's literacy learning. In the following vignettes, I (Jim) report my observations of parent mediation and interaction as parents worked at centers during the session in Chestnut Grove Elementary School that we mentioned in the introduction to this chapter.

OBSERVATION FROM JANUARY 16, 2009

About 30 parents and other caregivers circulate among the 8 or so learning centers that the facilitators have set up reflecting today's theme, Literacy and Play. Caregivers include mothers and fathers, grandparents, older siblings, and aunts. The majority of the participants are Punjabi speakers, some of whom are recent immigrants and others who have lived in Canada for some time. Several Karen-speaking families also attend; refugees from Myanmar, many of them have lived in camps prior to coming to Canada and many of them have limited or no schooling.

I sit at one of the centers, carefully documenting the way that different dads interact, especially paying attention to how the adults support the child they are accompanying. One child is painting his name on butcher paper placed neatly on an appropriately sized easel. His mother carefully has her hand over the child's hand and carefully guides each movement, including dipping the brush carefully into the paint so as not to overload it. The name is impeccably neat and both the mother and child smile, obviously pleased at their product. Shortly after, another child about the same age comes to the easel, accompanied by her mother. The mother stands about a foot and a half behind the child, obviously very pleased by the child's painting but saying nothing. When the child finishes her painting, she looks at her mother, who without saying anything, smiles approvingly.

I direct my attention to the second easel where a child and her father are standing. I notice that the father holds one of his daughter's hands while she paints her name neatly with the other. I am unable to understand his occasional comment in Karen but it appears that he is both encouraging the child for her efforts and providing comments/suggestions when she needs them. I turn my attention back to the first easel at which a mother and her son each have a brush and have divided the paper so that each has about one-half of it to work on. They talk continuously in Punjabi. Afterward, I ask the mother what it was they were saying and she indicates they were offering support and suggestions to each other, commenting on the shape, neatness, use of color, and so forth.

After this pair completes their painting and removes the paper and hangs it to dry, a grandmother and her grandson approach the easel. The grandmother clips the paper on the easel and directs the child to get a brush and to begin painting. She sits next to the child and talks continuously. The child looks to her for direction and she appears to suggest improvements and need for corrections and adjustments that the child immediately does. After about 10 minutes, the child's painting is completed and he and the grandmother appear to be quite pleased with it.

CULTURAL-BASED WAYS OF SCAFFOLDING

In the scenario described above, all of the children were being supported but in different ways. And although some of the adults were providing the verbal "scaffolding" (Bruner, 1978) that is highly promoted in Western education, others provided support differently. For example, the hand-over-hand guidance that one of the caregivers provided might be seen as anathema, as it is contradictory to the exploratory, risk-taking perspective promoted by North American educators (e.g., Gunderson & Anderson, 2003). Likewise, the parent who stands beaming behind the child as she paints is also expressing her support, albeit in a nonverbal manner. But we need to remember, that in some cultural groups, nonverbal communication is as powerful as the verbal praise that many middle-class parents tend to heap on children for their efforts and accomplishments.

As Rogoff (2003) pointed out, "human development is a cultural process" (p. 3); however, "to date, the study of human development has been based largely on research and theory coming from middle-class communities in Europe and North America" (p. 4). Furthermore, we contend that Vygotsky's notion of adult support has largely come to mean *an adult talking with a child*, leading teachers sometimes to ignore other forms of interaction that might be equally important (Rogoff, 2003). As North American society becomes increasingly diverse, it is imperative that we as teachers acknowledge the diverse ways that families support their children (e.g., Gregory, 1997) and enact culturally responsive literacy practices in our classrooms to support the knowledge, skills, and strategies that children bring to school and preschool with them.

As we have worked with families from different cultural and language groups, we have had to de-center our own thinking in many ways. In addition to learning the many ways that caregivers and caregivers support learning, we have had to be careful not to assume essentialist stances, assuming that all East-Asian parents hold particular beliefs or that Chinese caregivers behave in particular ways with children. And this is hard work, as Fiona now explains.

FIONA

As a teacher-facilitator in the program, my background in early childhood education and my bias toward a play-based program is often challenged. When I meet with families in the adult-only part of the PALS program I encourage the families to follow their child's lead and to resist doing the activity for the child. Too often I have experienced the adult taking the scissors away from the child in order to speed up the process and make it look neat!

As I read and reflect upon Jim's observations and the many diverse ways families are supporting their children's literacy development, I am struck by the need for me to examine my assumptions. I struggle with the dilemma of honoring who families are and what they bring to the program and my deeply held beliefs about how young children learn and a pedagogy that supports developmentally appropriate practices that reflect Western notions of child development and learning.

Add into the mix the cultural practices and background experiences of the immigrant and refugee families. How do I come to know what they are? As a facilitator who sees the families for approximately 2 hours every few weeks for 10 to 15 sessions, I am struck by how much I have to learn about each family within these time constraints. It takes time to build trusting relationships with families. How do I align all of these factors? Who am I to question the ways in which family members scaffold their young child's literacy development?

There is so much rhetoric in education. We are constantly telling parents, "You are your child's first and most important teacher." If I really believe that statement then why do I send the message to families, often implicitly and sometimes explicitly, that there is a "right" way to support learning (e.g., following the child's lead)? I have come to the conclusion that I need to carefully observe the competencies that families bring when supporting their children's literacy learning, build upon them, and provide a variety of models of learning and teaching for them to choose from.

Since families have told us that they want to learn about how the schools support children's learning (e.g., Anderson & Morrison, 2007), we believe it important to demonstrate and model for them the child-centered pedagogy of the school. For example, if I observe a grandmother using the hand-over-hand technique with scissors with her 3-year-old grandson while cutting during a particular craft activity, I might invite them to try dual-handed scissors next. I would then provide grocery flyers or newspapers and appropriate scissors for the age of the child for them to take home so the child could "practice" independently. In each PALS session we try to offer several examples of ways families can support their children's learning that reflect the "school ways" that the children can expect in kindergarten. PALS center activities become a bridge between home practices and school ones (Pahl & Kelly, 2005). In order to establish this bridge, we have found it necessary to combine careful observation and scaffolding for the families. But perhaps most importantly, we need to recognize that there are many pathways to literacy (Gregory, Long, & Volk, 2004), and we must always recognize, value, support, and build on what families are already doing to support young children's language and literacy learning.

This work leaves me humbled and despite having more than 30 years experience in working with young children and their families, I am reminded that this work is complex, it is nuanced, and it is a delicate dance.

CONCLUSION

We have learned much from our work with families from different cultural and linguistic groups, and this has shaped our own practices. We not only need to be *kid-watchers*, but *family-watchers*. Families' ways of interacting in the PALS program taught us much about the expectations and behaviors of caregivers and children around learning. It alerted us to the fact that learning and teaching are culturally situated and that as educators, we must be aware that our ways are not the only ways of doing things. We not only need to accept these differences, but we can be more conscious about making school-ways of learning and interacting more transparent for caregivers and children.

MAKE THIS HAPPEN IN YOUR CLASSROOM

- Learn about the literacy practices of the families and communities with whom you work. For example, some families value and practice storytelling rather than storybook reading at bedtime with their children. In addition to affirming with families that storytelling is a valuable language and literacy activity, introduce *storytelling*, in addition to storybook reading, into your classrooms.
- Tell families explicitly that they are important in their children's literacy development and that the school values what they are already doing.

- Bring culturally relevant texts into the classroom, as did the teacher we mentioned earlier who had families share Farsi poems, songs, and rhymes.
- Help families realize the things they are doing to support children's early learning. For example, use statements beginning with *I noticed that.*
- For teachers working in the context of family literacy programs, such as PALS, provide a range of take-home materials in addition to books. For example, we provided the Farsi families a deck of playing cards at the Early Mathematics session; the parents indicated that their children enjoyed using the kings, queens, and jacks to make up stories in addition to using the cards for counting, sorting, and so forth.
- Become familiar with professional resources for teachers that provide support in working with children and families from culturally and linguistically diverse homes and communities. For example, in addition to some of the resources referred to in this article, other practical resources, such as JoBeth Allen's (2007) *Creating Welcoming Schools: A Practical Guide to Home-School Partnerships with Diverse Families*, are available from professional organizations such as the International Reading Association.

ACKNOWLEDGMENTS

We would like to acknowledge the collaboration and support of 2010 Legacies Now in the PALS in Immigrant Communities. Sincere appreciation is also extended to the families, teachers, and administrators with whom we work and from whom we learn.

REFERENCES

Allen, J. (2007). *Creating welcoming schools: A practical guide to home-school partnerships with diverse families.* New York: Teachers College Press.

Anderson, J., & Morrison, F. (2007). "A great program . . . for me as a Gramma": Caregivers evaluate a family literacy initiative. *Canadian Journal of Education, 30,* 68–89.

Anderson, J., & Morrison, F. (2010). *Parents as literacy supporters (PALS).* Vancouver, BC: 2010 Legacies Now.

Bruner, J. (1978). The role of dialogue in language acquisition. In A. Sinclair, R. J. Jarvelle, & W. J. M. Levelt (Eds.), *The child's concept of language.* New York: Springer-Verlag.

Gregory, E. (1997). *One child, many worlds: Early learning in multicultural communities.* New York: Teachers College Press.

Gregory, E. (2005). Guiding lights: Siblings as literacy teachers in a multilingual community. In J. Anderson, M. Kendrick, T. Rogers, & S. Smythe (Eds.), *Portraits of literacy across families, communities and schools: Intersections and tensions* (pp. 21–39). Mahwah, NJ: Erlbaum.

Gregory, E., Long, S., & Volk, D. (2004). *Many pathways to literacy: Young children learning with siblings, grandparents, peers and communities.* New York: Routledge-Farmer.

Gunderson, L., & Anderson, J. (2003). Multicultural views of literacy learning and teaching. In A. Willis, G. Garcia, R. Barrera, & V. Harris (Eds.), *Multicultural issues in literacy research and practice* (pp. 123–144). Mahwah, NJ: Erlbaum.

Moll, L., Amanti, C., Neff, D., & Gonzalez, N. (1992). Funds of knowledge for teaching: Using a qualitative approach to connect homes and classrooms. *Theory into Practice, 31,* 132–141.

Mui, S., & Anderson, J. (2008). At home with the Johals: Another look at family literacy. *Reading Teacher, 62,* 234–243.

Pahl, K., & Kelly, S. (2005). Family literacy as a third space between home and school: Some case studies. *Literacy, 39,* 91–96.

Rogoff, B. (2003). *The cultural nature of human development.* Oxford, UK: Oxford University Press.

Ruggiano Schmidt, P., & Ma, W. (2006). *50 strategies for culturally responsive teaching K–8.* Thousand Oaks, CA: Corwin.

Taylor, D., & Dorsey-Gaines, C. (1988). *Growing up literate: Learning from inner-city families.* Portsmouth, NH: Heinemann.

Williams Shealy, M., & Callins, T. (2007). Creating culturally responsive literacy programs in inclusive classrooms. *Instruction in School and Clinic, 42,* 195–197.

Part IV

BUILDING ON STUDENTS' LINGUISTIC STRENGTHS

Most of us are bilingual. We often use different language forms to communicate with our families, friends, teachers, spiritual leaders, and employers. The language we use depends on our audience (Au, 1993). In the United States, the African American vernacular is a recognized language form (Delpit, 1988). Appalachian Dialect is spoken along the Eastern mountain region of the United States, and traces its origins to Elizabethan England. Spanish, Italian, and many other languages also possess dialects (Dial, 1969).

In our schools, standardized English is the language form valued in schools. However, when students with differing languages and dialects enter our classrooms, it is important that they maintain a strong connection with their home languages and dialects as they learn more standard forms of English (Gunderson, 2009). Language differences should not be recognized as language deficits. Children who learn to speak English in this manner maintain a positive self-concept and are more likely to succeed academically and socially (Banks, 2001; Diaz, 2001; Garcia, 2002). We must adopt the additive perspective in our classrooms and schools, a perspective that honors the languages and cultures of those groups new to this country, as well as those members of the "First Nation People," the authentic first inhabitants of the North American continent and the enslaved African Americans; both groups recently began to gain equal rights.

Therefore, to become culturally responsive literacy teachers, we must connect students' languages and cultures with English literacy development. The teachers in this section artfully make those connections in elementary and secondary schools.

REFERENCES

Au, K. H. (1993). *Literacy instruction in multicultural settings.* Orlando: Harcourt Brace.

Banks, J. A. (2001). *Cultural diversity and education: Foundations, curriculum, and teaching* (4th ed.). Boston: Pearson.

Delpit, L. D. (1988). The silenced dialogue: Power and pedagogy in educating other people's children. *Harvard Educational Review, 58,* 280–298.

Dial, W. P. (1969). The dialect of the Appalachian people. *West Virginia History, 30*(2), 463–471.

Diaz, C. F. (2001). *Multicultural education for the twenty-first century.* New York: Longman.

Garcia, E. (2002). *Student cultural diversity: Understanding and meeting the challenge* (3rd ed.). Boston: Houghton Mifflin.

Gunderson, L. (2009, February). *Where are the English language learners?* Paper presented at English Language Learner Institute at the annual convention of the International Reading Association, Phoenix, AZ.

CHAPTER 11

Teaching Through Language

Using Multilingual Tools to Promote Literacy Achievement Among African American Elementary Students

Heidi Oliver O'Gilvie, Jennifer D. Turner, and Harry Hughes

As African American literacy educators, we believe that culturally responsive pedagogy is essential for promoting the literacy development of the African American students in today's elementary schools. Much of the work on culturally responsive pedagogy has focused on the instructional materials, methods, and activities (Ladson-Billings, 1994; Smith-Maddox, 1998) that encourage teachers to recognize and validate African American Vernacular English (AAVE) and use it to help students acquire an additional language code—standardized English (Delpit & Dowdy, 2002; Morrell, 2002). It is not well known how teachers use other related discourses—such as hip-hop/rap (Morrell, 2002) or those derived from the institutions within the African American community such as the church and boys and girls clubs (McMillon & McMillon, 2004)—to strengthen students' literacy abilities. In this chapter, we highlight how a 5th-grade teacher, Mr. Harry Hughes, uses these language tools to accomplish this goal.

We begin with a discussion of the theoretical framework as a way to contextualize Harry's use of multiple language discourses as teaching tools. Next, we will briefly explain the literacy practices and strategies Harry employed to design rich literacy lessons that are inclusive of skills needed to interact and understand various texts. More specifically, we reveal the types of language tools that he uses to build upon the communication styles and patterns his African American students bring forth within the

141

learning community. Finally, we conclude with implications for teaching African American students using multilingual strategies.

BACKGROUND

Our work is grounded in a social constructivist view of literacy and literacy learning (Au, 1998, 2006; Vygotsky, 1978). Social constructivist perspectives "see literacy, first and foremost, as a social practice always embedded within structures of power" (Hammerberg, 2004, p. 649). According to Larson (2003), language tools are important pedagogical factors to consider because "literacy learning is mediated by language use in face-to-face interaction in specific contexts, for specific audiences and purposes" (p. 90). In classroom contexts, then, language tools are used by teachers to "position students as objects or subjects in relation to text construction and how that relationship to text mediates access to participation in literacy activities" (Larson, 2003, p. 91).

To better understand the complex relationships between language, literacy, and schooling, we briefly describe three distinct "languages" that may be spoken by African American students. We believe that these three languages represent "multilingual teaching tools" that are utilized by culturally sensitive literacy teachers striving to promote the literacy development of African American students.

Much of what we know about African American students' language centers on AAVE, a language that is common across the African American population and often transcends racial, geographic, generational, and even some social class boundaries (Perry & Delpit, 1998). AAVE is a rule-governed, complex language system, which represents the integration of African and European linguistic conventions and traditions (Smitherman, 1998). As Smitherman (1998) eloquently notes, AAVE is "neither 'broken English' or 'sloppy speech' nor some bizarre lingo spoken only by baggy-pants-wearing Black kids . . . rather . . . [it is] the Africanization of American English" (p. 30).

Teachers who are culturally responsive recognize AAVE as a legitimate language. They know how to embrace their African American students' affinity for AAVE, and can engage in open dialogue about its appropriate contextual usage. In other words, culturally responsive literacy teachers help African American students learn to use language and literacy in meaningful and purposeful ways by teaching them how to "code switch" or change linguistic codes and conventions depending upon the audience and intent of the message (Howard, 2001). For example, in his study of powerful pedagogy, Howard (2001) reported that the four African American teachers worked tirelessly to "structure their teaching in ways that allowed African American students to take advantage of their verbal skills and discourse styles" (p. 190). Because all four teachers were multilingual themselves, they easily moved back and forth between AAVE and standardized English during their lessons. Equally important, these teachers discussed the importance of "code-switching" with their African American students, and explicitly modeled this strategy as part of their literacy curriculum.

POPULAR CULTURE DISCOURSES AS LANGUAGE TOOLS

Although it may not be readily apparent that popular culture has its own language practices, popular culture has been shown to have its own conventions, idioms, and norms, which describe particular ways of life and express specific meanings and values through people's behavior and their participation in societal institutions (Morrell, 2002). Hagood (2002) defines popular culture as "the large-scale acceptance of and pleasure in a particular text produced for audience consumption" (p. 248). Popular culture is generally characterized as various texts, including print (e.g., book, comics, magazines), nonprint (e.g., music videos, images), or texts that combine both (e.g., video games/manuals, movies) (Xu, 2004).

One example of a popular culture discourse that is strongly associated with African American youth is hip-hop/rap music. Quinn (2005) characterizes rap music using three distinct categories. *Gansta Rap*, which represents what rappers see in their communities, often reflects (and may exacerbate) numerous problems facing African American communities and young men in general such as violence, drugs, and unemployment. *Back Pack Rap* or *Critically Conscious Rap* includes the infusion of a critical analysis of systems into their lyrics. *Popular Rap* is considered a "faddish" style of rap music, which sounds like and is often included in the rhythm and blues genre of music. African American youth—and other young people from various ethnic and racial backgrounds—consume all three types of rap music.

Because hip-hop/rap music represents such a strong force in popular culture, literacy researchers like Ernest Morrell (2002) have begun to investigate how teachers may be able to draw upon this music to teach language arts. Morrell, who has done extensive studies of various ways to include hip-hop in the traditional literacy classroom, created a hip-hop course for urban high school students that linked hip-hop to poetry. Morrell's course included an in-depth exploration of poetry and the historical periods in which the poems were written, and students were expected to read both poetry and hip-hop lyrics with a critical eye. Students were also required to write their responses to these texts and generated pieces that provided critical social commentary and encouraging action for social justice. Based upon his work, Morrell concluded that teachers who use hip-hop as a pedagogical tool can improve the literacy achievement and global understanding of urban students because these types of language practices are situated in their lived experiences and communities. Morrell's approach is similar to cultural modeling (Lee, 2007)—students are asked to interpret culturally familiar literacies (hip-hop lyrics) and apply the same reasoning abilities to make sense of texts that may be unfamiliar (Shakespeare and other canonical texts)—although cultural modeling focuses more on helping students understand the conceptual skills that are used to make sense of these texts.

COMMUNITY DISCOURSES AS LANGUAGE TOOLS

According to McCollough (2000), "African American students often display unique linguistic patterns. Their speech may be characterized as vibrant and expressive, with extreme variety in rhythm, meter, tone, and style" (p. 5). This colorful style of linguistic communication is often used within numerous community-based organizations like the Boys and Girls Clubs, churches, and after-school programs (McMillon & McMillon, 2004). African American community leaders, including preachers, politicians, and business leaders, often draw upon the Black oral tradition because of its "verbal adroitness, the cogent and quick wit, the brilliant use of metaphor and the facility in rhythm and rhyme" (Perry & Delpit, quoted in Bohn, 2003, p. 689).

We use the term *community discourses* to represent several linguistic forms that are common within the social institutions located within the African American community (e.g., churches, recreation centers, Boys and Girls Clubs). Based on language research (Perry & Delpit, 1998; Smitherman, 1998) we include four language acts within the community discourse:

- call and response, in which the speaker talks and encourages the audience to "talk back" with appropriate responses
- proverbializing, in which the speaker teaches ideals and values (e.g., truth, freedom) through brief statements

- narrativizing, in which the speaker tells stories based on personal and/ or historical lived experiences
- signifying, in which the speaker uses exaggeration, irony, and humor as a way of saying something on two different levels at once

In many social organizations and institutions within the African American community, these four linguistic forms are the basis of "the rituals, routines and practices . . . that helped Black language speakers become fluent readers, writers, and powerful speakers" (Perry, 1998, p. 13). And because African American children are active within their local communities, they are familiar with these highly sophisticated ways of communicating and interacting. Thus, when culturally responsive teachers use community-based language tools in their classrooms (e.g., call and response, proverbializing), they promote and support the literacy learning and development of their African American students (McMillon & Edwards, 2000; McMillon & McMillon, 2004).

SCHOOL CONTEXT AND STUDENTS

Harry Hughes worked in a culturally and linguistically diverse school located in an urban center along the eastern corridor of the United States. During the 2005–2006 school year, PS-5 (a pseudonym) served more than 300 students. Eighty-nine percent of the school population was African American, while 10% were Hispanic. Ninety-five percent of the student body were eligible for free and reduced-price meals. Like many urban schools, PS-5 also had a fairly high mobility rate (12%).

The school building was in dire need of renovations. According to district records, the school was constructed more than 70 years ago. The three-level structure had only two restroom facilities (one for girls, one for boys) for the entire student body. The school relied on radiator heat and did not have central air conditioning; many windows did not open. Although there were some computers in fair condition, establishing and maintaining Internet connectivity in classrooms was always a challenge. Like many of the dilapidated schools in Kozol's (1988) book, the facilities at PS-5 were generally deplorable: Floor and ceiling tiles were damaged, the furniture was old and broken, and few of the chalkboards were functional.

Harry had 18 students in his 5th-grade classroom during the 2005–2006 academic year. Sixteen students were African American; 2 were Hispanic. There were 11 boys and 7 girls, and the students' reading abilities ranged from 3rd grade to 7th grade. Many parents worked hard to maintain employment and some parents struggled with substance abuse and other addictions that impact parenting and children's educational outcomes. Despite difficult circumstances, these families cared deeply about their children's educations, and many worked diligently to find resources that helped to create opportunities for their children that would assist with social preparation for years to come.

A MASTER TEACHER: MR. HARRY HUGHES

Harry Hughes, an African American man in his early 30s, is passionate about teaching in an urban community. His approach to teaching is strongly grounded in his past experiences as an African American male student in suburban schools. As a result of past discriminating experiences in his early education, Harry turned to music in an effort to make connections to the larger society that resonated with him. He became an avid listener and admirer of hip-hop and the hip-hop culture, and this love blossomed at the University of Virginia. During his studies as a history major, Harry joined an organization that paired mentors with youth at risk for academic failure. Soon after graduation, he changed his focus from pursuing law school to elementary education. He attributes this significant life decision to his youth mentoring experience. After completing a 1-year certification program, Harry began teaching in an urban school.

After 7 years of teaching 4th and 5th grades, Harry has earned the respect given to a master teacher. He is admired and emulated by administrators, teachers, parents, and students. His literacy pedagogy is thoughtful and engaging during the daily 90 minutes of literacy development. The time is structured to provide students with authentic yet meaningful literacy learning opportunities. Harry utilizes writing and computer centers that promote self-regulated learning and independent thought (Pressley, 1995). The students also have seat work and small-group instruction.

In addition, Harry implements Book Club Plus, an approach to literacy development geared toward engaging students more fully in conversations about books (Raphael, 2000). In book clubs, Harry encouraged his students to read and generate rich discussions about the text.

Harry also emphasized comprehension instruction and relied on coaching techniques, which involved scaffolding and using supportive actions to move either an individual or a group of students to the next level of independence with respect to completing a task, strategy, or activity (Taylor,

Pearson, Peterson, & Rodriquez, 2003). During the literacy block, Harry allowed students to select texts based on their individual preferences, encouraged students to read more information and expository text, incorporated critical literacy, and engaged students in thoughtful discussion about text. Furthermore, Harry used direct instruction, as well as preview and predict strategies.

Finally, vocabulary instruction in Harry's classroom combined several different lesson formats to promote students' vocabulary development. For instance, he introduced students to vocabulary words for both reading and social studies instruction. They were given semantic maps called "vocabulary quilts" or "word maps." On these quilts and maps students wrote terms and definitions and other related words that helped them construct meaning. During Book Club Plus, Harry disseminated sets of vocabulary terms all related to the chapters that were taught, giving the children pre-exposure to core vocabulary for the comprehension of story content.

LANGUAGE TOOLS FOR TEACHING LITERACY

In addition to the effective instructional practices discussed in the previous section, we identified three language tools that Harry consistently used to teach school literacy to his 5th-graders: code-switching (moving between AAVE and standardized English), rappin' about hip-hop, and preachin' and teachin'.

Code-Switching

To help his students to begin to develop this linguistic skill, Harry often talked to them about code-switching. Harry encouraged students to always consider context prior to speaking. For example, in the classroom, Harry discouraged the use of Ebonics during lessons and learning activities (e.g., small-group discussions). Although AAVE is an important part of African American students' home language patterns, Harry eloquently explained why he limited its use in the classroom:

> It is okay for them [students] to talk freely at appropriate times. But it is also important for them to learn standard forms of English. When students are speaking to adults in schools or other professional settings, or potential employees, they cannot say stuff like "I'm here to rap 'bout that joint you advertised in the paper, homie." They must be able to clearly express themselves in Standard English.

Although Harry rarely allowed the use of AAVE in the classroom, he helped his African American students acquire standardized English (SE) in a manner that did not belittle. For example, students often misconjugated verb forms, such as *to be* in this example: "Is we going to recess today?" Harry would often explain to his African American students what the appropriate form would be in SE (e.g., "Son, because you are speaking about more than one person going to recess, it is 'Are we going to recess today?' Do you understand that?"). Through this type of response, Harry wanted his African American students to understand that using SE was appropriate for formal settings, and he wanted to ensure that they knew the "rules" of SE so that they would be able to use this language proficiently.

Interestingly, there were times when Harry relied on AAVE to communicate with his African American students. For example, one morning Harry reprimanded students that were having trouble settling down by saying "Look Joe [slang for anyone's name] you can't be comin up in the spot [slang for place, meaning classroom] clowning at 8 in the morning, save that mess for later son, aight [alright]?" (O'Gilvie, 2007). After hearing this, students hurried to empty their backpacks and find their seats. Harry's use of AAVE required no explanation; because his African American students spoke this language, they understood and responded accordingly. By using AAVE, Harry was able to draw upon the power of their cultural connectedness to help his African American students to settle down, rather than appealing to the official teacher authority vested in SE. Thus, Harry used AAVE and SE as multilingual ways of communicating with his African American students for varying purposes (e.g., teaching, discipline).

Rappin' About Hip-Hop

As an avid hip-hop fan, Harry used the "language" of hip-hop (e.g., names of popular rap artists and songs, using slang, promoting critique) and was able to effectively use it to spark critical discussions with his African American students. Harry knew that his African American students loved hip-hop, so he took every opportunity to use this language tool in the classroom:

I like to use hip-hop and music that is relevant to my students 'cause it is engaging. They are really interested and everyone participates. You know I really think that they feel safe 'cause there is usually no right or wrong answer. So all of my kids participate. Actively. (Interview, 4/20/06)

Harry drew upon the language of critique to provide the African American students in his class with opportunities to read and respond to hip-hop "texts." He explained how the class would critically explore a song by Kanye West:

> All right folks, we are going to end today's lesson with a critical exploration of music and lyrics. How many of you like Kanye West? (all hands are raised) Okay then, we are going to not only listen to "Hey Mama" by Kanye West, we are going to read the lyrics and analyze them. By analyze I mean, we are going to try to figure out what Kanye is saying. Last time we did this, you all told me that rappers and singers have hidden messages and we discovered throughout this year that authors and many others do too. I am going to pull up the words to Kanye's song on the smart board so that we can all see them. I will also give you a copy. I used a marker to mark out curse words. (O'Gilvie, 2007)

During this lesson, students listened to the lyrics and took notes. To begin the conversation, Harry prompted students to think about the overall message being conveyed by Kanye West and asked them to discuss the words to the song with a partner in a think-pair-share. Harry then facilitated a whole-group discussion, with students sharing their own personal critiques of the song. The list below captures the thoughts and feelings of the students after analyzing the lyrics.

I think Kanye is trying to tell people that he is really proud of his mother.

Kanye is telling his fans that his mother really wanted him to finish school.

Kanye is saying that his mother always took care of him, like when she made him that homemade chicken soup, and put training wheels on his bike.

I think Kanye is thanking his mother, because he don't mention his father at all. So I think his mother did everything, just like my mother.

Kanye going to buy his mom a car for all that she has done for him.

He thinks his mom is an angel.

He says his mom is like poetry, and poems are beautiful and nice.

Kanye said it don't have to be no special time to thank his mother for being a good mother.

He said his mother worked late at night so she could keep the lights on in the house.

I think he think his mom is strong because he said words like unbreakable and thing that don't break are strong.

They used to live somewhere else, then they move to the Chi [Chicago] when he was 3.

He is telling his mother that he sorry for acting up and stuff.
He did the opposite of what his mother told him, but she still loved him
    anyway.
He really loved his mother.
He didn't like his father, because he only thanks his mother.

Harry effectively orchestrated this literacy lesson using the language of hip-hop and, more specifically, identifying the concept of critical analysis as one that is important to listening to hip-hop. Just as critics for popular hip-hop magazines like *Vibe* and *The Source* critique the rappers' messages in songs, Harry used the language of critique (e.g., "By analyze I mean we are going to try to figure out what Kanye is saying"; "rappers and singers have hidden messages") to help his African American students to deconstruct these messages and to develop their own opinions about the artist's intentions.

Preachin' and Teachin'

The third language tool that Harry used in his classroom is what we call *preachin' and teachin'*. This language tool depends upon an individual's personality, and Harry was able to utilize it well, because he was a charismatic and dynamic urban educator. He was constantly in motion, teaching lessons from the front, back, and all sides of the room. He was so magnetic that his students often swiveled in their seats, because they did not want to take their eyes off Harry or miss a word that he said.

As an African American educator, Harry drew upon language tools that are similar to those used by community leaders in the African American community (e.g., ministers, youth workers). He used *call and response,* the use of repetition to help his students recall information and generate solutions to problems:

> OK class, let's use one of our strategies before we start this chapter.
> Repeat after me "preview and predict," "preview and predict,"
> "preview and predict," "preview and predict." I need you all to look at
> the first section of this chapter. Take your time. Look at the pictures,
> read the subtitles, look at the words in italics and bold. Take about 3
> minutes to do this. (Field notes, 2/6/06)

Here, Harry had his students "respond" to him when he called "preview and predict." As a language tool, call and response can be very powerful, because the rhythm, the intonation of voice, and the stress on certain words and syllables resonates strongly with Black oral traditions that evoke participation and interaction between speakers and the audience (Smitherman, 1998). Harry further explained why the call and response style can improve African American students' learning:

> When I have my students repeat after me, I find that they remember the steps better. It is much like rapping or singing. They remember the words to songs, so they can also remember the steps to solve problems or write down categories from the reading story map. During tests and quizzes, I usually see a few of them mumbling to themselves. I smile inside when I see this. (Field notes, 2/6/06)

Just as many African American preachers use call and response to help the congregation remember critical ideas from the sermon (e.g., "Turn to your neighbor and tell them that their blessing is on the way" and the congregation turns to two or three people and repeats these words), Harry used call and response as a tool for reinforcing important reading strategies for his African American students.

Finally, Harry often used the mini-sermon to emphasize important ideals and life lessons. Smitherman (1998) characterizes this language tool as proverbializing, because the messages that are "given" by the speaker are brief, but they have strong moral content. Harry's students were accustomed to this strategy and everything was silent when Harry began one of his mini-sermons. For example, after students spent weeks preparing for an academic competition, Harry gave this mini-sermon:

> Boys and girls, I just want to congratulate you on a job well done. You all prepared well, studied hard, and most of all came together as a team. I want you to remember how it feels to be champions and remember how much work it takes to be victorious. Now when we see our opponents, we need to tell them good game, 'cause that's what good people with good sportsmanship do. (O'Gilvie, 2007)

The mini-sermon resonated with students since many of them were able to make verbal connections with Sunday services. Similar to many African American ministers, Harry's tone, inflection and pitch captivated his African American students.

CONCLUSION

This chapter explores the multilingual tools that Harry Hughes utilized to teach literacy to his African American 5th-graders. Similar to other culturally responsive teachers (Ladson-Billings, 1994; Strickland, 1994), Harry recognized that African American students come to school having had many rich experiences with language, and these experiences may be different from academic language (e.g., school literacy). By advocating an additive approach (Cummins, 2000), Harry was able to embrace the multiple languages that African American students were familiar with and used his students' home languages as bridges to school literacy. His students responded favorably because they were not required to leave their language at the door; rather, they were encouraged to dialogue with the teacher and their peers, to challenge texts, to share perspectives, and ultimately, to speak with authentic voices.

We believe that teachers, even though they may not be "linguistic insiders" with respect to African American communities, can learn to use multilingual tools with the African American students in their classrooms. This involves: (a) learning about African American culture and language through current reading research; (b) becoming familiar with African American students' language through literature; and (c) using technology to support the use of African American students' language.

MAKE THIS HAPPEN IN YOUR CLASSROOM

- Learn about African American culture and language. The list below includes researchers who have written about African American children, and whose work may be helpful for teachers who want to learn more about culturally responsive pedagogy, language diversity, and African American students.

Delpit, L. (1995). *Other people's children: Cultural conflict in the classrooms.* New York: New Press.

Delpit, L., & Dowdy, J. K. (Eds.). (2002). *The skin we speak: Thoughts on language and culture in the classroom.* New York: New Press.

Diller, D. (1999). Opening the dialogue: Using culture as a tool to teach young African American children. *The Reading Teacher, 52,* 820–828.

Edwards, P. A., McMillon, G. T., & Turner, J. D. (2010). *Change is gonna come: Transforming literacy education for African American students.* New York: Teachers College Press.

Gray, E. S. (2009). The importance of visibility: Students' and teachers' criteria for selecting African American literature. *The Reading Teacher, 62,* 472–481.

Hammond, W., Hoover, M., & McPhail, I. (Eds.). (2005). *Teaching African American learners to read: Perspectives and practices.* Newark, DE: International Reading Association.

Hefflin, B., & Barksdale-Ladd, M. (2001). African American children's literature that helps students find themselves: Selection guidelines for grades K–3. *The Reading Teacher, 54,* 810–819.

Turner, J. D. (2005). Orchestrating success for African American readers: The case of an effective third-grade teacher. *Reading Research and Instruction, 44,* 27–48.

- Become familiar with African American students' language through literature. Children's literature is a wonderful source of information about African American linguistic traditions. Hefflin and Barksdale-Ladd (2001) contend that high-quality African American literature often uses "language that is authentic and realistic, particularly dialogue that correctly portrays African American dialect appropriate to the character" (p. 814). Picture books and chapter books that focus specifically on the experiences of urban African American children and young adults may be particularly engaging. The inclusion and use of texts that capture the stories of people of color are especially important for intermediate students because during these years, most school districts are required to utilize mandated curricula that may not capture the stories of African American people.
- Use book clubs. We encourage teachers to use children's and young adult literature in a variety of ways in their classrooms. Like Harry, many teachers have discovered that the book club approach (Raphael, 2000) is very useful because this format allows for deep classroom conversations and critical analysis of culturally conscious texts. The following is just a small sampling of books that teachers can use as references:

Curtis, C. P. (1995). *The Watsons go to Birmingham—1963.* New York: Delacorte.

Curtis, C. P. (1999). *Bud, not Buddy.* New York: Delacorte.

Draper, S. (2008). *Copper sun.* New York: Atheneum.

Feelings, T. (1996). *The middle passage: White ships/Black cargo.* New York: Dial.

Forman, R. (2007). *Young cornrows callin out the moon.* San Francisco: Children's Book Press.

Giovanni, N. (Ed.). (2008). *Hip hop speaks to children.* Naperville, IL: Sourcebooks Jabberwocky.

Howard, E. F. (1991). *Aunt Flossie's hats (and crab cakes later).* New York: Clarion.

Mitchell, M. (1993). *Uncle Jed's barbershop.* New York: Aladdin.

Myers, W. D. (1997). *Slam.* New York: Scholastic.

Pinkney, S. L., & Pinkney, M. (2000). *Shades of Black: A celebration of our children.* New York: Scholastic.

Ringgold, F. (2004). *Cassie's word quilt.* New York: Dragonfly.

Schotter, R. (2008). *Doo wop pop.* New York: HarperCollins.

Steptoe, J. (1988). *Mufaro's beautiful daughters.* New York: HarperCollins.

Thomas, L. (2007). *Turning White: A memoir of change.* Troy, MI: Momentum.

- Use technology to support the use of African American students' language. Technology can be a critical resource to teachers who want to use a variety of multilingual tools to teach African American literacy learners. Teachers who want to use hip-hop or other popular songs in their classrooms should review the lyrics on Web sites such as lyrics.com or azlyrics.com. Not only will teachers be able to ensure that the song lyrics are appropriate for their students, but these Web sites enable teachers to print out the lyrics or to project them so that the students can see them as well.

REFERENCES

Au, K. (2006). *Multicultural issues and literacy achievement.* Mahwah, NJ: Erlbaum.

Bohn, A. P. (2003). Familiar voices: Using Ebonics communication techniques in the primary classroom. *Urban Education, 38,* 688–707.

Cummins, J. (2000). *Language, power, and pedagogy: Bilingual children in the cross-fire.* Clevedon, UK: Multilingual Matters.

Delpit, L., & Dowdy, J. K. (Eds.). (2002). *The skin we speak: Thoughts on language and culture in the classroom.* New York: New Press.

Hagood, M. C. (2002). Critical literacy for whom? *Reading Research and Instruction, 41*(3), 247–266.

Hammerberg, D. (2004). Comprehension instruction for socioculturally diverse classrooms: A review of what we know. *Reading Teacher, 57,* 648–658.

Howard, T. C. (2001). Powerful pedagogy for African American *students:* A case study of four teachers. *Urban Education, 36*(2), 179–202.

Kozol, J. (1988). *Savage inequalities: Children in America's schools.* New York: HarperPerennial.

Ladson-Billings, G. (1994). *The dreamkeepers: Successful teachers of African American children.* San Francisco: Jossey-Bass.

Larson, J. (2003). Negotiating race in classroom research: Tensions and possibilities. In S. Greene & D. Abt-Perkins (Eds.), *Making race visible: Literacy research for cultural understanding* (pp. 89–106). New York: Teachers College Press.

Lee, C. D. (2007). *Culture, literacy, and learning: Taking bloom in the midst of the whirlwind.* New York: Teachers College Press.

McCollough, S. (2000). Teaching African American students. *Clearinghouse, 74,* 5–6.

McMillon, G. M. T., & Edwards, P. A. (2000). Why does Joshua hate school, but love Sunday school?: *Language Arts, 78,* 111–120.

McMillon, G. M. T., & McMillon, V. (2004). The empowering literacy practices of the African American Church. In F. B. Boyd, C. H. Brock, & M. S. Rozendal (Eds.), *Multicultural and multilingual literacy and language: Contexts and Practices* (pp. 280–303). New York: Guilford.

Morrell, E. (2002). Toward a critical pedagogy of popular culture: Literacy development among urban youth. *Journal of Adolescent and Adult Literacy, 46,* 72–77.

O'Gilvie, H. P. (2007). *Excellent teaching of literacy in an urban school: Including new literacies and youth development*. Unpublished doctoral dissertation. University of Maryland College Park, College Park, MD.

Perry, T. (1998). "I'on know why they be trippin'": Reflections on the Ebonics debate. In T. Perry & L. Delpit (Eds.), *The real Ebonics debate: Power, language, and the education of African American children* (pp. 3–16). Boston: Beacon Press.

Perry, T., & Delpit, L. (Eds.). (1998). *The real Ebonics debate: Power, language, and the education of African American children.* Boston: Beacon Press.

Pressley, M. (1995). More about the development of self-regulation: Complex, long-term, and thoroughly social. *Educational Psychologist, 30,* 207–212.

Quinn, E. (2005). *Nuthin but a "G" thang: The culture and commerce of gangsta rap.* New York: Columbia University Press.

Raphael, T. (2000). Balancing literature and instruction: Lessons from the Book Club Project. In B. M. Taylor, M. F. Graves, & P. Van Den Brock (Eds.), *Reading for meaning: Fostering comprehension in the middle grades* (pp. 70–94). New York: Teachers College Press.

Smitherman, G. (1998). Black English/Ebonics: What it be like? In T. Perry & L. Delpit (Eds.), *The real Ebonics debate: Power, language, and the education of African American children* (pp. 29–37). Boston: Beacon Press.

Smith-Maddox, R. (1998). Defining culture as a dimension of academic achievement: Implications for culturally responsive curriculum, instruction, and assessment. *Journal of Negro Education, 67,* 302–317.

Strickland, D. (1994). Educating African American at-risk learners: Finding a better way. *Language Arts, 71,* 328–336.

Taylor, B. M., Pearson, P. D., Peterson, D. S., & Rodriguez, M. C. (2003). Reading growth in high-poverty classrooms: The influence of teacher practices that encourage cognitive engagement in literacy learning. *Elementary School Journal, 104,* 3–28.

Vygotsky, L. S. (1978). *Mind in society: The development of higher psychological processes.* Cambridge, MA: Harvard University Press.

Xu, S. (2004). Teachers' reading of students' popular culture texts: The interplay of students' interests, teacher knowledge, and literacy curriculum. In C. Fairbanks, J. Worthy, B. Maloch, J. V. Hoffman, & D. L. Schallert (Eds.), *53rd Yearbook of the National Reading Conference* (pp. 417–431). Oak Creek, WI: National Reading Conference.

CHAPTER 12

Working with Diverse Language Speakers in an Early Childhood Setting

Sunita Singh

The biggest child-specific demographic change in the United States over the next 20 years is predicted to be the increase in the number of children who speak English as a second language (Cochran, 2007). In early childhood settings where the physical, social, emotional, and cognitive domains of learning are interrelated, the challenges are manifold. Therefore, culturally responsive teaching (Ladson-Billings & Tate, 1995) becomes a necessity—a means of connecting known information to the new information, so that children and their families can better understand the educational system in the United States and learn a new language in a risk-free, respectful environment.

When English language learners (ELLs) enter a school, they face the dual challenge of learning a new language and also trying to fit in with the new academic routines both socially and academically (Peregoy & Boyle, 2001). Providing ELLs with resources to support language and literacy development in their first language in addition to their second language is beneficial and culturally responsive. Supporting literacy in the first language will not only lead to successful bilingual and biliteracy development, but will also enhance the development of literacy skills in the second language (Bernhardt, 2003; Gregory & Kenner, 2003) by encouraging transfer (Kenner & Gregory, 2003). Researchers have discussed positive aspects of bilingualism and biliteracy (Gregory & Williams, 2000; Ruggiano Schmidt, 1998; Williams & Snipper, 1990). Additionally, researchers proposing a social and constructive model of second language literacy encourage "additive" bilingualism in opposition to "subtractive" bilingualism (Moll, Sáez, & Dworin, 2001; Williams & Snipper, 1990) for development of biliteracy.

ROLE OF THE CLASSROOM TEACHER

The classroom teacher is seen to be the most important element in the creation of effective instruction, especially for children speaking English as a second language in an English-dominant classroom (Abbott & Grose, 1998; Blanton, 2002). If staff working with young bilingual children support and use languages other than English, children will feel confident about using both languages. Children who do not have a positive feeling about the use of their home language and who are not supported by staff may lose the ability to speak in their home language and become "receiving bilinguals" (Siraj-Blatchford & Clarke, 2000, p. 29–30). The classroom teacher's expertise in connecting to the second language learners and providing them with developmentally appropriate instruction is significant. It is not required (and also not possible always) that the teachers be from the same ethnolinguistic community (Jiménez, Gersten, & Rivera, 1996). But, even if instruction in the main classroom is in the second language (English), the learners must be provided with adequate support in their first language so they can develop as successful bilinguals and biliterates. This implies a professional need to explore how teachers might be responding to these developments, in an effort to better support them in their culturally responsive literacy practices.

According to the position statement by the National Association of Education of Young Children, "Teachers bring each child's home culture and language into the shared culture of the learning community so that the unique contributions of that home culture and language can be recognized and valued by the other community members, and the child's connection with family and home is supported" (2009, p. 20).

Based on the theoretical insights highlighted above, this chapter focuses on the instructional practices of Lucy, a White, monolingual, early childhood educator who served culturally and linguistically diverse kindergartners in a small Midwestern town. Lucy provided manifold opportunities for use and support of all languages spoken by her class, namely, English, Japanese, Korean, Spanish, and Vietnamese, in addition to the regular instruction that she was providing in English. She was a culturally responsive teacher. In this chapter, I will focus on areas of her literacy program that supported English language learners in their first language.

LUCY

Lucy was a monolingual teacher of European-American descent who grew up in a small Midwestern community with little diversity. She had 10 years of teaching experience at the preschool level, a master's degree in guidance and counseling, was certified in early childhood education, and in the generalist category from the National Board for Professional Teaching Standards. As a preschool teacher, Lucy had been involved in the preschool's Even Start program and had gained an opportunity to work with families who spoke little or no English. She had herself enrolled in classes to learn Spanish and had developed basic communication skills. Every year that Lucy taught, there were at least four different languages spoken in the classroom, with no assigned time in the schedule for incorporating languages other than English into the curriculum. Lucy had developed a program that offered all children the opportunity to be exposed to all languages spoken in the classroom, provided opportunities for all children to develop positive attitudes to other languages and language users, and provided children with the opportunity to learn another language. Her first step in this process was building a relationship with the parents of the students in her classroom. As she said,

> I think a lot of teachers feel uncomfortable dealing with the parents. It's like if I am having a problem, I am going to talk to the parents. They are almost intimidated to develop a relationship with parents. Some teachers have an attitude of "this child is at school now and so home life doesn't come into the classroom." And I think it does.

Lucy was a strong advocate of native language instruction for the second language learners in her classroom. She firmly believed that supporting children in reading and writing in their native languages was important for literacy development in their second language, English, and for maintaining their linguistic and cultural identity. She also believed that the teacher and the school should advocate for and find appropriate resources to support such services. Her curriculum was child-centered and she adapted the balanced literacy approach to the needs of her multilingual classroom so that all the children could work and learn at the level of their full potential.

CLASSROOM SPACES

In Lucy's classroom, the process of incorporating all the languages spoken began in the morning and continued throughout the day. She used different languages during circle time, learned basic expressions in the languages spoken by the children in her class, included relevant children's literature, invited guest speakers who could read books in different languages in the classroom, and also invited parents for holiday celebrations of other countries and cultures. She turned to the "parents as a natural resource as much as possible," finding it especially invaluable for her ELL children. She said she really looked forward to parents visiting the classroom and always recognized the help they could provide.

Lucy's first step in providing culturally responsive instruction was to represent all languages spoken by the children in the physical spaces of the classroom. Her classroom was recognizable by a big stuffed "pink panther" that sat outside the room, and the children's lockers, visible from the classroom, were labeled and decorated by each child. The classroom was divided into 12 centers (Blocks, Meeting Area, Computer, Housekeeping, Listening, Reading, Science, Discovery, Math, Work Bench, Art, and Writing) and were labeled in English and Spanish. The major activity area for the children was the circle time area that was defined by a bright carpet with numbers and letters of the alphabet in colorful large squares. In the center of the room were three tables with the children's names on them and chairs. Also, small, lined pieces of paper had imprints of two hands, and on the imprint of each hand were written the words "left" and "right." For the English speakers, it was written in English and for the Spanish speakers, in Spanish. In every learning center of the classroom, there were stationery items for the children to write and books for them to read. The classroom wall had the alphabet in English, Spanish, Japanese, and Vietnamese. Additionally, the small multicultural classroom library collection included books in all languages spoken in the classroom.

BUILDING A CULTURALLY RESPONSIVE COMMUNITY

The first 45 minutes of the school day, from 8:45 to 9:30 a.m., was reserved for sign-in, the pledge, and circle time activities. The focus during this time was mainly community building, but literacy instruction was an integral part. Lucy's aim always was to build a classroom community that allowed her students to think of themselves as a "classroom family." Typically, the day began with "sign-in," when the children signed their names on a paper as they came into the classroom by looking at their name cards. This routine was followed by "circle time" activities that were done as a whole class. These activities included greeting one another, singing a classroom hello song, selection of line leader for the day (saying the letters in the student's first and last names and clapping the syllables in the names), calendar routine (including counting of the day, date, and month), signing rhymes with movement, and math. Show-and-tell was also included during the circle time and children could bring in items from home to share with the class and the class could ask them questions about the item. The following vignette exemplified a typical morning routine in Lucy's kindergarten classroom.

> As the children arrived in the morning, they greeted Miss Lucy, collected their laminated Zaner-Bloser 4x7 name cards, and gravitated toward the kidney-shaped table at the rear end of the classroom. Some took longer, as they shared their excitement from the previous day with Miss Lucy. The kidney-shaped table had several sheets of lined or unlined 9x11 papers spread across with the dates on them. The name cards had the children's names written in English and also in Japanese and Vietnamese, depending on the native language of the child. Using the name cards as a model, children "signed-in" their names in one or two languages. After a brief period of morning chatter and playing with manipulatives, they gathered on the carpet for circle time routine. Circle time routine began with a "hello song" in English and Spanish. Miss Lucy asked Aiko, "How do people in your house greet each other when they have not seen each other for some time?" Aiko replied, "*konnichiwa.*" All children said "*konnichiwa*" to one child as they sat holding hands in a circle. Circle time proceeded with the line leader and calendar routines for which children chose the language they wanted to do the routines in.

Aiko was a Japanese-speaking student in Lucy's class one of the years. Lucy initiated contact with her parents and asked them about basic greetings in Japanese. Later during the semester, she asked Aiko to do the calendar routine in Japanese with a Japanese calendar made by Aiko's mother. After the routine, all children thanked her in Japanese by saying "*Arigato.*"

The languages spoken in the classroom also influenced children. According to Lucy, the children responded to all the languages and cultures in the classroom with great interest and enthusiasm and continued to incorporate them until the end of the school year. Children were also eager to use any of the languages spoken in the classroom. Following is an observation of circle time where Hae-Yung, a Korean-speaking child does the calendar routine in Spanish with help from Lucy:

As Hae-Yung stands near the calendar, children continue talking. After children settle down, Lucy asks children if they wanted to say the calendar in English or Spanish. Children choose Spanish. Lucy helps Hae-Yung, the Korean-speaking child to say the month, day and date in Spanish. The class also sings "Days of the Week" and counts the number of days in the month in Spanish. Beata does the patterns in Spanish. Maria, the bilingual aide, also comes to the classroom and leads the remainder of the calendar routines in Spanish.

During one of the circle time routines, children wanted Akeiyla, an English-speaking child, to say the letters in her name in Japanese. Lucy then asked Aiko if she would write Akeiyla's name in Japanese. As she wrote, everyone bent down to see what she was writing. Lucy explained to the class that Japanese uses characters. Ultimately, Akeiyla said the letters in her name in Spanish. According to Lucy,

> here we have some English-speaking kids who don't even know the letters in English practicing in Spanish! I am like okay! And so I just do it anyway, because they are motivated and I don't want to turn it off. Somebody would probably say it is wrong, but it's okay.

There were also times when children came to Lucy's classroom not using their native languages. In cases like these Lucy turned to the parents or other resource personnel for support. Such a student in Lucy's classroom was Nancy, a Vietnamese-speaking child who was not using her native language at all. Later during the semester, Lucy mentioned that Nancy had started using Vietnamese whenever she could. As Lucy said,

> It is good to see that this is a child who had earlier totally disassociated herself from her language and her culture. If you talked to her in Vietnamese, she would answer in English. And now if I ask her, "Nancy, how do you say that in Vietnamese?" She tells me instantly. She is teaching the calendar and she tells them in Vietnamese.

Overall, there was an increase in the awareness of the languages spoken and in the respect shown to speakers of other languages in the classroom by all children. Lucy also acknowledged her own limitations. As she said, "Having ESL students, you have to be so aware of the names because you can't do the sounds of the names. It takes me a long time to learn." Lucy's assessment of the children's progress was ongoing, as she said, with respect to the sign-in sheets,

> I think a lot relates to community learning. I put numbers on the sign-in sheets because I wanted to see what happens if you put numbers. Now all of a sudden the children want to write their last names. Brittney, John, can write their last names even though their name cards don't have their last names. What is important is that they are not putting spaces in the names. They will do that when they get their name cards with their last names and spaces in between them. They know the capital. I say, "what word, not name does it spell?" when I show the name card.

The main purpose of morning routine was building community, but Lucy continued to support all languages while assessing children's growth in literacy learning and her own goals for teaching.

CULTURALLY RESPONSIVE LITERACY INSTRUCTION

Lucy incorporated all the key elements of the district's balanced literacy curriculum in her instruction (e.g., modeled reading and writing, shared reading and writing, interactive reading and writing, guided reading and writing, and independent reading and writing), adapting them as best she was able to her children's needs and levels. The literacy activities in the classroom were scheduled during literacy block (9:30–10:25) and literacy center time (10:50–11:20), after circle time. Literacy block included mainly whole-class activities related to writing and reading. The writing activities included writing the morning message (modeled writing), interactive writing, and independent journal writing. The reading activities included read-aloud and shared reading. In addition to these, Lucy also included activities related to the children's names, making classroom books, and singing rhymes. The purpose of the literacy centers was to encourage children to work with each other and also independently. Some of the prominent centers in the classroom were listening, reading, writing, computers, and science. The activities for these centers included listening, guided reading, buddy reading, independent reading, interactive writing, making dictionaries, writing rainbow words, sight words, writing ABC words, writing around the room, building a sentence, writing a message, identifying letters, computer, literacy games, and science. Lucy wanted each child to take part in one reading and one writing center every day.

The literacy time was mainly in English, but Lucy encouraged the use of Spanish, Japanese, and Vietnamese also as a means to stimulate the interests of the children to whom she taught literacy at that time. During this time, Lucy invited resource personnel she knew from the district, tutors, or parents, at least once a week, to provide instruction to all children in a language spoken in the classroom, in addition to the half hour of tutorial support provided by the district to individual children.

Reading Instruction

Lucy encouraged children to bring books to school that they read at home, irrespective of the language. She would allow them to read or pretend to read the book to the class during the literacy time, or later in the day, during free-choice time or sharing time. Once a month, Lucy also invited a resource person to the classroom to read a book in one of the languages spoken in the classroom other than English. Once, she invited the Vietnamese-speaking librarian to read a story in Vietnamese to the whole class. All children listened to the story with attention even though the Vietnamese-speaking child Nancy was the only one who could understand it. At the end of the story children learned some greetings in Vietnamese (e.g., "goodbye" and "thank you"), which they then used with each other. Lucy also asked Aiko's parents to send books that Aiko could read in the classroom, and her parents sent three Harry Potter books in Japanese, which Aiko then read during the course of the semester. At the same time all students, including ELLs, were provided with support in English literacy instruction so that they could read independently, starting with simple texts used for guided reading.

Lucy also initiated reading instruction in Spanish by asking Maria, a part-time bilingual aide in the school, to come to the classroom once a week so the children could learn Spanish from her. The two followed a pattern of concurrent translation in which Lucy first read a poem or story in English and Maria then read the poem or story in Spanish.

The following illustrates how the instruction was coordinated between the two. Lucy had a rhyme written on pocket charts and asked the children to read it aloud as she pointed to the words herself. Lucy brought in a candlestick for this routine. She also substituted each child's name for Jack as s/he jumped over the candlestick: "Jack be nimble, Jack be quick, Jack jump over the candlestick." Lucy then asked Maria to say the same rhyme in Spanish. Following the suggestions, Maria produced the following:

Muy ágil es Gil, que sin quemarse, salta encima del candil.

In this manner, Lucy incorporated Spanish reading into her balanced curriculum for the English-speaking children, despite the fact that there was no requirement to do so.

Writing Instruction

Instruction in writing was a significant part of Lucy's balanced literacy curriculum. In journal writing, also known as independent writing, children were asked to think of a story, draw a picture about it, and write it using invented spellings. Lucy generally asked them to read their story to her by pointing to the words. Children could also share their journals during sharing time. Later, she modeled the writing using conventional spellings, saying, "This is how big people write," thus, modeling the conventional form and yet validating their own writing. In case of students who wrote in a different language, Lucy let them follow the same process even though she herself could not model the conventional form for them.

On days when Maria was present in the classroom, Lucy and Maria followed the same pattern of instruction for journal writing in Spanish. Maria worked with children who had drawn pictures or written stories in their Spanish-language journals and read to her, pointing to the words. Maria modeled the conventional form of writing for them.

Lucy encouraged Aiko to write in Japanese in her journal and read Japanese texts during independent reading, in an effort to ease Aiko's transition to her new school environment. During the first 3 months of school, Aiko had no tutor, hence, no support for native language or ESL instruction. Later in the semester, Aiko was assigned a tutor, Todd, who helped her with Japanese and ESL. She could not speak English at all initially, so Lucy encouraged her to write in Japanese in her journals because Lucy had learned from the parents that Aiko could read and write in Japanese. With assistance from Lucy, Aiko was also writing in English by using sight words and invented spellings. During sharing time, Aiko shared her journals in Japanese. Children were excited and fascinated by the new language in the classroom and Lucy said with respect to this new development in her classroom,

You know what? Japanese has been popping up in their writing. They ask Aiko during journal writing to write in Japanese. Today Nancy had written a whole page of Japanese and was asking Todd what it was . . . Todd read it out. Whatever she had written made sense to Todd.

One of the other writing-related activities in the classroom was writing a brief reflection about a story children had read in the class, either as a read-aloud or independent reading. One of the stories that were read in the class was *Henny Penny*. The children's interest in learning other languages was evident, especially in Hae-Yung's spelling of the word *penny* with *ñ*s, instead of *n*s (peññy), using *ñ*s as he had seen in the Spanish writing being used in the classroom. He also regularly made an effort to read and write in Spanish.

Lucy thus provided space for children's expressions in their native language and literacy by accommodating their own constructions of literacy (Levy, 2008). This allowed children to maintain and develop language and literacy skills in their native language as they were beginning to develop the same in English. Additionally, this reflected Lucy's understanding of the social construction of motivation (Nolen, 2007), thus, motivating children to read and write using their social contexts.

CONCLUSION

Although literacy block and literacy centers were the main periods for literacy instruction in Lucy's classroom, culturally responsive practices occurred throughout the day. During movement time Lucy varied the music that she played, respecting the diversity of students in the classroom. Similarly, she included books for read-aloud and rhymes in the classroom that were culturally responsive and also popular with children. She included small celebrations in her classrooms on special occasions, for example, on the occasion of Kwanza, Martin Luther King's birthday, Day of the Dead, Christmas, and so on. Sometimes she invited parents to these celebrations. Celebrations could be in the form of bringing treats for the children, baking together in the classroom, or making tortillas. Always, there was a literacy component included in the celebration, for example, writing a journal entry about the celebration or reading a book about the holiday. The books read during the celebration were later available for children to read on their own during independent reading time. Lucy's support of the students who spoke English as a second language was reflected in the physical, social, and academic spaces in the classroom. The focus of instruction in the classroom was English, yet encouraged development of biliteracy skills (Reyes & Azuara, 2008).

- During the initial contact with parents inquire about the language and literacy routines in their homes and ask them to send materials in their native language that can be displayed on the classroom walls.
- Invite parents to the classroom to read a book, for holiday celebrations, and for other classroom routines if their schedule permits.
- Learn some basic greetings (hello, goodbye, thank you) in the languages spoken in the classroom by the children.
- Allow children to use their native language in the classroom, especially if there is more than one child who speaks that language.
- Enrich your classroom by prominently displaying literature from diverse languages and cultures.

REFERENCES

Abbott, S., & Grose, C. (1998). "I know English so many, Mrs. Abbott": Reciprocal discoveries in a linguistically diverse classroom. *Language Arts, 75*(3), 175–184.

Bernhardt, E. (2003). Challenges to reading research from a multilingual world. *Reading Research Quarterly, 38*(1), 112–117.

Blanton, L. L. (2002). Seeing the invisible: Situating L2 literacy acquisition in child–teacher interaction. *Journal of Second Language Writing, 11*, 295–310.

Cochran, M. (2007). *Finding our way: The future of American early care and education.* Washington, DC: Zero to Three.

Galdone, P. (1968). *Henny Penny.* New York: Clarion.

Gregory, E., & Williams, A. (2000). *City literacies: Learning to read across generations and cultures.* New York: Routledge.

Gregory, E., & Kenner, C. (2003). The out-of-school schooling of literacy. In H. Hall, J. Larson, & J. Marsh (Eds.), *Handbook of early childhood literacy* (pp. 75–84). Thousand Oaks, CA: Sage.

Jiménez, R. T., Gersten, R. M., & Rivera, A. (1996). Conversations with a Chicana teacher: Supporting students' transition from native to English language instruction. *Elementary School Journal, 96*(3), 333–341.

Kenner, C., & Gregory, E. (2003). Becoming biliterate. In H. Hall, J. Larson, & J. Marsh (Eds.), *Handbook of early childhood literacy* (pp. 178–188). Thousand Oaks, CA: Sage.

Ladson-Billings, G., & Tate, W. F. (1995). Toward a critical race theory of education. *Teachers College Record, 97*(1), 47–68.

Levy, R. (2008). "Third Spaces" are interesting places: Applying "third space theory" to nursery aged children's constructions of themselves as readers. *Journal of Early Childhood Literacy, 8*(1), 43–66. doi: 10.1177/1468798407087161

Moll, L. C., Sáez, R., & Dworin, J. (2001). Exploring biliteracy: Two student case examples of writing as a social practice. *Elementary School Journal, 101*(4), 435–449.

National Association for the Education of Young Children. (2009). *Developmentally appropriate practice in early childhood programs serving children from birth through age 8: A position statement of the National Association for the Education of Young Children.* Retrieved March 13, 2010, from http://www.naeyc.org/files/naeyc/file/positions/PSDAP.pdf

Nolen, S. B. (2007). The development of motivation to read and write in young children: Development in social contexts. *Cognition & Instruction, 25*(2), 219–270.

Peregoy, S. F., & Boyle, O. F. (2001). *Reading, writing and learning in ESL—A Resource Book for K–12 teachers.* New York: Longman.

Reyes, I., & Azuara, P. (2008). Emergent biliteracy in young Mexican immigrant children. *Reading Research Quarterly, 43*(4), 374–398.

Ruggiano Schmidt, P. R. (1998). The ABCs of cultural understanding and communication. *Equity and Excellence in Education, 31*(2), 28–38.

Siraj-Blatchford, I., & Clarke, P. (2000). *Supporting identity, diversity and language in the early years.* Philadelphia: Open University Press.

Williams, J. D., & Snipper, G. C. (1990). *Literacy and Bilingualism.* White Plains, NY: Longman.

CHAPTER 13

Cross-Cultural Connections

Developing Teaching Principles Through Stories

Mario E. López-Gopar

Dear Elena:

I hope this e-mail finds you well. It was lovely to have you here in Oaxaca. I wish you were here, so we could talk more about our students. Even though you're teaching in Oregon and I'm teaching in Oaxaca, I think that we have a lot of things to discuss and that we could learn from one another, don't you?

Well, I'll let you go. I have to help Manuel, who is preparing dinner today. We're eating the black *mole* that you loved. We'll think of you while we eat.

A big hug,
Margarita

Dear Margarita:

I wish I could be there having some of that *mole* with you. After my trip to Oaxaca, I have been asking a lot of my students where they're from in Mexico, and many of their families come from Oaxaca! Can you believe it? Let's continue exchanging e-mails because as you said, we can help each other a lot.

I have to run, too. I have to go grocery shopping. Who knows, I may find that delicious black *mole* here.

XOXOXO,
Elena

Elena and Margarita are "fictional" characters and so are the e-mails. However, they are inspired by teachers with whom I have collaborated in my teaching and research career and from data I have collected in different research projects. I worked with teachers in Oregon for 4 years, working as an elementary school teacher for the first 2, and the other 2 as a literacy and English language development coach. In Oregon, I worked in a small rural community. Sixty percent of the school district's population was of Mexican origin. Many of the students were recent immigrants or first-generation Mexican Americans. I have also worked with teachers and student teachers in Oaxaca, Mexico, for the last 5 years both in teaching preparation programs and research projects. In Oaxaca, which is located in the southern part of Mexico, I have worked with urban and semi-urban schools. Oaxaca is the most culturally and linguistically diverse state in the country with 16 indigenous languages officially recognized by the government, including Chinanteco, Chatino, Mazateco, Mixe, Mixtec, Triqui, and Zapotec.

I am using e-mail exchanges—dialogues or stories—as part of this chapter to underscore the fact that teachers construct theories and/or teaching principles dialogically across different contexts. Bruner (1990) argues that narrative or stories play a key role in the development of hypotheses or theories. We learn to see the world and our teaching, in this case, based on the different stories that we hear from others. Teachers are many times seen as consumers of theories and knowledge presented in their teaching preparation programs and/or professional development workshops (McLaren, 2003). Contrary to this technical view of teaching, I consider teachers to be individuals who can create theories and/or teaching principles before, while, and after they teach. Teachers develop theories when they engage in dialogue with other teachers, tell each other stories about their students, appropriate each other's beliefs and practices, and connect them to the literature they encounter in professional development courses and/or programs that they seek on a personal basis (López-Gopar, 2009). In addition, these e-mails will reflect that teachers' practice does not occur in a vacuum. It is connected to the historical and sociopolitical milieu they live in and to their own personal lives.

The purpose of this chapter is to present the co-construction of principles and strategies for teaching multilingual elementary students by two elementary school teachers: one teaching in Oaxaca, Mexico, and the other teaching in Oregon, USA. Through e-mail exchanges, these teachers will discuss and reflect upon the following themes: (1) My students are bilingual and multilingual people! (2) My students are readers and writers! (3) Celebrating students' translanguaging practices; (4) Multiple discourses: Multiple worlds; and (5) Authors in the classroom. These themes will be introduced by these teachers' e-mail exchanges interspersed with my analysis.

MY STUDENTS ARE BILINGUAL OR MULTILINGUAL PEOPLE!

Dear Margarita:

I hope this e-mail finds you well. I'm excited and nervous with my new position. This year I'm working as a reading specialist. I'm excited because I'm helping children learn to read and write in Spanish because we have a dual immersion program in our school. However, I'm also nervous because other teachers at my school don't consider me a "specialist." Well, I'll do my best!

Remember I told you that I've been finding out that there are a lot of students from Oaxaca in Oregon. Well, I have a story to tell you about one of these students. His name is Jaime and he's in 2nd grade. His teacher sent Jaime to me because he's having problems reading in Spanish. Well, I had Jaime read several books to me. I noticed that he didn't understand all the words in the story and that he was omitting some final sounds in certain words, especially words in plural. I thought he was not paying attention to the final letters. However, I later noticed that he was doing the same when he was speaking. I was about to refer him to the speech therapist when I remembered that you told me that in Oaxaca there are many people who speak an indigenous language. Well, I talked to Jaime's parents, and guess what? Jaime's first language is *not* Spanish. His first language is Mixtec. No wonder he didn't understand all the words in Spanish either. I feel very bad now because I almost sent Jaime to the Special Ed teacher. Now, I feel that I should send him to the TAG (talented and gifted) teacher. Jaime is trilingual!! He speaks Mixtec and is learning to read and write in Spanish and English!

Well, I must go and tell Jaime's teacher the news. I'm sure she will be surprised.

A big hug,

Elena

Elena's story is not atypical. With the development of nation-states like Mexico, the United States, Bolivia, and Brazil, to name a few, many minority and indigenous languages have been devalued and pushed to the private domains (May, 2001). Consequently, one tends to assume that only one language is spoken in each country (e.g., Spanish in Mexico and Bolivia, Portuguese in Brazil, and English in the United States). Nevertheless, in many countries around the world, there are different minority and indigenous languages spoken. Hence, next time you receive a student from Mexico, do not assume that she will speak Spanish. More importantly, do not rush into labeling students as "Special Ed" without learning about their linguistic background first. Cummins (1984) analyzed numerous psychologists' reports on ESL students' performance and showed how their reports placed students in deficit models and mislabeled them as "Special Ed" students. These psychologists, Cummins (1984) argues, simply ignored the fact that they were dealing with children who were adding an additional language to their linguistic repertoire.

In order to establish culturally responsive literacy teaching practices, knowing about your students' personal and linguistic background is a must. Viv Edwards' (1998) book *The Power of Babel: Teaching and Learning in Multilingual Classrooms* offers very practical classroom ideas as to how to bring the multilingualism present in today's classrooms to the forefront. One way is to have the students conduct surveys on the different multilingual practices their families engage in. Children interview one another and their family members about the language(s) they speak, who they speak these languages with, and so forth. These surveys can also include questions regarding literacy practices connecting them to the different languages spoken by the family. You will be surprised how complex students' multilingual and literacy practices are. In the following section, Margarita will tell us a story about one of her students' literacy practices.

MY STUDENTS ARE READERS AND WRITERS!

Dear Elena:

Good luck with your new position. I completely understand how you feel about being judged by other teachers. You'll do just fine, I'm sure.

I totally understand how you feel about Jaime, too. I also feel bad when I assume something about my students and later discover that my assumptions were wrong. I have a rather similar story. During my teaching practicum, I taught at a school where children from different indigenous communities came together. At this school, I also had the opportunity to do some research with children whose parents had no or limited formal schooling.

In that class, I had a student named Zenén. He was a student from a Zapotec-speaking community. His father was in the USA and his stepmother was not able to read and write alphabetically. My host teacher used to sit Zenén in the row with the low-achieving children. During my practicum, I encouraged my 6th-grade students to read for pleasure. I would bring books to the class, read to them, and encourage them to take a book home every day. I noticed that Zenén didn't want to check books out. I thought he was one of those reluctant readers. I also assumed that he didn't do much reading and writing at home either since he didn't have any role models. Thus, I concluded that his low grades in school were connected to all this.

One day, as part of the research we were conducting, I had the chance to interview Zenén about his literacy practices at home and in the community. I was so surprised! He told me that he runs a grocery store pretty much by himself because his dad is in the USA and his mother (I am happy he calls her that because he lost his birth mother when he was 3 years old) can barely read and write alphabetically. Zenén keeps a record of the things he sells on a daily basis, places the orders with the different grocery providers he deals with, and even keeps a notebook with the people who buy things "*fiado*" (you know, when people do not have money, they buy things at the grocery stores and pay later). Zenén told me that he also reads the Bible to his mother. He even chats with his cousin on MSN Messenger. Can you believe it? I asked him directly why he didn't want to take home any of the books that I brought to class. Zenén told me that he has a younger brother and that he was afraid that his younger brother might damage the books and that he would have to pay for them. I then figured out that my "reluctant" reader was a businessman who didn't want to risk his hard-earned money and that his teacher and I were simply underestimating his abilities and not making connections to Zenén's current literacy practices.

I guess that we need to constantly learn about our students in order to avoid making false assumptions, right?

Well, I must go. I have to attend a committee meeting. Wish me luck!

All the best,

Margarita

Margarita's (mis)conceptions about what counts as literacy practices are embedded in a historical and sociocultural context. In Mexico, as in many parts of the world, many people do not consider themselves to be readers because comics, short stories with pictures, and stories and legends told by grandmothers are not considered good literature or even literature at all (Garrido, 2004; López-Gopar, 2006). To be considered a reader, you must read books related to school or the classics. This is a very narrow view of literacy. "Do you read?" or "Are you a reader?" are no longer suitable questions because students engage in multiple literacy practices beyond books assigned at school. Heath (1983) demonstrated how working families in the United States engaged in different literacy practices. More recently, the Cultural Practices of Literacy Study coordinated by Victoria Purcell-Gates (2007) provided a series of case studies of literacy practices in different sociocultural communities that have been historically discriminated against. All these case studies, similar to Zenén's story, prove that people engage in different literacy practices. However, whether or not these practices are considered legitimate depends on the beliefs and power relations existing in these communities. You can access these case studies at the following Web site: http://cpls.educ.ubc.ca/

In Margarita's case, she had the opportunity to learn about Zenén's literacy practices through an interview. I am aware that teachers often do not have the time to sit down with each and every one of their students to learn about their linguistic and literacy practices. One thing that you can try is to have your students write in their journals about these practices. First, however, you need to let your students know that there are many literacy practices, besides reading school-related texts, and that you approve of those practices. Once you establish an atmosphere in which all literacy practices are validated, students will start sharing what they and their family read and write at home and in their community. You, as the teacher, will then be able to build on those practices, which are part of the funds of knowledge (Moll, Amanti, Neff, & González, 1992) that students bring to school. In the next section, you will see how linguistic practices go beyond language borders.

CELEBRATING STUDENTS' TRANSLANGUAGING PRACTICES

Dear Margarita:

I hope this e-mail finds you well. The days of proving myself are over. The teachers trust me now and we talk all the time about how to meet our students' needs.

Thanks for sharing Zenén's story. It is certainly an eye-opener. It is amazing how once we learn about our students' personal lives and we start seeing them as intelligent people, they perform as such, right? Jaime is blossoming now that I openly admire his multilingualism.

One thing I would like to discuss with you is my students' use of the different languages both in speaking and in their writing. For instance, when we're working in Spanish, sometimes they speak English among themselves. Other times, when they're speaking Spanish, they code-switch. They say, "*Orale, tú* (Hey, you), get the book." Also, when they're writing in Spanish, they use English words and transform them into Spanish. They sometimes write, "*Estaba corriendo y él me* puchó" (I was running and he *pushed* me)."

What do you think of this? Do your bilingual students do the same?

Well, let me know when you have a chance. I heard that you may go on strike. I read it on the online news Web site you sent me. I hope your demands are met, so you don't miss any classes.

Un fuerte abrazo,
Elena

Dear Elena:

It was great to hear from you. Thanks for your kind wishes. Our situation is complex. On the one hand, I don't want to miss any school days. On the other, if we don't pressure the government, they'll never pay attention to our demands. I wish we could be independent from the International Monetary Fund (IMF). The IMF lends Mexico money, but it imposes restrictions on how this money is used. One thing the IMF does not like is for Mexico to use money on social projects, like education. I think the IMF wants Mexican children to be undereducated, so that they'll always be dependent on them. The IMF is also pushing education toward privatization. Can you imagine, only rich kids will be able to afford higher education?

Anyhow, regarding your question about switching between languages, my students do it all the time. A couple of weeks ago, we were comparing words in Spanish and Zapotec, and they also transformed different words. Here is the list they came up with:

Spanish	**Zapotec from the Sierra Sur**
cruz (cross)	*crus*
plato (plate)	*guian*

escalera (ladder)	*scaler*
mesa (table)	*mes*
frijol (beans)	*mé*
culebra (snake)	*mal*

As you can see, the words for *cross*, *ladder*, and *table* are very similar to Spanish. The word *cross* certainly was brought by the Spanish *conquistadores*. So, it was not part of the vocabulary of the Zapotecs since they had other gods.

There are some teachers here who think that students should not do that because they are "contaminating" or "butchering" the language. In my case, I let them do it because we can all understand it. I'm not sure whether I'm right or not, though. Let me know if you find out something and what other people think.

Well, take good care and let's keep in touch.

Margarita

The issue that Elena and Margarita addressed is certainly complex, especially because monolingualism has been taken as the norm. Cummins (2008) and García (2009) argue that monolingual and monoglossic beliefs have prevailed in literacy education programs, especially bilingual programs. In other words, teachers and children are expected to keep languages separate. However, according to García (2009), bilingual and multilingual people move in and out of different languages as they engage in language and literacy practices. They can, for instance, read a text in English, discuss it orally in Spanish, and then write a summary in English. They can also code-switch. García (2009) refers to this as a translanguaging practice. Cummins (2008) also argues that students increase their metalinguistic awareness when they use multiple languages and that the students' knowledge transfers across multiple languages.

Translanguaging practices are not only performed by students, they are certainly used by the media, advertising companies, and businesses to sell products. You can find many examples of texts that use multiple languages or combinations of these languages in the book *Linguistic Landscape: Expanding the Scenery* edited by Shohamy and Gorter (2008). You and your students can become sociolinguists and sociocultural literacy researchers and explore the use of translanguaging practices in conversations and in written texts. With this activity you will not only validate your bilingual students' translanguaging and literacy practices, but you will also expose your monolingual students to the new types of texts available in their surroundings. If we are to prepare students to critically comprehend "real" texts, then we need to start bringing these texts into the classroom. In the next section, we will connect the use of translanguaging practices to the concept of discourses.

MULTIPLE DISCOURSES: MULTIPLE WORLDS

Dear Margarita:

I hope this e-mail finds you well. I'm sorry that I haven't been in touch. I caught the flu and so did my two children. We're fine now, but we all had to go to the clinic. That was a hassle. Well, I shouldn't complain because there are millions of people without medical insurance here in the USA. Many of the children's parents have never set foot in a hospital here.

I'm glad your strike is over. I hope you got what you wanted. Regarding our previous conversation, I started talking to other colleagues about code-switching and "our" use of multiple languages. We all agreed that we also do it all the time. One of my colleagues pointed out that even academics do it. For instance, authors use phrases in Latin like *sine qua non* (an essential element) or phrases in French like *par excellence* or *in lieu of*. We concluded that they probably just want to show how smart they are.

One of my colleagues told me that she also allows her students to translanguage. However, she said that she also makes her students aware that there are times when you need to use only one language because people may not understand the two languages or because people may not approve of it. She also told me that she constantly tells her students to think of the audience while they are writing and to think about how to best get their point across so they get what they want. She told me about this wonderful book *Click Clack Moo: Cows That Type* by Doreen Cronin. In this story, the cows use writing to negotiate with the farmer to obtain better living conditions, and they even give the farmer a strike ultimatum. This book is available in Spanish, too. If you want to use it with your students, the title is *Click Clack Moo: Vacas Escritoras*.

Bottom line, I think that we need to prepare our students for real life, don't you? We need to celebrate their unique linguistic and literacy practices, but we also need to make them aware that they have to play "by the rules" if they want to get by in the different worlds they will encounter.

Well, take good care and give my best to your wonderful family.

Elena

Elena's message is highly relevant. Elena and her colleague are well aware that literacy practices are embedded in power relations and that students need to "play by the rules" if they want to succeed in the different social groups that they belong to. These "rules," Gee (1989) argues, are dictated by social institutions such as churches, schools, and government agencies. Gee (1989) points out that one should talk, write, and act in certain ways in these institutions if one wants to have access and get what one wants. He calls these combinations of acts (saying, writing, doing, being, and valuing) *Discourses*. Students then must develop multiple discourses if they participate in different social institutions.

Cummins (2001) argues that critical literacy is essential if students are to unveil how language intersects with power in different social institutions. Delpit (1988) has argued that it is through constant observation of language use that children can find out how certain genres of power work. Kaufman (1998) provides a good example. She narrates how she discussed writing job application letters with her students. A lot of her class time was devoted to how companies operate, what they value, and how they expect people to write and speak. They then focus on what companies look for in a letter of application and how it is organized, so that their letter is not dismissed immediately. Kaufman's students realized that if they write that they had no job experience right at the beginning, they would most likely not get the job. However, if they highlight all their strengths at the beginning of the letter and state their lack of experience at the end, they may have a better chance. Delpit (1988) also argues that once children know how these genres work, they can use language more strategically to generate new knowledge and act on social realities, and that it is the teacher's job to point this out to the student if they do not know how these genres operate.

AUTHORS IN THE CLASSROOM

Dear Elena:

I hope this e-mail finds you well and that you and your family are over that flu. It's been terrible here as well.

Thanks for sharing your colleague's perspective on the use of multiple languages. Your colleague is right. We have to let students know how certain social institutions work and what language should look like in those cases. We've learned this the hard way when dealing with the secretary of education and government institutions here in Oaxaca. It seems that we need to speak *their* language and write the way *they* want in order to get things approved.

For this reason, I have my students do a lot of writing. I have them create their own texts. When we do that, we also focus a lot on the audience and the purpose of our texts. We write different types of texts: letters, pamphlets, storybooks, posters, and many others. This has worked very well for me, especially because it's my students' work and it seems that their life is reflected in those texts. They're very proud of their texts and seem to be very interested in each other's texts. They also take them home. Lots of parents have come to me to tell me how proud they are of their children's work and how much they have learned from these texts as well.

Well, talking about writing, I have to let you go. We, as a school, are writing a letter of complaint to the federal government. Can you believe that our students now have to take a standardized test created at the federal level? I don't know what type of children the creators of this exam had in mind, but it's certainly not our students. It gets even worse. If our students don't do well, we may not get any funding from the federal government. This is starting to sound like what's happening in your school with the absurd law you told me about passed by Bush a few years ago. It seems that Mexico is following this misguided trend. Well, what keeps me going is knowing that I can make a difference in my children's lives, and that someday they might become the leaders who are finally able to turn this crazy world around.

Well, I guess this is our last e-mail this school year. I'm glad you will be in Oaxaca again during the summer, so that we can continue sharing our complaints and our teaching adventures in person.

A big hug,

Margarita

Margarita's e-mail introduces what ought to be a pedagogical cornerstone of our teaching in today's diverse classrooms—creating authors in the classrooms. Botelho (2004) argues that only a very small percentage of children's books reflect the lives of underrepresented groups in the United States. This is also the case in many other countries where multiculturalism has become the norm in schools. One of the ways to meet this challenge is to ask students to create their own texts. Students have different realities depending on where they live, who they are, and where their parents come from. Creating multilingual and multimodal texts (books, paintings, plays, songs, poems, Web pages, etc.) with children is a powerful way to make them feel that their talents and identities are recognized, valued, respected, and affirmed in the classrooms (Ada & Campoy, 2004; Cummins, Bismilla, Chow, Cohen, Giampapa, Leoni, Sandhu, & Sastri, 2005). It is in these texts that students invest their identities and, thus, become not only authors but protagonists as well.

Ada and Campoy's (2004) book *Authors in the Classroom* gives excellent examples of texts created by both teachers and students, which reflect the struggles, emotions, and dreams of their authors. You can also visit the Multiliteracies Project (http://www.multiliteracies.ca) conducted across Canada to see examples of "identity texts" created by students. Cummins (2006) defines identity texts as the products of students' creative work or performances realized within the pedagogical space of the classroom. He states that "students invest their identity in these texts . . . that then hold a mirror up to students in which their identities are reflected back in a positive light" (p. 60). Along similar lines, Kamler (2001) argues that "it is through the processes of designing [stories or identity texts] that writers produce new representations of reality and at the same time remake themselves—that is, reconstruct and renegotiate their identities" (p. 54). Elena and Margarita are doing exactly this with their students; they are creating new representations of their students and see them as intelligent and creative, not as deficient learners in need of fixing. This in turn may work toward the development of new and more egalitarian schools and societies.

MAKE THIS HAPPEN IN YOUR CLASSROOM

In this chapter, I have used e-mails to present the teaching principles created by teachers with whom I worked. These principles derived from many teachers' knowledge and experience of what has worked for them in their respective contexts. One of the underlying concepts behind these principles is the fact that we must learn from and about students on a daily basis. It is our job as educators to learn about the languages, knowledge, and skills that all students bring into the classroom. Cummins (2001) maintains that "if teachers [do not] learn much from their students, it is probable that their students [will] not learn much from them" (p. 4).

I encourage you to try the following in order to reinvent your own principles so that they speak to your particular sociocultural context:

- Learn about your students' linguistic practices. Monolingualism is
  no longer the norm, and your students are most likely bilingual or
  multilingual people who use their languages in multiple contexts and
  for multiple reasons.
- Learn about your students' literacy practices. Children *do* engage in
  numerous literacy practices. These practices may not be the ones
  valued or promoted in schools. Nevertheless, these practices are what
  children bring to school, and school literacy practices should be built
  on them.
- Acknowledge and value your students' translanguaging practices.
  With the recent increase of migration, different ethnolinguistic groups
  have come into contact with each other. Language borders are being
  crossed and languages are becoming complex. Your students are
  creative individuals who use and mix different languages in order to
  navigate among the different social groups they belong to.
- Prepare your students for the multiple discourses they may
  encounter. Linguistic and literacy practices are always embedded in
  power relations depending on the institutions in which they occur.
  If students are not able to act, speak, and write in the way these
  institutions require, they will become alienated.
- Create authors in the classrooms. In today's culturally and
  linguistically diverse classrooms, there are no materials, textbooks,
  or syllabi that will speak to *all* the children in your class. By creating
  authors in the classroom, not only can we reach *all* of our students in
  our class, but we can also create opportunities for children to become
  the protagonists of their stories and to work toward creating more
  egalitarian institutions and societies.

REFERENCES

Ada, A. F., & Campoy, I. (2004). *Authors in the classroom: A transformative education process.* New York: Pearson.

Botelho, M. J. (2004). *Reading class: Disrupting power in children's literature.* Unpublished doctoral thesis, University of Massachusetts Amherst.

Bruner, J. (1990). *Acts of meaning.* Cambridge, MA: Harvard University Press.

Cummins, J. (1984). *Bilingualism and special education: Issues in assessment and pedagogy.* Clevedon, UK: Multilingual Matters.

Cummins, J. (2001). *Negotiating identities: Education for empowerment in a diverse society* (2nd ed.). Los Angeles: California Association for Bilingual Education.

Cummins, J. (2006). Identity texts: The imaginative construction of self through multiliteracies pedagogy. In O. García, T. Skutnabb-Kangas, & M. E. Torres-Guzmán (Eds.), *Imagining multilingual schools* (pp. 51–68). Toronto, Ontario, Canada: Multilingual Matters.

Cummins, J. (2008). Teaching for transfer: Challenging the two solitudes assumption in bilingual education. In J. Cummins & N. Hornberger (Eds.), *Encyclopedia of language education, Vol. 5: Bilingual education* (pp. 65–75). New York: Springer.

Cummins, J., Bismilla, V., Chow, P., Cohen, S., Giampapa, F., Leoni, L., Sandhu, P., & Sastri, P. (2005). Affirming identity in multilingual classrooms. *Educational Leadership, 63*(1), 38–43.

Delpit, L. D. (1988). The silenced dialogue: Power and pedagogy in educating other people's children. *Harvard Educational Review, 58,* 280–298.

Edwards, V. (1998). *The power of Babel: Teaching and learning in multicultural classrooms.* Reading, UK: Trentham.

García, O. (2009). *Bilingual education in the 21st century: A global perspective.* Malden, MA: Wiley-Blackwell.

Garrido, F. (2004). *Para leerte mejor: Mecanismos de la lectura y de la formación de lectores.* Mexico: Planeta.

Gee, J. P. (1989). Literacy, discourse, and linguistics: Introduction. *Journal of Education, 171,* 5–17.

Heath, S. B. (1983). *Ways with words: Language, life, and work in communities and classrooms.* New York: Cambridge University Press.

Kamler, B. (2001). *Relocating the personal: A critical writing pedagogy.* New York: State University of New York Press.

Kaufman, A. M. (1998). *Alfabetización temprana . . . y ¿después?* Buenos Aires, Argentina: Santillana.

López-Gopar, M. E. (2006). *Mi viaje como promotor de la lecto-escritura. Entre Lectores* (Gaceta del Programa Nacional de Salas de Lecturas del CONACULTA), 2(3), 15, 19.

López-Gopar, M. E. (2009). *"What makes children different is what makes them better": Teaching Mexican children "English" to foster multilingual, multiliteracies, and intercultural practices.* Unpublished doctoral dissertation, University of Toronto, Toronto, Canada.

May, S. (2001). *Language and minority rights.* Harlow, UK: Pearson.

McLaren, P. (2003). *Life in schools* (4th ed.). New York: Allyn and Bacon.

Moll, L. C., Amanti, C., Neff, D., & González, N. (1992). Funds of knowledge for teaching: Using a qualitative approach to connect homes and classrooms. *Theory into Practice, 31*(2), 132–141.

Purcell-Gates, V. (Ed.). (2007). *Cultural practices of literacy: Complicating the complex.* Mahwah, NJ: Erlbaum.

Shohamy, E., & Gorter, D. (Eds.). (2008). *Linguistic landscape: Expanding the scenery.* New York: Routledge.

CHAPTER 14

The Words We Need

A Culturally Responsive Approach to Scaffolding English Learners' Vocabulary Development

Julie Coppola,
Maryellen Leelman, and Rosanne Barbacano

Morning Verse

> We come together from many different places to learn, to work and to play. . . .

The work in this chapter took place in an elementary school in Lexington, Massachusetts, a large suburban community west of Boston, in two print-rich classrooms filled with the sights and sounds of children reading, writing, listening, and talking. Their teachers, Rosanne, a 2nd-grade teacher, and Ellen, a 4th-grade teacher, regularly plan multiple and varied opportunities for their students to participate in whole-class and small-group discussions, talk informally with their teachers and peers, and read for enjoyment to gain new information and skills. Students routinely write to share their thoughts and feelings and demonstrate what they have learned. Opportunities to learn about words, acquire new words, and use newly learned words, orally and in writing, are throughout the school day, woven systematically into it.

Yet, despite Rosanne's and Ellen's best efforts to ensure that all their students would develop their oral and written language skills, there were several children in each classroom who struggled to become part of these vibrant word-learning communities. These children often were silent during whole-class discussions or participated minimally in small-group work. Their written work reflected a lack of or limited understanding of words that their grade-level peers were able to identify easily as they read or use as they talked and wrote. In each case, the teachers noted that the child was a member of a growing group of students in their school and community—English learners, children who were learning a new language at the same time they were expected to use this language to participate in daily classroom life and to achieve academically.

Similar to many school districts throughout the United States, Lexington was experiencing unprecedented growth in the number of students who require special assistance to achieve in English. To better serve these students, Maryellen, a school-wide speech and language specialist, and Rosanne enrolled in Julie's graduate course in teaching literacy to English learners. Here they undertook an in-depth study of second language vocabulary assessment, teaching, and learning. In addition, Maryellen, Rosanne, and Ellen enrolled in their school district's Sheltered English Language Learning course in which they learned how to plan and deliver instruction that targets English learners' language and content-area learning needs. Although these inservice courses focused on different aspects of teaching English learners, a common theme was the importance of scaffolding students' participation in ongoing classroom instruction through a culturally responsive approach to assessment and instruction, that is, they learned the importance of planning activities that (a) acknowledge and connect with students' language and cultural backgrounds and (b) include opportunities for students to share and build upon their background knowledge and experiences (Ruggiano Schmidt, 1998). Ellen invited Maryellen and Rosanne to her classroom to see one outcome of attending to these particular components of effective instruction for English learners: a poster presentation by two of her English-learning students about their native lands, Puerto Rico and the Dominican Republic, to their 4th-grade classmates after a North American geography unit.

These shared inservice and classroom experiences prompted Maryellen, Rosanne, and Ellen to consider ways they might collaborate to strengthen their instruction of English learners. The result was a content-based literacy unit that included opportunities for English learners to research and share information about their home countries and cultures and to acquire academic vocabulary. Throughout the unit, 4th-grade students mentored 2nd-grade students as the 2nd-graders researched countries from around the world, collected and learned new geography words, and practiced word-learning strategies. Although all the children in the two classrooms participated in the unit, we provide a brief description of the six English learners in Rosanne's 2nd-grade classroom of 20 and two English learners in Ellen's 4th-grade classroom of 20. Then we turn our attention to the steps Maryellen and the teachers took to reach their goals of promoting English learners' active participation in ongoing classroom instruction in general and their acquisition of academic vocabulary in particular.

ENGLISH LEARNERS
IN ALL-ENGLISH CLASSROOMS

Like most English learners in all-English classrooms, the children spend the majority of their school day in their grade-level classrooms surrounded by the demands of English. And, like most English learners, the children were at different stages of learning English. In addition, the children had varying levels of language and literacy skills in their home languages, and they received varying levels of extra language instruction both inside and outside of school.

In Rosanne's class, one child, Kemen, is at the beginning stage of learning English, speaks Spanish at home, and receives pull-out English as a second language (ESL) instruction 2 hours per week. Three of the children, Meena, Naoko, and Hei, are at the intermediate stage of learning English, and they receive pull-out ESL instruction for 1.5 hours a week. Outside of school, these three children speak English and their home languages, Tamil, Japanese, and Korean, and they receive formal instruction in their home languages. Two of the English learners in Rosanne's classroom, Chen and Dae-Ho, Taiwanese speakers, no longer meet the criteria for receiving ESL instruction, yet they continue to struggle with grade-level language demands. For example, providing a written or oral response to an abstract question in a math journal, such as, *Which of the following are likely to happen?* continues to present a challenge. Similarly, instructional vocabulary used routinely by their teacher and peers, such as writing about "small moments" (Calkins, 2003). or personal anecdotes during writer's workshop, is misunderstood frequently.

In Ellen's 4th-grade classroom, only one student, Paloma, a native-Spanish speaker, receives extra language services at school in the form of pull-out ESL instruction. This takes place during two 30-minute sessions each week. Another student, Dania, a Spanish-speaker from the Dominican Republic, does not receive ESL instruction but relies heavily on extra support from Ellen to meet the language demands of the classroom. Typical of many English learners, these students struggle with words with multiple meanings and homophones.

There are also children in each classroom who are either bilingual or in the process of becoming bilingual in their home language and English. Additional home languages represented in Rosanne's and Ellen's classrooms include Armenian, Chinese, and Hebrew.

WHAT WE KNOW ABOUT TEACHING VOCABULARY TO ENGLISH LEARNERS

English learners need to know many word meanings to thrive socially and academically. Research in effective vocabulary instruction for English learners suggests that teachers can meet this need through a combination of direct instruction in word meanings and teaching students word-learning strategies such as using context cues and analyzing word parts (Carlo et al., 2004; Kieffer & Lesaux, 2007). Teaching students about cognates or words that share common Greek and Latin roots and teaching useful words or words that students will encounter in a variety of contexts (Calderon & Wasden, 2009); supporting students' understanding of word meanings by the use of visual aids (Silverman, 2007); and embedding discussions about words in read-alouds (Collins, 2010) are all steps that teachers can take to promote English learners' vocabulary development. Connecting the learning of new English words to concepts and words already gained in the first language is another important contributor to success for English learners (Grognet, Jameson, Franco, & Derrick-Mescua, 2000).

According to Graves and Watts-Taffe (2008), all students can benefit from the opportunity to develop word consciousness, the awareness of and interest in words, and they propose an instructional framework designed to help students achieve this goal. The essential elements are "(a) create a word-rich environment, (b) recognize and promote adept diction, (c) promote wordplay, (d) foster word consciousness through writing, (e) involve students in original investigations, [and] (f) teach students about words" (p. 186). Finally, like all learners, English learners need multiple, rich, and varied opportunities to use their newly acquired words and to practice word-learning strategies.

In the following section, we share the steps Maryellen and the teachers took to promote the students' vocabulary development and increase the students' participation in ongoing classroom instruction.

OUR PLAN: DAY ONE IN ELLEN'S 4TH-GRADE CLASSROOM (45 MINUTES)

Maryellen met with the 4th-graders to let them know that they would have an opportunity to mentor 2nd-grade students by helping them learn the meanings of new geography words. Maryellen introduced a new word she had encountered when she saw a huge, black woodpecker with a gorgeous red crest. She discovered it was a Pileated Woodpecker, and she asked the students to brainstorm how they might discover the meaning of this interesting word. Together, Maryellen and the students created a list of all the strategies they use to learn new words such as using context cues, thinking about word parts, using the dictionary, using the Internet, identifying the part of speech (e.g., How else could this word be used? Do you think it is a noun?"), making a prediction about the word's meaning, making a picture about what they think the word means, writing a sentence to help remember the new word, or generating synonyms.

Students decided the dictionary was the best choice to learn about *pileated*, and after consulting the dictionary the students worked with Maryellen to complete a (commercially available) graphic organizer in which each listed the target word, an example, their own definitions, and a non-example.

Then, Maryellen returned to the list of word-learning strategies and asked the students to think about how they might help a 2nd-grader use one or more of the strategies. She asked the students to begin to create their own graphic organizers that they could use to help a 2nd-grader learn the meanings of new words the 2nd-graders found as they researched their countries.

DAY TWO IN ELLEN'S 4TH-GRADE CLASSROOM (30 MINUTES)

In this session, the students completed their graphic organizers. As shown in Figures 14.1 and 14.2, the students paid particular attention to writing word-learning strategies in a way that would be helpful for the 2nd-graders. For example, in Figure 14.1, in addition to asking a student to make a prediction about a word's meaning, one student added, "how you think it [the word] could be used." In Figure 14.2, another student encouraged the 2nd-graders to look for "little words" within the new word. One 4th-grader thought using context cues would be a great help. Yet, not certain that the 2nd-grader would understand how to find the context cues, he added, "write the sentence and highlight the words around your word." Also during this class session, the two English learners worked individually to prepare posters that included important geography words and defini-

FIGURE 14.1. Helping 2nd-Graders Determine Word Meanings

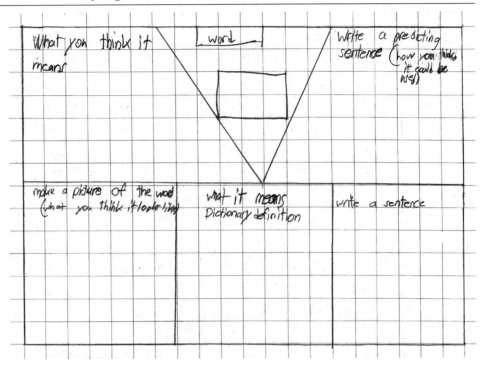

FIGURE 14.2. Looking for Little Words

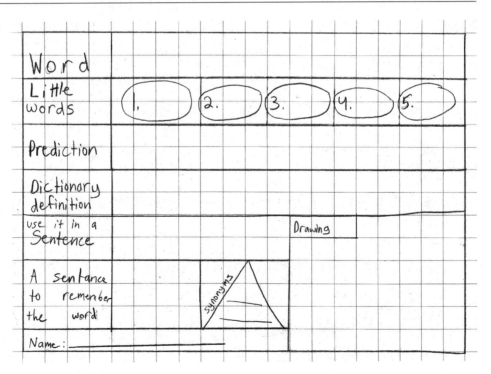

tions from their previous presentations about the Dominican Republic and Puerto Rico.

DAY THREE WITH 2ND- AND 4TH-GRADERS COMBINED (60 MINUTES)

All the students gathered in Rosanne's 2nd-grade classroom, and Ellen's two students presented their posters. They shared their maps of Puerto Rico and the Dominican Republic that included their new geography words, and they related information about daily life routines in their native lands such as going to the local open-air food markets. The students also used the opportunity to stress a major difference between their home countries and their new home in Lexington: "We don't have as much things as we do in this country." Yet, the students emphasized, "We enjoy food, cooking, dance, parties or festivals, laughing and fun!" The 2nd-graders asked many questions, such as, "How many languages are there in Puerto Rico?"

Next, to help all the students recognize the richness and variety of countries and cultural backgrounds represented by the children in the two classrooms, Rosanne asked all students to share their or their families' home countries, and she recorded the information on newsprint. China, Colombia, France, Greece, Hungary, Israel, Lithuania, and Scotland were some of the countries listed. Then, Rosanne paired a 4th-grader with a 2nd-grader and sent students off to complete an interview to learn as much as they could about their partner, including their country of origin. Students then gathered in a large group and several pairs of students reported what they had learned about each other. They then arranged themselves into small-groups to continue relaying information about their partners. Rosanne was able to add several additional countries to the list, including countries such as Ireland and Italy.

DAY FOUR WITH CLASSES COMBINED (60 MINUTES)

Maryellen explained to the students as they met in Rosanne's classroom, that today, as they read with their partners, their goal was to stop while they were reading, and if there was a new word to "collect it" and "learn what the word means." In preparation for the unit, Rosanne gathered multiple copies of the *A Visit To* series (Taylor & Pearson, 2009), a nonfiction series about countries around the word. She used one text from this series to model how the 4th-graders could collect words with their 2nd-grade partners:

> You each have a piece of poster paper, and you will write the name of your country and your name and your partner's name as the researchers. Now let's pretend you are with your partner, and you are reading a book about Mexico. When you come across the word *neighbor*, you will ask your partner, "Do you know what a neighbor is?" The 2nd-grader might answer, "Yeah, I have a neighbor that is a friend next door, but how can Mexico, a whole country, be a neighbor?" So if your 2nd-grader does not know what the word *neighbor* means in that context and in this text, you will write the word on your word-collection chart, then write the word on a sticky note and place it on your country poster. You should also add the word to our class word-collection chart in the back of the room. Then you will look at your graphic organizer that has the strategies you brainstormed to help the 2nd-graders learn their new words. If drawing a picture is the strategy you decide to use, please add the picture. If your 2nd-grader needed the whole sentence, *Mexico is a neighbor to our country,* then the sentence and a little picture with the USA next to Mexico will go on your poster as well.

Then before the students moved to tables to work in pairs, Rosanne displayed a completed country poster with geography words and definitions to guide the students as they worked. Each pair of students received a copy of a country book that had a personal or family connection to the 2nd-grader wherever possible. Each pair of students also received a large piece of construction paper for their poster, sticky notes to record their words, and a word-collection chart to keep track of all the words they were collecting. The 4th-graders also received copies of the graphic organizers they had generated.

As students read and collected words at the tables, teachers and students added to the class word collection. Examples of geography words collected during the first day included *delta, humid, monsoon, crops,* and *ash.* Students also worked in pairs to complete their graphic organizers. For example, as seen in Figure 14.3, 4th-grader Larry taught his 2nd-grader partner the meaning of *settled* by first making a prediction about the meaning. Next, he showed his partner how to take the word apart. They ended their work with *settled* by putting it in a sentence and confirming the definition using the dictionary.

FIGURE 14.3. Determining the Meaning of *Settled*

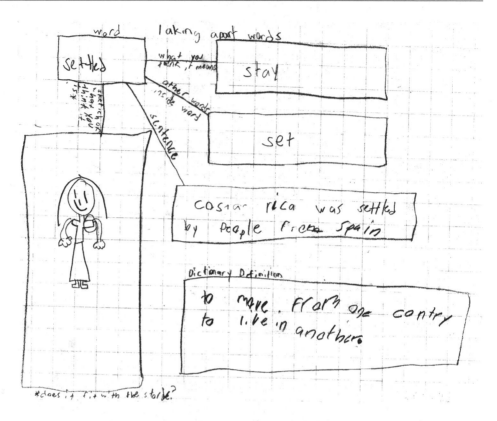

DAY FIVE WITH CLASSES COMBINED (60 MINUTES)

The two classes met in Rosanne's classroom and continued exploring their countries, by rereading their country books, gathering new words, and practicing word-learning strategies. As the class word-collection chart grew (Figure 14.4), Maryellen, Rosanne, and Ellen kept notes about what students were learning about words as they worked with their partners. For example, two students reported they learned the word for the Cambodian language, Khmer, and when 2nd-grader Kemen associated the word *coast* with riding his bicycle, his partner drew a picture to help him clarify the meaning in a geographic context, which was "edge of land." The students continued to learn about each other as they worked together. For example, one 4th-grader reported that he learned that his partner was from Taiwan and that "[Taiwan] is different from China."

FIGURE 14.4. Class Word-Collection Chart

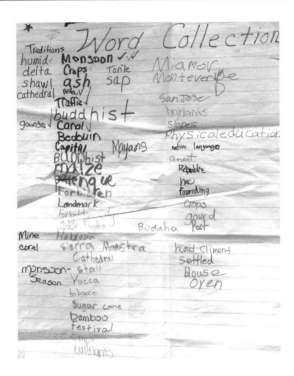

DAY SIX WITH CLASSES COMBINED (30 MINUTES)

In this class session, the students completed a quick write to share what they had learned about their partners and the strategies they were using to collect and learn new words. Next, the 2nd-graders, with help from their partners, completed the self-assessment shown in Figure 14.5 about their knowledge of the words that had been collected to date by the class.

DAYS SEVEN AND EIGHT WITH CLASSES COMBINED (60 MINUTES EACH)

Two days were devoted to working on country posters in which students displayed examples of newly learned words and their meanings along with interesting facts about their countries (see Figure 14.6). Students shared with the class their posters with their new words as a culminating activity. When the 4th-graders returned to their classroom, they had one last op-

FIGURE 14.5. I Know This Word . . .

portunity to share an important geography word and its meaning with the 2nd-graders (Figure 14.7).

CONCLUSION

Developing students' vocabulary and their interest in and awareness of words is a long-term process. Thoughtful attention to assessing and teaching vocabulary was evident in each classroom prior to implementing this unit. However, implementing this unit brought attention to the need to not only teach new words to English learners, but accelerate their overall learning of words and the use of word-learning strategies. The unit provided many opportunities for teachers and students to accomplish these goals as students identified new words and strategies to learn word meanings. Students also had authentic opportunities to talk about and use their new words. Ongoing informal assessment provided the teachers with repeated opportunities to assess the extent to which students were learning new

FIGURE 14.6. "China Is a Great Place" Poster

FIGURE 14.7. Sharing Word Meanings

Forest

A forest is an area of land where there are a lot of trees. Mosses, ferns and a lot of other plants grow there, too. Some forests are very big and thick.

words. For example, students were assessed on their use of the key vocabulary terms in informal conversations and as they completed their country posters. Although the focus of the unit was learning new content words, the teachers also became more aware of the importance of ongoing attention to providing opportunities for English learners to acquire words that are part of their English-speaking peers' "everyday" language. For example, in one of the partner activities it was striking to find that one English learner did not yet have the word *jeans* when he wanted to write about what his partner was wearing.

We also found that when teachers plan a culturally responsive unit that provides their English learners with opportunities to build upon and share their background knowledge and experiences such as information about their home countries and cultural practices, they are eager to do so. We observed English learners talking about these topics in whole-group and small-group settings and as they worked to learn new words with a partner. In one particularly poignant example, Rosanne observed Kemen, who was largely silent in the 2nd-grade classroom, animatedly teach his 4th-grade partner the word *mariachi* as they talked about music.

The English speakers benefited as well from this culturally responsive unit, as these students were so intrigued by their English-learning classmates' countries, cultures, and languages that the English-speaking students became motivated to learn more about their own heritages. They also expressed amazement about their classmates' growing bilingual/bicultural abilities. As one 4th-grader wrote, "My partner, Chen, is from Tywan [*sic*], and he knows a lot of vocabulary!"

One of the greatest challenges teachers face is finding ways to support English learners' efforts to show their competence. Overall, we found that providing authentic opportunities to read, write, talk, and play with words, as students learn about each other, benefited all the students in these classrooms. We hope that our experience of planning a culturally responsive approach to vocabulary teaching will encourage all teachers to infuse opportunities for their English-learning students to share what they know and can do in their classrooms.

MAKE THIS HAPPEN IN YOUR CLASSROOM

- Seek out a colleague or group of colleagues to collaborate as you plan effective instruction that supports not only your English learners' vocabulary development but also that of all the students.

- Research on effective schools (e.g., Taylor & Pearson, 2002) demonstrates that when teachers and specialists collaborate, all students benefit.
- Select a topic that lends itself easily to providing a scaffolding or spiraling learning opportunity. For example, learning about other countries is a topic that appears at several grade levels. As the 2nd-graders were introduced to the topic, the 4th-graders applied and practiced their newly learned skills.
- Use a series of nonfiction leveled texts appropriate to the learners. The text selection contributed to the success of this unit because all students had easy access to texts that included engaging photographs and a variety of other nonfiction text features such as maps and glossaries. These text features supported rich whole-class and partner discussions and provided opportunities for students at all reading levels to access information presented at their level.
- Some other resources for students that we recommend:

    Culturegrams. This multimedia reference provides current information about the customs and lifestyles of people in more than 200 countries around the world. The site is reviewed regularly for accuracy by in-country experts and may be found at http://www.culturegrams.com

    Time Incorporated. (2010). *Time for kids around the world.* New York: Author.
- For teachers we highly recommend:

Bear, D., Helman, L., Templeton, S., Invernizzi, M., & Johnston, F. (2007). *Words their way with English learners: Word study for phonics, vocabulary, and spelling instruction.* Upper Saddle River, NJ: Pearson/Merrill Prentice Hall.

REFERENCES

Calderon, M., & Wasden, R. (2009). Preparing middle and secondary school teachers to teach reading, language, and content: A look at professional development programs. In J. Coppola & E. Primas (Eds.), *One classroom, many learners: Best literacy practices for today's multilingual classrooms* (pp. 251–269). Newark, DE: International Reading Association

Calkins, L. (2003). *Small moments: Personal narrative writing.* Portsmouth, NH: Heinemann.

Carlo, M., August, D., McLaughlin, B., Snow, C., Dressler, C., Lippman, D., et al. (2004). Closing the gap: Addressing the vocabulary needs of English-language learners in mainstream and bilingual classrooms. *Reading Research Quarterly, 39*(2), 188–215.

Collins. M. (2010). ESL preschoolers' English vocabulary acquisition from storybook reading. *Early Childhood Research Quarterly, 25,* 84–97

Graves, M., & Watts-Taffe, S. (2008). For the love of words: Fostering word conscious-ness in young readers. *Reading Teacher, 62*(3), 185–193.

Grognet, A., Jameson, J., Franco, L., & Derrick-Mescua, M. (2000*). Enhancing English language learning in elementary classrooms.* Arlington, VA: Center for Applied Linguistics and Delta.

Kieffer, M., & Lesaux, N. (2007). Breaking down words to build meaning: Morphology, vocabulary and reading comprehension in the urban classroom. *Reading Teacher, 61*(2), 134–144.

Ruggiano Schmidt, P. (1998). *Cultural conflict and struggle: Literacy learning in a kin-dergarten program.* New York: Peter Lang.

Silverman, R. (2007). Vocabulary development for English-language and English-only learners in kindergarten. *Elementary School Journal, 107*(4), 365–383.

Taylor, B., & Pearson, P. D. (Eds.). (2002). *Teaching reading: Effective schools, accom-plished teachers.* Mahwah, NJ: Erlbaum.

A visit to (Series, 2nd ed.). Portsmouth, NH: Heinemann.

Part V

BECOMING CULTURALLY RESPONSIVE LITERACY TEACHERS

Since most teachers in North America are from middle-class, European-American origins and have had few relationships with diverse groups of people, they often have great difficulty connecting with the diverse families and communities of their children (Lazar, 2004; Ruggiano Schmidt, 2002). This lack of experience with others who are culturally different from themselves allows stereotypes in the media to become embedded. Therefore, it is the objective of strong teacher education programs to help teachers understand, appreciate, and celebrate diversity in their classrooms (Pattnaik, 1997).

Reflective practice (Schön, 1987) seems to be a key component in the development of culturally responsive teachers. The adage, "Know thyself and understand others," epitomizes the need for teachers to look carefully at their own backgrounds in relation to family, education, religion, interests, talents, victories, disappointments, and challenges. Additionally, present and future teachers must study their own professional development and perform careful self-analyses . . . these processes become most effective when writing, reading, listening, observing, and talking occur in a safe environment (Lazar, 2004; Osborne, 1996; Ruggiano Schmidt, 2005).

Next, teachers should see their children and families as sources of information for learning that can be explored in the classroom and connected to the curriculum (Edwards, 2004). Teachers are unable to do this if they are uncomfortable working with diverse groups of people. Therefore, teacher preparation programs that offer opportunities and assignments to learn while working with people from diverse backgrounds may help present and future teachers become comfortable with differences, and ultimately to cherish them. This next section brings us teachers who are growing professionally as they learn about themselves and others through multiple cultural lenses.

REFERENCES

Edwards, P. A. (2004). *Children's literacy development.* Boston: Pearson.

Lazar, A. (2004). *Learning to be literacy teachers in urban schools: Stories of growth and change.* Newark, DE: International Reading Association.

Osborne, A. B. (1996). Practice into theory into practice: Culturally relevant pedagogy for students we have marginalized and normalized, *Anthropology and Education Quarterly, 27*(3), 285–315.

Pattnaik, J. (1997). Cultural stereotypes and preservice education: Moving beyond our biases. *Equity and Excellence in Education, 30*(3), 40–50.

Ruggiano Schmidt, P. R. (2002). *Cultural conflict and struggle: Literacy learning in a kindergarten program.* New York: Peter Lang.

Schön, D. (1987). *Educating the reflective practitioner.* San Francisco: Jossey-Bass.

CHAPTER 15

Encountering the ABCs and Meeting the Challenges

Patricia Ruggiano Schmidt, Fernando Rodriguez, and Laura Sandroni

This chapter focuses on Multicultural Literacy Methods, a state-required graduate course that deals with the complexity of developing literacy within cultures of home, school, and community as well as the structural aspects of language (Cummins, 1986; Edwards, Pleasants, & Franklin, 1999; Ruggiano Schmidt, Gangemi, Kelsey, LaBarbera, McKenzie, et al., 2009; Vygotsky, 1978). This course is based on the four principles of critical race theory (CRT) (Ladson-Billings, 1999; Ladson-Billings & Tate, 1995; Nebeker, 1998).

The first principle of CR teaching claims that societal structure has made race invisible due to the realities of White privilege. The second legitimates experiential storytelling and promotes listening to the voices of those who have been discriminated against as part of the social order. The third proposes that meaningful social change can occur only when there is a radical change in existing social structures. The fourth principle questions civil rights legislation since it seems to be de jure rather than de facto, thus ultimately maintaining White supremacy (Jenson, 2005). Finally, critical race theory exhorts educators to take action and begin changing the social structure of schools. One way to do this is through culturally relevant or culturally responsive pedagogy (Ladson-Billings, 1999). Preparing educators for culturally responsive teaching requires that they develop an ability to make connections with home, school, and community for literacy development. However, most teachers have not had sustained relationships with people from different ethnic, linguistic, and cultural backgrounds or from lower socioeconomic backgrounds. (This is likely to be true for future teachers enrolled in the course as well.) As a result, much of their knowledge about diversity has been influenced by media stereotypes (Pattnaik, 1997; Tatum, 1997). Additionally, school curriculum, methods, and materials usually reflect only European-American or White culture and ignore the backgrounds and experiences of students and families from lower socioeconomic levels and differing linguistic, ethnic, and cultural backgrounds (Boykin, 1978; Gunderson, 2007; Howard, 2001; Lazar, 2007; Nieto, 1999; Ruggiano Schmidt & Ma, 2006).

Often, teacher education programs that attempt to address the need for culturally responsive teaching use reading, writing, listening, viewing, and speaking by assigning autobiographies, biographies, reflections on diversity issues, and discussions of cross-cultural analyses (Cochran-Smith, 1995; Florio-Ruane, 1994; Lazar, 2007; Noordhoff & Kleinfield, 1993; Osborne, 1996; Spindler & Spindler, 1987; Tatum, 1992). However, Multicultural Literacy Methods, the course discussed in this chapter, requires additional activities—in-depth cross-cultural self-analyses and creation and implementation of culturally responsive classroom ideas.

SETTING

Multicultural Literacy Methods was designed by Patricia Ruggiano Schmidt, a literacy professor at a small, liberal arts, religious-affiliated college in the northeastern United States. Ninety percent to ninety-five percent of the present and future teachers enrolled are from a European-American, middle-socioeconomic background. The course is required for certification in elementary education, secondary education, and TESOL (teaching English to speakers of other languages) and based on the model known as the ABCs of Cultural Understanding and Communication (Ruggiano Schmidt, 1998; Ruggiano Schmidt & Finkbeiner, 2006; Xu, 2000a). This model was created by me and evolved over the last 16 years in terms of the guiding principle "know thyself and understand others." Present and future K–12 teachers who experience the model's process often begin to successfully connect home, school, and community for literacy learning (Izzo & Ruggiano Schmidt, 2006; Leftwich, 2002; Ruggiano Schmidt, 1998, 1999; Ruggiano Schmidt & Finkbeiner, 2006; Ruggiano Schmidt & Ma, 2006; Xu, 2000a, 2000b). The following explains the model's five-step process.

1. *Autobiography*. Each graduate student writes a detailed autobiography with significant life events. Starting with earliest memories, they include family origins, education, foods, celebrations, fun, victories,

traumatic events, loves, honors, disappointments, and anything considered important. (They have actually begun their family histories.)

2. *Biography.* Each graduate student performs semistructured interviews (Spradley, 1979) and writes a biography of someone who is from a different culture from his or her own and includes significant life events, such as family origins, education, foods, celebrations, fun, victories, traumatic events, loves, honors, disappointments, and anything else considered important. Additionally, skin tone must be significantly different. The person's language and home community are also studied at three separate meetings scheduled for the interviews. Each meeting occurs on a different day and is at least 30 minutes in length.

3. *Cross-Cultural Analyses.* When performing cultural analyses (Spindler & Spindler, 1987), each graduate student compares and contrasts his or her own culture with the interviewee's culture. Lists of similarities and differences result in the form of charts or Venn diagrams.

4. *Cultural Analyses of Differences.* Students analyze the differences between themselves and the interviewees, explaining the differences that cause discomfort and those that are admired. After each difference, they individually explain, in detail, why they admire each difference or why that difference might make them feel a bit uncomfortable. They then connect their analyses to power issues related to dominant and nondominant communities. They must consider race, class, and equity issues and connect with articles they have read and discussed in class.

5. *Home–School Communication Design.* This includes detailed plans/ideas for the ABCs home/school connections for literacy development with modifications for classroom adaptation and implementation. The plan must have 40 lesson/unit ideas, suggestions, or concepts that attempt to integrate multicultural literacy. Each one is described in a paragraph detailing the literacy connections between home, school, and community and plan's relation to a particular content area. The ideas can be generated from sources online, readings, class discussions, and personal creativity.

In this course, writing the autobiography is considered interesting and fun by most students. The stories are not shared publicly and are given only to me, the professor, for perusal. Other professors teach the course and uphold the same confidentiality. Grading does not occur. Students often write painful, as well as happy memories. Most become so involved with thinking about their own lives that they write 20 to 30 pages and include photos.

The interviews are also enlightening experiences. Initially, students are tentative about the process, but the professor models the semi-structured interview (Spradley, 1979), and students practice with their classmates. Also, the list of similarities and differences is simple, yet informative; students easily see differences but tend to emphasize similarities when discussing their findings in class.

The analyses of differences produce epiphanies. Students begin to understand the meaning of ethnocentrism, a concept that describes a person's perceptions of the world in terms of his or her own cultural norms. They realize that there is much to admire in differences, but also, they are clearly uncomfortable about certain differences. These analyses help them reflect on why they admire and why they feel uncomfortable about certain differences. Students realize that power and equity issues permeate our society and these issues affect people's lives.

Finally, I encourage students to think about ways to communicate and connect with families and communities as they teach the required curriculums. They are then expected to create or adapt 40 lesson ideas related to their teaching areas and based on the *Seven Characteristics of Culturally Responsive Teaching* (Ruggiano Schmidt & Ma, 2006). These characteristics, described later in this chapter, emerged over years of observations of culturally responsive literacy teaching.

SAMPLES OF GRADUATE STUDENTS' PRODUCTS

Samples in this chapter are presented to demonstrate the power of the ABCs of Cultural Understanding and Communication in this college course. However, there are numerous books, chapters, and articles on the implementation of the ABCs in elementary and secondary classrooms (Ruggiano Schmidt, 1999, 2000, 2001, 2005; Ruggiano Schmidt & Finkbeiner, 2006; Ruggiano Schmidt et al., 2009; Ruggiano Schmidt & Ma, 2006; Xu, 2000b) that present pictures of teachers' successes with their students.

CULTURAL ANALYSES OF DIFFERENCES

Over the last 17 years, I have collected hundreds of graduate student reports of analyses of differences from ABCs projects. They almost unanimously demonstrate the personal growth of individuals as they reflect on feelings, in varying degrees, on their own discomforts and admirations. For example, a young African American male history teacher, named Ryan Deas, interviewed a woman in her 50s who described her Jewish background. He believed that age would be the greatest difference between them due to the civil rights and feminist movements in the United States. Instead, he found that they both had histories of atrocities related to slavery, civil rights violations, and the Holocaust, but both the Jews and the African Americans have persevered. He stated,

> Going through the ABCs model first, with my own autobiography, then with C's biography, and now the cross-cultural analysis have allowed me to see things in myself that I never before realized. I revisited many of the events in my life that have shaped me into who I am now. I was able to see how much of an impact each of those experiences has had on who I have become. That foundation and framework for life is something that really is the window that I look through when observing life. I definitely know that this ABCs model has enlightened me to the fact that these so-called "first impressions" will be taking place in my classroom. But if I can create an environment where students feel free to share and to listen to other students' experiences from different cultures, my classroom will become a place where diversity will enhance education, not hinder it.

Teachers grow through the ABCs project by taking an in-depth look at their own lives and by listening and learning from lives that appear very different from their own. The stories of two other cases follow in their own words. A Hispanic male's cultural analyses after interviewing a European-American male provides another set of powerful insights.

Case 1

> While completing the ABCs of Cultural Understanding and Communication Model (Ruggiano Schmidt, 1998), I interviewed Bob, a European-American male about my age. I thought my interview with Bob would be quick and a flash in the pan so to speak. I was dead wrong. My interviews with Bob gave me greater insight into myself and I hope to use this newfound information with my own students. The ABCs model is not confined within the walls of academia but can be applied to our personal lives.
> One of the first differences that stood out while conducting my interview was the closeness Bob had with his extended family. His

nuclear family was small like mine, a total of four members, but hearing him talk about his cousins, aunts, and uncles who lived across the street, I could feel the impact they had on his life. The late night cookouts, hanging out every day with his cousins, I felt jealous. I thought I had resolved my familial issues long ago, but talking with Bob flared them up again.

A long *long* time ago, my mom said something I didn't quite understand until now. She told me our family is cold. When I heard how involved Bob was with his, I now knew what she meant.

Both of my parents emigrated here from Ecuador. They had to relearn everything. Language. Social mores. Dress. Everything. In that process, I believe, they became more reserved. Not in the political sense, but socially. Now that I think about it, all of their friends were Hispanic. The only White people I came across were the ones on TV. As for African Americans I went to an elementary school that was predominantly African American. They didn't instill fear of any particular group, but because their social net seemed so closed, I think their behaviors contributed to my social awkwardness. When I'm around other Hispanics I feel at ease. Place me around anyone else and I begin to tense up. If I'm at a party I'm usually the one who's fenced away in a corner.

Bob, though, didn't have this. Based on his involvement in sports, being class president, partying in college, etc., I saw someone who was comfortable around any group of people, someone who could adapt to any social situation very easily, or at least with minimal effort. This "openness" is a trait I both admire and envy, one that's always been elusive. Granted, I'll always be an introvert, I think, but the ABCs gave me closure to that part of my life and will hopefully allow me to be less timid.

As I continued the interview, I became uncomfortable with Bob's inability to juggle both his social and academic life while growing up, and because of this he missed out on some epic opportunities. He revealed that his partying habits prevented him from completing many of the colleges he attended. He had to leave because he became delinquent in both his academic and swim team obligations. Since he was fortunate enough to get a scholarship for his swimming ability, I figured this was incentive enough for academic achievement.

I received a full ride at the university thanks to my mom, but I would have *never* gambled this grand opportunity away with partying.

Maybe it was a combination of guilt and academic obligation but it was my mission to graduate. My mom sacrificed so much for me to get there and if I got kicked out, for whatever reason, I wouldn't be able to face her again.

Another missed opportunity for Bob was the Olympics. At a very young age, Bob discovered he was given a gift in swimming. During high school he was either the captain or the co-captain of any swim team he was on. His ability was being encouraged by both coaches and family members. Deep down he knew his talent could take him to the Olympics. Partying, though, got in the way.

Teaching is a noble profession and I'm happy Bob is now focused and ready to pursue this career, but at the same time I feel frustrated because he was given a gift only a handful of others have. I'm not sure if it's typical of European Americans to disregard talents in lieu of hedonism, but with my family it's a bit different. My culture values religion. Admittedly, I'm in my agnostic phase, but growing up, my parents instilled the core tenets of the Christian faith. They taught me how important it was to be humble, but most of all, grateful for any opportunity that came our way. I attribute this to my family not having much while growing up. My grandparents were uneducated, but worked hard their whole lives to support their families. My parents were both uneducated though my mom eventually broke that mold. With me, though, they saw hope. For the first time, they were in a country that could provide everything they ever wanted but unfortunately could not grasp. This immigrant mindset, I call it, pushed my brother and me to not settle for anything less, to keep dreaming and at the same time to back it up with hard work.

Bob's family was educated. They were long established in the United States and as a result, I believe, became complacent in their goals. It is true that Bob's family has endured many medical issues and they should be commended for being strong survivors, but after generations of living in America that immigrant hunger seems no longer present. This is why I think Bob lapsed into his partying ways; there was lack of moral support.

My hope is that Bob has learned from his mistakes and in the future will not only help his children, but his students if he ever sees them heading down a wrong path. On the upside, though, his partying did exercise his social muscle, and although I see many negatives associated with it, some positives can be taken in as well.

Bob's partying ways allowed him to have fun. Because of my strict upbringing I denied myself this. When I was finally in a setting to have some actual fun, I didn't know what to do. Even now I struggle in social settings and I can't help but wonder if I should have been more reckless in my youth, enough so that I would let loose occasionally and not be so self-conscious around others.

Finally, the most revealing aspect of the ABCs model was the autobiography. It was there that I revisited and confronted many of the demons from my past. Unfortunately I spent a lot of my youth being ashamed of my culture and appearance. When I was out in public I made sure not to speak to my mom in Spanish, because we would get odd looks from others, in my head at least. After elementary school there was a sea of White in my classrooms and I was always *always* the one dark M&M that ruined this picturesque setting.

It was also hard recalling the events that involved my father but at the same time it felt like I was letting go of the old me. I thought I had long ago resolved my issues with my father. As I recalled those events, I noticed just how angry I was with him. There were even days when I didn't do anything else but recall past events. However, I placed myself in my father's shoes for the first time and began to understand where he was coming from, his anger, etc.

The ABCs model gave me the strength to reach out to my father since it had been years [since] we last spoke. Our initial conversation was awkward due to time. In the end I would be lying if there weren't any man-tears coming from [me].

I see the world differently now. My interviews with Bob showed me how my relationships with friends, acquaintances, family, specifically my father, were affecting my present behaviors. I realized it was time to let go. I realize now that beauty lies in human differences and the celebration of differences brings us to unity.

This teacher found that the process of analyzing similarities and differences provided better understandings of himself and a more forgiving attitude toward others. This change could have a powerful impact on his students. Next, are excerpts from a European-American female teacher who interviewed a Muslim woman.

Case 2

Leila was married by an Islamic spiritual leader (imam) in a very traditional Muslim wedding. Unlike a traditional American wedding, the bride and groom do not exchange vows with each other during the ceremony. The imam asks the bride's father and the groom to exchange vows. It made me uncomfortable to know that while her father and future husband vowed to take care of her for the rest of her life, she remained quiet. Were her intentions to commit herself to her husband not as important, or perhaps just assumed? In preparation for our wedding ceremony, my husband and I went through endless examples of wedding vows before finally choosing ones that we felt fit us.

Another part of the Muslim culture that I don't understand is why the husband has to give the bride a dowry (gift) of gold and gems at their wedding. Leila said that the average dowry is worth $60,000 in gold. Her husband's family struggled with money when he was growing up, so I was surprised to hear that he had enough money to afford a dowry worth that amount of money. Money struggles aside, who has this type of money at their young age? If you do have this type of money, why not put it down on a new home? I understand that the dowry is a demonstration that the husband is able to support his wife financially, however, does it have to be that extravagant a demonstration? Leila describes the Islamic religion as one that celebrates and rewards simplicity. How is $60,000 worth of gold and gems simple? When I asked Leila how often she wears the jewelry, she shared that, in her culture, women only wear this type of jewelry to wedding ceremonies. Leila keeps her jewelry in a safe at the bank. As a young married person, I can't help but wonder if the money might have been better spent on something a little more pragmatic.

Something else in Leila's past that I didn't quite understand is why her parents would send her to a Catholic school, if she practiced Islam at home. Leila was harassed by her peers and teachers every day for being Muslim and practicing Islam. Is the fact that the private school may offer a better education worth having your child bullied by teachers and students? I don't understand why Leila had to wait until 8th grade until her parents finally gave her permission to transfer to a public school. According to Leila, at that point, she had already come to the conclusion that she didn't fit into the American culture, and wanted to return to Palestine.

I have really enjoyed getting to know Leila, and can definitely see myself becoming good friends with her, but I am hesitant to "get too close" after learning that she wants to return to Palestine. It takes a lot of work in order to make good friends and nurture relationships at this stage in my life, especially the long distance ones. The fact that Leila wants to leave the country, because she feels as though she doesn't fit, causes me discomfort. I would like to think that immigrants who come to America are happy and want to stay and raise families. I find it difficult to grasp that after spending more than 20 years in America (the vast majority of her life), she still feels as though she fits in better with the Palestinian culture. I understand why and it saddens me, since it is based on mistreatment.

One of the things that I admire most about Leila is the fact that she is an avid traveler. I myself am more of a homebody. My husband and I prefer to spend any extra money that we have on our house, rather than on a vacation. I envy the fact that Leila has been able to visit her extended family in Palestine every summer. I would love to visit distant relatives in Ireland. Now that I have an 18-month old, I wouldn't have the courage to leave the country for an extended period of time with, or without, her. But Leila was smart to take every opportunity to travel to distant places such as Europe, the Caribbean, and Palestine while she was still young and had the freedom. If I could do it all over again, I would have traveled to at least one of those locations with friends, or my husband, prior to having our daughter.

Both of these teachers had rich experiences, typical of the analyses of differences. As a result, they began to see the significance of creating and adapting classroom ideas that connect home and school for culturally responsive literacy learning.

CULTURALLY RESPONSIVE LITERACY IDEAS

Multicultural Literacy Methods requires that teachers bring their curricula to class and pair up according to their content areas for designing their home, school, community connections. The pairs begin searching for ideas on the Internet, in research articles, textbooks, and in any other sources. Their ideas must be based on the following *Seven Characteristics of Culturally Responsive Teaching.* These were derived from previous classroom implementations of successful culturally responsive teaching

(Izzo & Ruggiano Schmidt, 2006; Ruggiano Schmidt, 2000, 2005; Ruggiano Schmidt et al., 2009).

Seven Characteristics for Culturally Responsive Instruction

1. *High expectations:* supporting students as they develop the literacy appropriate to their ages and abilities
2. *Positive relationships with families and community:* demonstrating clear connections with student families and communities in terms of curriculum content and relationships
3. *Cultural sensitivity:* reshaping curriculum mediated for culturally valued knowledge, connecting with the standards-based curriculum as well as individual students' cultural backgrounds
4. *Active teaching methods:* involving students in a variety of reading, writing, listening, speaking, and viewing behaviors throughout the lesson plan
5. *Teacher as facilitator:* presenting information briefly, giving directions, summarizing responses, and working with small groups, pairs, and individuals
6. *Student control of portions of the lesson, "healthy hum":* encouraging talking at conversation levels around the topic studied while completing assignments in small groups and pairs
7. *Instruction around groups and pairs; low anxiety:* maintaining a low-anxiety atmosphere in which assignments are completed individually, but students work in small groups or pairs and are given time to share ideas and think critically about the work

EXAMPLES OF CULTURALLY RESPONSIVE TEACHING IN THE CONTENT AREAS

The examples that follow are from many content areas and could be adapted for various ages and stages of learning:

Living Environment (Elementary or Secondary)

1. Students, in pairs, will be assigned scientists from diverse cultural backgrounds.
2. Students will research life stories and their impact on today's science.
3. Students will present scientists to the class by role-playing them.
4. Students will take questions from the class.

5. Students will talk about why science is important to their communities.

Example: The first open-heart surgery was performed by an African American surgeon, Dr. Daniel Hale Williams.

American History (Elementary or Secondary)

1. Students will interview relatives or family friends who participated in a war, soldier or civilian.
2. Class will prepare questions to be asked by the interviewers.
3. Interviewers may also invite interviewees to speak in class. Students will have questions prepared ahead of time to ask the people.
4. Students will then discuss wars and see how primary sources relate to the text.

Women's Contributions to Mathematics

1. Thompson (1981) believes that the cyclical nature of menstruation played a major role in mathematical development.
2. Lunar markings on prehistoric bone fragments show how women marked their cycles and thus began to mark time.
3. Women were also the first agriculturists while men were the hunters and gatherers. Therefore, women observed the periodicity of nature, and future scientific observations were based on their records.
4. Hypatia, first woman mathematician that we know of today, left us much knowledge about algebra.
5. Students research women mathematicians from diverse cultural backgrounds and report to the class.
6. With beans, pennies, or other small objects, present number patterns. Create triangular and square number patterns.
7. Find a formula that indicates how to find the squares of numbers. Write the explanation and then teach your idea to a partner.
8. Present in pairs why you think women's contributions and those of traditionally underrepresented groups have been largely ignored in modern mathematics.

Earth Science (Elementary and Secondary)

1. Visit the shores of a polluted lake in the United States with an environmental engineer and a geologist. Have them tell what needs to be done to clean up the lake.

2.   Invite a (Native American) clan mother or faith keeper to speak about the environment. Have questions prepared concerning how they would clean up the site.
3.   Create a class plan for cleaning up the lake and present to Congress and state legislature.

Language Arts (Elementary and Secondary)

1.   Students will photograph neighborhoods with disposable cameras.
2.   They will visit their own neighborhood and another that they consider completely different. Photos should illustrate what students see as their beliefs about the particular neighborhood.
3.   Teacher develops the pictures and students write about the significance of at least three of the photos from each of the two neighborhoods. They then present their ideas in class.
4.   The purpose of this exercise is to develop an appreciation for differences in communities. For example, in a farm community, the student might photograph a farm and the local town. In suburbia, a student might photograph an upscale development and a nearby urban neighborhood.
6.   Students discuss similarities and differences and then search for pieces of prose or poetry that describe these communities.

Social Studies

1.   Students brainstorm and construct a list of toys they played with as children.
2.   Student ask their grandparents, or an elderly person, what toys they played with as children and compare.
3.   Class lecture explains the conditions of World War II Germany and how children of this era fashioned toys out of rubble resulting from bombings.
4.   Class researches toys and brings information to school's technology teacher, where a prototype of one such artifact is constructed from scrap.

American History

1.   Class devises a list of nations that represents the students' family background and create a chart discussing each of these nations' roles in the Cold War and their experiences with communism.

2. A veteran of the Vietnam War (preferably from a student's own family) is invited to class and is asked to discuss the U.S. policy of containment and his or her opinions on the Vietnam conflict.
3. Students prepare a list of questions to ask regarding the veteran's experience with South Vietnamese culture.
4. Students write a reaction paper.

Social Studies

1. Class visits an area nursing home in search of anyone who has traveled outside of the country during the 20th century.
2. Students conduct interviews with those who traveled outside the country and gather information regarding the reason for and nature of the trip.
3. Class gathers information, plots interviewees' travel destinations on a map, creates a bar graph comparing the reasons for their travels, and summarizes their experiences in foreign lands.
4. Class reports their findings to the residents in a special presentation at the nursing home.

Physical Education and Language Arts

1. Students in groups research sports in ancient Egypt.
2. Each group chooses one type of sport, and researches where it was played and how.
3. Class meets the physical education teacher (who provides school's game resources) outdoors where each group demonstrates to the rest of the class how the sport was played.
4. Class writes reactions to the sport, including how each relates to modern-day variations and which of them they considered most fun.

I assess culturally responsive literacy ideas using the rubric on the following page that includes the seven characteristics. The lesson samples received 16 to 18 points because they included most of the seven characteristics of culturally responsive literacy classroom ideas.

INTERVIEW SUMMARIES

As the professor of this course, I had studied anonymous course evaluations, but believed that this class offered unusually thoughtful participa-

Rubric for Culturally Responsive Lesson/Unit Ideas

	Detailed Ideas for Multicultural Literacy Lessons in a Specific Content Area	Connecting Home, School, and Community	Literacy Learning and Content Area Connections	Sources of Lesson Ideas	Organization, Appearance, and Editing	Interest Level
3	Ideas have necessary information for lesson implementation	Obvious connections exist between the content area and ethnic, linguistic, and/or cultural diversity	At least 3 components of the literacy connection (reading, writing, listening, speaking, and viewing) are present in the implementation of these ideas	Lesson ideas for my content are from reliable sources (teachers, journals, text books etc.) and sources are identified	Overall organization, appearance, and editing appear perfect	The content area lesson ideas demonstrate great variety and active involvement of student
2	Ideas have some, but not adequate, information necessary for lesson implementation	Adequate connections exist between the content area and ethnic, linguistic, and/or cultural diversity	At least 2 components of the literacy connection are present in the lesson ideas	Most lesson ideas for my content area came from a reliable source or sources and sources are identified	The organization is difficult to follow due to appearance and editing	The lessons have little variety and active student involvement
1	Only the idea is presented	Does not demonstrate clear connections between the content area and ethnic, linguistic, and/or cultural diversity	At least one component of the literacy connection is present in the lesson ideas	I don't know where I got lesson ideas or didn't pay attention to the sources	The organization, appearance, and editing are not systematic enough to be able to easily implement ideas	The lessons lack motivational strategies since they incorporate repetitious activities with little student involvement

18 points=A; 14 points=B; 10 points=C; 6 points=D

tion that could not be assessed on the evaluations. So, I decided to interview four students, a few weeks after the course ended. During the last class, I asked for a group of practicing teacher volunteers who would be willing to share their thoughts about the course. I chose the first 2 males and first 2 females who raised their hands. As a focus group, they shared their reflections for an hour at the college snack bar. During that time, they seemed to speak clearly and honestly with each other as they dealt with questions prepared by me. My presence may have hindered them somewhat, but they knew their final grades and I had encouraged open expression of beliefs and attitudes throughout the semester. They responded to the following: (1) Tell me what you think you learned from this course. (2) How do you think you'll use this course in the future? (3) What would you like to see changed in the course?

All of the teachers claimed that the ABCs process was good in that it helped them think about their own lives and how their experiences had already affected their classroom teaching. The teachers also claimed to be confident in their abilities to connect with students and families from diverse economic, linguistic, and cultural backgrounds. Their culturally responsive literacy ideas were already being put into practice in their class-rooms. They also enjoyed meeting a clan mother and visiting the Onon-daga Nation School and said that during this field trip, they had acquired information that helped them learn the importance of making connections with cultural backgrounds. Finally, they stated that this course should be required for all students at the college. They believed that the ABCs pro-cess helped them reflect on themselves in ways that will make them much more sensitive in evaluating their own students. They also believed that they would be able to connect with members of their communities more easily and effectively in the future.

FINAL COMMENTS FROM THE FOCUS GROUP

Make the course two semesters long and periodically model or help us
    with lessons in our classrooms.
It's a phenomenal course, because it not only teaches you to be more
    sensitive, but it shows you how!
More work than most courses, but worth it.
I had time to reflect about who I am and what I could become as a teacher
    and a better person. Thank you.

CONCLUSION

Critical race theory (Ladson-Billings & Tate, 1995) exhorts us to go out and take action to change a world that discriminates on the basis of skin shades, religion, culture, language, and economic status. Therefore, cours-es that promote culturally responsive teaching and learning can help teach-ers change their classrooms and the world. We want our students to be different and willing to reach out and work with others, but first, teacher preparation institutions and inservice programs need to show them how. This type of cooperation and collaboration relate to survival of all that exists in our world. Consequently, teachers, as well as their students, require an understanding and appreciation of linguistic, ethnic, cultural, and economic differences in order to develop the critical literacy necessary for meaningful teaching and learning (Garcia & Willis, 2001).

MAKE THIS HAPPEN IN YOUR CLASSROOM

All teachers can challenge themselves by completing the ABCs of Cultural Understanding and Communication in their own way.

- Write your autobiography.
- Interview a challenging parent or family member of a student on neutral ground. Invite him or her for coffee and ask the following:
  a. What can I do to make this the best year of school for your child?
  b. What are your hopes and dreams for your child?
  c. How can the school help you realize these hopes and dreams for your child?
  d. When can we talk again and learn from each other?
- List similarities and differences between you and the parent.
- Complete your analyses of differences. What do you admire about the parent and why? What makes you feel uncomfortable and why?
- Create culturally responsive literacy lessons that follow the curriculum and connect home and school. Use the seven characteristics as a guide and then evaluate your ideas using the rubric in this chapter.

Finally, figure out how your students are responding. Are they reading, writing, speaking, and listening at a higher level? How are they working in class . . . are they interested and focused? Do they recognize similarities and differences in positive ways? How are they performing on your tests and standardized tests? What changes are evident? Have you met the challenge of culturally responsive literacy teaching in your classroom?

REFERENCES

Boykin, A. W. (1978). Reading achievement and the social-cultural frame of reference of Afro-American students. *Journal of Negro Education* 53(4), 464–473.

Cochran-Smith, M. (1995). Uncertain allies: Understanding the boundaries of race and teaching. *Harvard Educational Review, 65*(4), 541–570.

Cummins, J. (1986). Empowering minority *students:* A framework for intervention. *Harvard Educational Review, 56*(1), 18–36.

Edwards, P. A., Pleasants, H., & Franklin, S. (1999*). A path to follow: Learning to listen to parents.* Portsmouth, NH: Heinemann.

Florio-Ruane, S. (1994). The future teachers' autobiography club: Preparing educators to support learning in culturally diverse classrooms. *English Education, 26*(1), 52–56.

Garcia, G. E., & Willis, A. I. (2001). Frameworks for understanding multicultural literacies. In P. R. Ruggiano Schmidt & P. B. Mosenthal (Eds.), *Reconceptualizing literacy in the new age of multiculturalism and pluralism* (pp. 3–31). Greenwich, CT: Information Age.

Gunderson, L. (2007). *English-only instruction and immigrant students in secondary schools: A critical examination.* Mahwah, NJ: Erlbaum.

Howard, T. (2001). Telling their side of the story: African American students' perceptions of culturally relevant teaching. *Urban Review, 33*(2), 131–149.

Izzo, A., & Ruggiano Schmidt, P. R. (2006). Successful ABCs in-service project: Supporting culturally responsive teaching. In P. R. Ruggiano Schmidt & C. Finkbeiner (Eds.), *ABCs of cultural understanding and communication: National and international adaptations* (pp. 161–187). Greenwich, CT: Information Age.

Jenson, R. (2005). *The heart of whiteness: Confronting race, racism, and white privilege.* San Francisco: City Lights.

Ladson-Billings, G. (1999). Preparing teachers for diverse student populations: A critical race theory perspective. In A. I. Nejad & P. D. Pearson (Eds.), *Review of research in education, Vol. 24* (pp. 211–247). Washington, DC: American Education Research Association.

Ladson-Billings, G., & Tate, W. F. (1995). Toward a critical race theory of education. *Teachers College Record, 97,* 47–68.

Lazar, A. (2007). It's not just about teaching kids to read: Helping preservice teachers acquire a mindset for teaching children in urban communities. *Journal of Literacy Research, 39*(4), 411–441.

Leftwich, S. (2002). Learning to use diverse students' literature in the classroom: A model for preservice teacher education. *Reading Online, 6*(2). Retrieved November 10, 2005, from www.readingonline.org

Nebeker, K. C. (1998). Critical race theory: A White graduate student's struggle with the growing area of scholarship. *International Journal of Qualitative Studies in Education, 11,* 25–41.

Nieto, S. (1999). *The light in their eyes.* New York: Teachers College Press.

Noordhoff, K., & Kleinfield, J. (1993). Preparing teachers for multicultural classrooms. *Teaching and Teacher Education, 9*(1), 27–39.

Osborne, A. B. (1996). Practice into theory into practice: Culturally relevant pedagogy for students we have marginalized and normalized. *Anthropology and Education Quarterly, 27*(3), 285–314.

Pattnaik, J. (1997). Cultural stereotypes and preservice education: Moving beyond our biases. *Equity and Excellence in Education, 30*(3), 40–50.

Ruggiano Schmidt, P. R. (1998). The ABCs of cultural understanding and communication. *Equity and Excellence in Education, 31*(2), 28–38.

Ruggiano Schmidt, P. R. (1999). Focus on research: Know thyself and understand others. *Language Arts, 76*(4), 332–340.

Ruggiano Schmidt, P. R. (2000). Teachers connecting and communicating with families for literacy development. In T. Shanahan & F. Rodriguez-Brown, (Eds.), *49th National Reading Conference Yearbook* (pp. 194–208). Chicago: National Reading Conference.

Ruggiano Schmidt, P. R. (2001). The power to empower. In P. R. Ruggiano Schmidt and P. B. Mosenthal (Eds.), *Reconceptualizing literacy in the new age of multiculturalism and pluralism* (pp. 389–430). Greenwich, CT: Information Age.

Ruggiano Schmidt, P. R. (2005). Culturally responsive instruction: Promoting literacy in secondary content areas. *Adolescent Literacy*. Naperville, IL: Learning Point. Retrieved from January 13, 2006, http://www.learningpt.org

Ruggiano Schmidt, P. R., & Finkbeiner, C. (2006). *ABCs of cultural understanding and communication: National and international adaptations.* Greenwich, CT: Information Age.

Ruggiano Schmidt, P. R., Gangemi, B., Kelsey, G., LaBarbera, C., McKenzie, S., Melchior, C., et al. (2009). My language, my culture: Helping teachers connect home and school for English literacy learning. In J. Coppola & E. V. Primas, (Eds.), *One classroom, many languages* (pp. 227–250). Newark, DE: International Reading Association.

Ruggiano Schmidt, P. R., & Ma, W. (2006). *50 literacy strategies for culturally responsive teaching.* Thousand Oaks, CA: Corwin Press.

Spindler, G., & Spindler, L. (1987). *The interpretive ethnography of education: At home and abroad.* Hillsdale, NJ: Erlbaum.

Spradley, J. (1979). *The ethnographic interview.* New York: Holt, Rinehart & Winston.

Tatum, B. (1992). Talking about race, learning about racism: The application of racial identity theory in the classroom. *Harvard Educational Review, 62*(1), 1–24.

Tatum, B. (1997). *Why are all the black kids sitting together in the cafeteria?* New York: Basic Books.

Thompson, W. I. (1981). *The time falling bodies take to light.* New York: St. Martin's.

Vygotsky, L. S. (1978). *Mind in society: The development of higher mental process.* Cambridge, MA: Harvard University Press.

Xu, H. (2000a). Preservice teachers integrate understandings of diversity into literacy instruction: An adaptation of the ABCs Model. *Journal of Teacher Education, 51*(2), 135–142.

Xu, H. (2000b). Preservice teachers in a literacy methods course consider issues of diversity. *Journal of Literacy Research, 32*(4), 505–531.

CHAPTER 16

Unlearning Color Blindness and Learning from Families

Julie K. Kidd

With every new group of students who entered my classroom, I felt it was my responsibility to provide my husband with full, rich descriptions, so he would know them almost as well as I did. I would talk endlessly about the children—their interests, achievements, challenges, abilities, personalities, family backgrounds, and experiences, as well as the cute, funny, maddening, or perplexing things they did in the classroom. One year when I was teaching 4th grade, I noticed that my descriptions included information about their racial, ethnic, cultural, and linguistic backgrounds. I wondered what this meant. By talking about race, ethnicity, culture, and language, was I being racist? Wasn't I supposed to view all of my students as the same? Shouldn't I be blind to the color of their skin? Does it make a difference that Du Ho's (all names are pseudonyms) family was from Korea and Eduardo's family was from El Salvador or that Shernita is Black and that Lora is White? Does it matter that Juan speaks Spanish and very little English and that Malika speaks Urdo and English fluently? These were the questions that percolated in my mind as I confronted my own uneasiness around issues of race, ethnicity, culture, and language.

What I came to understand is that these things do make a difference because children's cultural and linguistic identities influence who they are, what they do, what they believe, and how they view the world (Banks, 2006). By taking a color blind stance, which disregards the color of their skin and the diversity of their backgrounds, I would be ignoring the individual experiences that influence what they bring to the classroom and overlooking the very essence of who they are. Culture plays an important role in children's development and learning (Espinosa, 2010). Therefore, as teachers, we must acknowledge and respond to the diversity of the students in our classrooms and avoid a color blind stance that overlooks students' identities.

The need to unlearn color blindness became clearer as I moved into a university position, working with preservice teachers preparing to enter the teaching profession at a time when many of their students would be from cultures different from their own and would often speak languages other than English. As I worked with the preservice teachers, I discovered that many had entered the program believing that a color blind stance was expected and even desired to ensure equity in the classroom. What they, like many teachers, didn't understand was that taking a color blind stance prevented them from responding to their students' unique experiences, abilities, and needs. They didn't realize that "when teachers use knowledge about the social, cultural, and language backgrounds of their students when planning and implementing instruction, the academic achievement of students can increase" (Banks, Cochran-Smith, Moll, Richert, Zeichner, et al., 2005, p. 232).

In this chapter, we will examine what is involved in unlearning color blindness and what can be learned from families to help us better understand and respond to students with cultures and languages different from our own. Through the words of eight White women entering the teaching profession, we will explore the value of avoiding a color blind stance by recognizing not only students' cultural and linguistic diversity, but also our own cultural backgrounds. We will consider the importance of recognizing and addressing our biases and assumptions. This will help us to reflect on ways we can unlearn color blindness, which is a mindset necessary for teaching in culturally responsive ways. Finally, we will explore ways to learn from and bring families into our own classrooms. Libby, Mary, Lindsay, Jessica, Laura, Katie, Dana, and Beth will be our guides as we contemplate ways to respond to and build upon our students' rich cultural and linguistic backgrounds to promote achievement in all of our students.

UNLEARNING COLOR BLINDNESS

Semester One, I proposed in a curriculum class that preschoolers were color blind, that in ignoring color differences we were teaching children to be accepting and equitable. As my journey progressed, I realized more and more that color blindness prevented seeing children who were culturally and linguistically diverse. —*Libby*

Like Libby, many preservice teachers entered our teacher preparation program believing that taking a color blind stance was the most equitable course of action a teacher could take. Likewise, many admitted to holding biases and assumptions about cultures different from their own that prevented them from seeing the strengths children brought to the classroom and kept them from capitalizing on the diverse perspectives and practices that were prevalent (Kidd, Sánchez, & Thorp, 2004a, 2004b, 2005). However, through a journey that involved (1) readings centered on issues of race, culture, poverty, and social justice; (2) internships with students from diverse backgrounds; (3) interactions with diverse families; (4) critical reflection; and (5) discussion and dialogue, the preservice teachers found that their understandings of their own culture as well as other cultures shifted in ways that reduced the assumptions they held about cultures different from their own and enabled the teachers to provide instruction that responded to the individual strengths and needs of their students (Kidd, Sánchez, & Thorp, 2008). They discovered that understanding their own culture, addressing their biases and assumptions, and responding to their students' diverse cultural and linguistic backgrounds were essential to becoming the teachers they wanted to be. Whether we are novice or experienced teachers, we can learn from these preservice teachers' experiences as we continually move toward providing a more socially just environment for learning that promotes achievement by all children.

UNDERSTAND OUR OWN CULTURE

Over the past 2 years, I have worked to understand myself and my family in order to understand the meaning behind my actions. According to Gary Howard (2005), "Transformationist teachers also know that educational equity and school reform, in large part, depend on white educators' willingness to engage in the process of our own personal and professional growth" (p. 123). The first step toward transformation is being consciously aware of my own values and cultures. In doing so, I have been increasingly able to learn from and work with people of other cultures and backgrounds. Additionally, knowing myself has enabled me to fight against former assumptions and biases and work toward a greater understanding of my role in society.—*Lindsay*

In her discussion of her own journey toward cultural awareness and responsiveness, Lindsay helps us to see the importance of understanding our own cultural and family backgrounds and the influence our prior experiences and cultural knowledge have on our teaching and interactions with students and families. Lindsay became consciously aware of her assumptions and biases about people from cultures different from her own as she explored her own cultural background and reflected on her interactions with others from diverse cultural backgrounds. Through gathering stories about her childhood from family members and sharing stories with her peers about her own upbringing and family experiences, she was able to recognize the ways her family practices influenced her values, beliefs, practices, and interactions with others. As she interacted with students and families from cultures different from her own and listened to the stories they shared about their lived experiences, she grew to understand differences in beliefs, values, and practices between herself and the students and families she served. Reading articles and books like the one she cited above by Gary Howard (2005) provided her with opportunities to make connections between her family practices and cultural background and their influence on her beliefs, values, practices, and interactions with all of her students and their families.

When we are cognizant of our own cultural values and practices, we become aware of the arbitrary nature of the way we act and the ways we view the world. This awareness enables us to "see the variability in others' value systems without compromising our own" (Chamberlain, 2005, p. 205). It also helps us to recognize the ways our actions and interactions are guided by our own cultural beliefs and practices and how mismatches between our cultural expectations and those of our students might occur. This is illustrated in a story shared by a teaching intern from Korea who was working with a White middle-class American family:

> In working with one of my focus families, I taught a child named Emily who had a physical disability. Due to her [poor] gross and motor coordination, Emily would fall frequently and hurt herself. My first and natural instinct was to run to her rescue; however, Emily's parents felt quite differently. They wanted her to be independent and strong. If she fell, she fell. They wanted their daughter to learn to get back up all on her own. As I examined my cultural lens, I realized how my culture embodied interdependence. In our culture, the idea of interdependence is frequently represented in our relationship with young children. It is in our nature to want and need to tend to young children, especially if they are distressed. To confess, there were several times when I followed my cultural beliefs and helped Emily up when no one was looking. (Kidd et al., 2008, p. 322)

This intern's recognition of the differences between her values and those of the child's family enabled her to respond to the child in a culturally responsive manner, while at the same time helping her to better understand the inner conflict she experienced as she interacted with the child in ways that differed from her own upbringing. She realized that to meet the needs of the child and the goals the parents had for their child, she had to suspend her own beliefs and acknowledge that independence was valued by the parents and it was her role to support this goal even though it was counter to her own cultural belief that interdependence should be fostered between children and caregivers. Too often teachers believe there is one right way or preferred way to approach a task without realizing that what they believe or value may be based on their own perspectives, experiences, family upbringing, and cultural knowledge. Exploring and reflecting on our own cultural beliefs, values, and practices enables us to recognize the validity of multiple perspectives and practices, including our own as well as the students in our classrooms. This awareness helps us examine the influence our cultural backgrounds have on our teaching practices and our interactions with students and families (Kidd, Sánchez, & Thorp, 2008). It also provides us with opportunities to examine, as Lindsay did, the biases and assumptions we hold about cultures and families different from our own.

RECOGNIZE AND ADDRESS ASSUMPTIONS AND BIASES

> My cultural awareness and advocacy for cultural diversity and understanding of differences has changed very much since I began the program. I have made remarks and assumptions based on stereotypes in my beginning teaching experiences, prior to my critical thinking and time spent reflecting after intense discussion. I think I have come to a new understanding about culture and my role as a teacher for my culturally diverse students. My desire is to learn through my past, present, and future experiences with the people I come in contact with.—*Jessica*

Like Lindsay, Jessica's assumptions and biases changed as she engaged in critical reflection and discussions with peers on her own cultural background as well as through interactions with families from cultures different from her own and readings focused on culture, poverty, and social justice. As Jessica interacted with families, she grew to know them as individuals and not by the stereotypes she had held about the cultural group or groups to which they belonged. She found that some of the beliefs she held, especially the deficit beliefs she considered to be true, were not substantiated by her experiences with the families. For example, she found that parents cared about their children's well-being and academic progress and supported their children's achievement in a variety of ways. She discovered that there were rich literacy practices in homes where she had believed none existed. And she realized that her assumptions and biases had kept her from seeing families as a valuable resource and partner in educating the children.

The importance of identifying our assumptions and biases and working to address them is a valuable message Jessica shares. The way we view and work with others is influenced by our recognition that cultural differences exist and that even within identified cultural groups variations exist from family to family and from individual to individual (Chamberlain, 2005). Our work with students is also affected by the biases and assumptions, or stereotypes, we hold about cultures different from our own. These assumptions often lead to teachers' deficit beliefs about students with diverse backgrounds (Risko, Roller, Cummins, Bean, Block, et al., 2008) and limit "their ability to provide quality instruction for all children in their classroom" (Lin, Lake, & Rice, 2008, p. 193). This intern's experience illustrates the difficulty and importance of facing one's own assumptions and biases:

> It was horrible to be faced with that ugly part of myself, and for the first time, I was conscious of the assumptions that I was bringing with me into the classroom. My negative assumptions about this child were wrong, and I was ashamed of my thoughts but at the same time happy that I was able to see that I did have assumptions. I am confident in saying that this was the most pivotal moment for me. Admitting to myself and acknowledging that I did bring assumptions into the classroom helped me to deal with my own biases, and I think that made me a better teacher. (Kidd et al., 2005)

This intern, like Jessica and many others, possessed a deficit view of the children in her classroom. The assumptions and stereotypes she held about children who live in poverty led to negative beliefs about the children's families. When she had an opportunity to visit one child's family at their home, she was confronted with a reality quite different from the reality she had created about the child and family. She discovered that the negative views she thought of as true were not accurate at all. Following the home visit, she felt ashamed by what she had been holding on to as true, and realized these ideas were driven by the assumptions and biases she held about families living in poverty.

Challenging our assumptions may not always be easy, but it is necessary. We need to examine the assumptions that guide our practice, become more knowledgeable about cultures different from our own, and learn to build on students' cultural knowledge. Until we do so, we may be unable to meet the needs of our diverse students and may continue to contribute to the achievement gap, especially the literacy achievement gap, that exists between White middle-class students and students of color (Au, 2006; Gay, 2000; Nieto, 2002). As Au explains, "Students of diverse backgrounds may have difficulty learning in school because instruction does not draw on the knowledge, values, and standards for behavior of their own culture and community" (p. 22).

RESPOND TO STUDENTS' CULTURAL AND LINGUISTIC BACKGROUNDS

> Culture is everything; it's our language, it's the food we eat, it is our music, it is our identity. Before entering [the early childhood education program], I was one of those people who would say that I was not racist because I treated everyone the same. I didn't realize that by saying everyone is the same you are taking away who they are, their race, their identity, and their life experiences. It is like you are erasing everyone who is different and all you are left with is the White culture. That was not my intention, and I now understand that we are all different and that difference should be both respected and celebrated. I can now provide a classroom where my students and their families feel comfortable, where they see pictures of themselves and their culture, and feel proud to share their culture with their classmates. —*Mary*

Mary's shift from taking a color blind stance to recognizing and valuing children's cultural diversity began during a discussion with peers when she declared how proud she was of herself for seeing all children as the same and not noticing the differences in the color of their skin or their family backgrounds. Until challenged, she did not see how pretending there were no differences among her students could have damaging effects on their well-being and achievement. As she reflected on the discussion that opened her eyes and her interactions with the diverse children in her classroom, her understanding of the importance of responding to, respecting, and valuing children's linguistic and cultural backgrounds emerged.

Mary encourages us to think about the important role culture and language play in the development and achievement of our students. Just like Lindsay reminds us that as we all have rich cultural and family backgrounds that influence our perspectives and practices, so do our students. Our students' cultural knowledge, linguistic backgrounds, and family experiences affect what they know, the ways they act, and the ways they learn (Gay, 2000). To ignore these differences is to pretend that all students learn in exactly the same way. Therefore, as teachers, we need to recognize our students' cultural and linguistic differences and figure out ways to build upon their strengths as we work to meet their individual needs. This involves getting to know our students and their families and being open to multiple perspectives and practices (Garmon, 2004, 2005; Kidd et al., 2008). It also means engaging in a reflective process that enables us to develop our self-awareness as well as our awareness and understanding of cultures different from our own (Garmon, 2004, 2005; Kidd, Sánchez, & Thorp, 2008).

DEVELOP CULTURAL AWARENESS AND RESPONSIVENESS

In looking at my history, my family, my culture, and my values, I have been able to increase my understanding of my role in society. I have seen the quality of my reflections grow as I learned more about myself. Combining my knowledge of my own background with an understanding of my role within a greater context has enabled me to critically reflect on my interactions, relationships, and practices. Knowing myself has helped me to empathize with people from other backgrounds and cultures, ultimately building stronger relationships out of mutual respect. —*Lindsay*

As Lindsay learned more about herself, she also came to know her students better. This reflective process was supported and encouraged in her preservice teacher preparation program. Through assignments that asked her to reflect critically on readings and experiences and discussions with peers that pushed her to examine her own beliefs, values, motivations, and practices, Lindsay became a reflective practitioner. Using a journal, she recorded her observations and thoughts and often referred back to these entries as she discussed in writing and orally with peers changes in her thinking and behavior. She used the journal as a vehicle for thinking through challenging situations and to help her reframe her ideas in light of what she was learning about working with students and families from diverse cultural, linguistic, and socioeconomic backgrounds.

As teachers committed to serving students with diverse cultural and linguistic backgrounds, we know that we must continually expand our knowledge and awareness of issues related to race, culture, poverty, and social justice. As Lindsay notes, doing so will lead to the development of stronger relationships with our students and their families, which will ultimately lead to culturally responsive teaching practices that enhance students' achievement. Preservice teachers have indicated that interacting with and learning from families, key readings, critical reflection, and discussion helped to develop their cultural awareness and culturally responsive teaching practices (Kidd, Sánchez, & Thorp, 2008). In the sections below, we will explore each of these types of experiences and the ways they interact to develop our cultural awareness and responsiveness.

INTERACT WITH AND LEARN FROM FAMILIES

When I was teaching preschool, parental communication was a huge part of my role as a teacher. Each day, I would be expected to have mini-conferences about how their child was interacting in the classroom. While this process was a bit intimidating at first, as I only wanted to say positive things about their children, I began to form relationships with the families and felt more comfortable expressing concerns I had about their children. This opportunity to share views and opinions through the creation of a relationship, not only helped the parents learn more about their children, but I was also able to hear stories and gain insight I might not have gotten through my interactions with the children. —*Katie*

As Katie discovered, building relationships with families is critical. Our interactions with families can yield information and insights that develop our understandings of cultures different from our own and help us get to know our students (Kidd et al., 2005). As we spend time with families, we hear their stories. These stories provide insight into their lived experiences, family practices, and cultural knowledge. Their stories are windows into their cultural experiences that can help us understand values, beliefs, and practices that may differ from our own. If we listen to these stories, we can use what we learn to not only develop our own cultural understandings but also provide instruction that builds on students' prior knowledge and experience and helps them make meaningful connections to the curriculum (Kidd, Sánchez, & Thorp, 2005).

READ TEXTS THAT FOCUS ON ISSUES OF RACE, CULTURE, POVERTY, AND SOCIAL JUSTICE

I had . . . never given much thought to the value of getting to know children and families outside of school. Reading Lisa Delpit (1995) got me thinking about looking at the whole child and the role of considering, as she says, "who sits before us" (p. 179). She argues that it is impossible for teachers to truly understand the children we teach unless we are successfully able to connect with families and the communities in which we are working. Families are enmeshed in communities and children are enmeshed in their families, and so I consider them to be valuable sources of information about the children I am spending my days with. —*Laura*

Laura helps us to see the influence reading can have on our beliefs as well as our teaching practices. As teachers, we need to search for readings that get us out of our comfort zone and stimulate our thinking about issues of race, culture, poverty, and social justice. Books like *Why Are All the Black Kids Sitting Together in the Cafeteria? And Other Conversations About Race* by Beverly Tatum (1997) prompt us to consider issues of race and White privilege. Jonathan Kozol's (2005) *Shame of the Nation* focuses our attention on poverty and the inequities in our schools. And Mary Cowhey (2006), in her book *Black Ants and Buddhists: Thinking Critically and Teaching Differently in the Primary Grades*, inspires us to integrate race, culture, and social justice into our classroom curriculum. Reading texts that promote critical reflection of our beliefs, assumptions, and teaching practices helps us to expand our knowledge, challenge our thinking, and make instructional decisions that foster learning in all students (Kidd, Sánchez, & Thorp, 2008).

REFLECT CRITICALLY ON YOUR PRACTICE

Not only is it important to look at each situation with fresh eyes, but to remember that teachers are the key role models in the classroom. Our position of power demands that we not only reflect on our own ideas, values, and assumptions, but also the situations we find ourselves in and our roles in how those situations resolve. In fact, reflection is key in uncovering our own prejudices, beliefs, and attitudes about people who are different from ourselves and can help us realize that our perceptions of those different from us come through our own "culturally clouded vision" (Delpit, 1995, p. xiv). I expect that my future classrooms will be full of children who come from different cultural and racial backgrounds from me, and I see it as my responsibility to examine myself and my own presumptions in terms of my relationship with them. —*Laura*

As Laura notes, critical reflection is essential to being teachers who respond to students' diverse backgrounds (Garmon, 2004, 2005; Kidd, Sánchez, & Thorp, 2008). Interacting with others and reading texts that stimulate thinking about race, culture, poverty, and social justice are not enough. We need to reflect on these experiences and contemplate how the information we gather interacts with our own values, beliefs, and practices. We need to consider how what we learn from families and texts contradicts our assumptions and biases. And we need to use our new understandings of families and cultures to inform our interactions with others, develop culturally responsive teaching practices, and create a more socially just environment for our students.

TALK ABOUT ISSUES OF RACE, CULTURE, AND POVERTY WITH OTHERS

Collaboration with peers through meaningful dialogue is inextricably connected to reflection, as some of the most meaningful reflection is guided by conversations with peers. [H]earing my own words provided me clarity, and receiving feedback from others helped me to understand multiple perspectives on the situation. According to Freire (2007), "Dialogue cannot exist, however, in the absence of profound love for the world and for people" (p. 89). It is important for me, when dialoguing, to understand that the end goal for all dialogues and reflections is ultimately to create a better world. The more perspectives and heightened understanding of issues that come with dialogue, the more I will be able to understand the significance behind my actions in decisions within the greater context of society. Dialogue, collaboration, and reflection should be deliberate and strategic in order for it to be productive. Reflection will increase intentionality behind decisions made in the classroom, deepening my understanding of my role as an educator and expanding my pedagogy.
—*Lindsay*

Lindsay reminds us that although much of our critical reflection may take place internally, dialogue about issues of race, culture, poverty, and social justice can be a meaningful way to more deeply reflect on these issues and their implications for our classrooms (Garmon, 2005). Through dialogue with our colleagues and members of cultures different from our own, our thoughts are challenged, our ideas are more fully developed, and our understandings of the issues evolve (Kidd, Sánchez, & Thorp, 2008). Through the give-and-take inherent in meaningful dialogue, we can develop, change, and strengthen our understandings of and convictions toward creating inclusive classrooms and providing culturally responsive instruction.

Developing our understandings of cultures different from our own enables us to enact practices that recognize and respond to the diversity of the students in our classrooms and promote inclusive classrooms. Within an inclusive environment that draws upon the students' family and cultural backgrounds and knowledge, we can get to know families and use what we learn to provide curriculum and instruction that builds upon students' prior experiences and cultural knowledge as well as their abilities, interests, and needs (Au, 2006; Kidd, Sánchez, & Thorp, 2008). The next section includes ideas for ways to respond to the diversity of the students in our classrooms.

CONCLUSION

Working toward a better society will never be finished, and any successes will be overshadowed by an ever present need for change within a greater context. Going into teaching, I thought, "Even if I can just change one life, that is a person's whole life, their whole world, that can be better because of me." Today my mindset is not only less patronizing but also much less willing to settle. My vision for myself today is to be part of a movement for a greater society, one that comes from working with communities for a greater good. —*Lindsay*

Listening to Libby, Mary, Lindsay, Jessica, Laura, Katie, Dana, and Beth as they began their journeys as teachers helps us to see the important role we play as we build upon our students' diverse cultural and linguistic backgrounds to foster achievement. Their honest reflections and our own communication with students and their families helps us examine our own assumptions and biases about cultures different from our own and consider ways to create inclusive environments that respect, appreciate, and respond to our students' diversity. Our classrooms can become models for creating a more socially just world as we bring families and their experiences into the classroom and discuss rather than avoid racial, cultural, and linguistic differences. In addition, we can provide curriculum and instruction that taps into students' cultural knowledge and addresses individual abilities, interests, and needs when we listen to and learn from what families share about their children and their lived experiences. By reflecting critically on our experiences and maintaining an openness to learning from the experiences of others, we can unlearn color blindness and instead respect, appreciate, and respond to our students' diverse backgrounds in ways that promote achievement in all students.

MAKE THIS HAPPEN IN YOUR CLASSROOM

As teachers committed to creating a more socially just society that embraces and responds to the diversity of the population, it is our responsibility to figure out ways to address issues of race, culture, poverty, and social justice in our own classrooms. We can do this by avoiding a color blind stance that ignores the diversity in our classrooms and, instead, embracing the cultural and linguistic differences that add to the richness of our classrooms. A first step toward a culturally responsive classroom is creating an environment that is inclusive of all children and families. We can do this by bringing families into the classroom and by using what we learn from families to inform our curriculum and instruction. In the following sections, Beth, Mary, and Dana share their thoughts about ways to make this happen in your classroom.

1. Create an inclusive environment

> I believe that the context you bring to your classroom is more important then the content in the curriculum. Making your class a place where everyone's social and cultural views are respected and accepted makes learning that much more meaningful for students. By connecting the curriculum to the students' lives they feel included and equally relevant in the classroom. This in return can promote learning. This can allow me as a teacher to stay connected with the community. Creating a classroom that respects social and cultural norms will help the students open up and feel more responsible in the classroom. I want my students to feel that they have a voice in my classroom and that their experiences matter. —*Beth*

Beth shares with us the importance of creating an environment that reflects the diversity of the children in our classrooms and promotes respect for diversity of perspectives and practices, including those not represented in the classroom. By creating an inclusive classroom, Beth conveys to all students and families that their cultural knowledge and experiences are valued. She also provides opportunities to promote learning in ways that draw upon students' prior knowledge. Several ways we, as teachers, can create and maintain inclusive classrooms that promote culturally responsive practices include the following:

- Provide opportunities for students to share their experiences and cultural knowledge.
- Connect the curriculum to students' lived experiences.
- Select literature, informational text, and multimedia that expose students to cultures represented in the classroom as well as those that are not.
- Display and use materials and resources that represent cultures in nonstereotypical ways.
- Initiate conversations related to issues of race, culture, poverty, and social justice.

When students believe their ways of knowing and acting are accepted and their voices are heard, they feel more involved in the classroom community and more engaged in their learning. Au (2006) explains, "Culturally responsive practice, in which teachers draw on interactional patterns familiar to students from the home, reduces resistance and helps students feel comfortable about participating in classroom literacy activities" (p. 93). Providing a learning environment that is safe, inviting, and draws upon familiar practices and exposes students to others' ways of knowing and being is important.

2. Bring families into the classroom

> While teaching [preschool] I learned a valuable lesson in how we are different. My students were between the ages of 3 and 5 years old. We were learning about families, so I sent home a large piece of paper and asked parents to make a poster with their child about their culture. I had the assignment translated so that everyone could be involved. Almost all of my students returned their posters, it was then that I realized how diverse my classroom really was. My students were from Guatemala, Bolivia, Ghana, El Salvador, Africa, Pakistan, and many other places. As a class, we learned so much about different countries and several of us wanted to travel to Ghana after seeing some of the pictures that students had brought to share. We had fun learning about each other and the children were very proud of themselves and their families. I displayed the posters around the classroom and the children loved to look at them, and it made the classroom environment more welcoming to the students and their families. —Mary

Bringing families into the classroom can be accomplished in a variety of ways. In this example, Mary chose to ask families to complete an assignment outside of school that would be shared during the instructional day.

She also found ways to include family members in the classroom by inviting them in to share stories related to the curriculum. Making connections between home and school, like Mary did, is important for developing a culturally responsive classroom. The following are some ideas of ways we can bring families into the classroom:

- Invite family members into the classroom to share their stories and experiences.
- Encourage students to bring photographs into the classroom to share and discuss.
- Ask students to bring in artifacts that represent their family's experiences and culture.
- Encourage students and families to write stories, make books, and create posters to share with classmates.

3. Use what is learned from families to plan instruction

> My assessment of [one] child's language . . . was directly connected to the feedback I received from his family. I asked [the] child about his native language and he was very reluctant to even admit that his family speaks another language. I then asked the family of [this] child about the use of his native language at home. I was told that he did not speak his native language at home. In visiting with the family, I noticed that they speak their native language to their children, but the younger child [the child in my classroom] responds in English. It was at this point that my interpretation centered around his motivation and comfort in using his language. With this understanding, I provided opportunities for him and the other students in the classroom to associate pride and success with their native languages. —*Dana*

Dana's point is an important one. We often hear that families are children's first teachers. If we keep in mind that families know their children better than anyone, we open ourselves up to learning valuable information that might help us provide instruction that better meets their needs. The following are ways we can get to know families:

- Visit students' homes and communities.
- Listen to families' stories and what they share about their children.
- Use what is learned from families to make the curriculum more relevant and meaningful.

- Provide instruction that builds on their prior knowledge, strengths, and interests.

REFERENCES

Au, K. (2006). *Multicultural issues and literacy achievement.* Mahwah, NJ: Erlbaum.

Banks, J. A. (2006). *Cultural diversity and education: Foundations, curriculum, and teaching* (5th ed.). New York: Pearson.

Banks, J. A., Cochran-Smith, M., Moll, L., Richert, A., Zeichner, K., LePage, P., et al. (2005). Teaching diverse learners. In L. Darling-Hammond & J. Bransford (Eds.), *Preparing teachers for a changing world: What teachers should learn and be able to do* (pp. 232–274). San Francisco: Jossey-Bass.

Chamberlain, S. P. (2005). Recognizing and responding to cultural differences in the education of culturally and linguistically diverse learners. *Intervention in School and Clinic, 40*(4), 195–211.

Cowhey, M. (2006). *Black ants and Buddhists: Thinking critically and teaching differently in the primary grades.* Portland, ME: Stenhouse.

Delpit, L. (1995). *Other people's children: Cultural conflict in the classroom.* New York: New Press.

Espinosa, L. (2010). *Getting it right for young children from diverse backgrounds.* New York: Pearson.

Freire, P. (2007). *Pedagogy of the oppressed.* New York: Continuum.

Garmon, M. A. (2004). Changing preservice teachers' attitudes/beliefs about diversity: What are the critical factors? *Journal of Teacher Education, 55,* 201–213.

Garmon, M. A. (2005). Six key factors for changing preservice teachers' attitudes/beliefs about diversity. *Educational Studies, 38,* 275–286.

Gay, G. (2000). *Culturally responsive teaching: Theory, research, and practice.* New York: Teachers College Press.

Howard, G. R. (2005). *We can't teach what we don't know: White teachers, multiracial schools* (2nd ed.). New York: Teachers College Press.

Kidd, J. K., Sánchez, S. Y., & Thorp, E. K. (2004a). Listening to the stories families tell: Promoting culturally responsive language and literacy experiences. In C. M. Fairbanks, J. Worthy, B. Maloch, J. V. Hoffman, & D. L. Shallert, (Eds.), *Fifty-Third Yearbook of the National Reading Conference* (pp. 246–263). Chicago: National Reading Conference.

Kidd, J. K., Sánchez, S. Y., & Thorp, E. K. (2004b). Gathering family stories: Facilitating preservice teachers' cultural awareness and responsiveness. *Action in Teacher Education, 26*(1), 64–73.

Kidd, J. K., Sánchez, S. Y., & Thorp, E. K. (2005). Cracking the challenge of changing dispositions: Changing hearts and minds through stories, narratives, and direct cultural interactions. *Journal of Early Childhood Teacher Education, 26*(4), 347–359.

Kidd, J. K., Sánchez, S. Y., & Thorp, E. K. (2008). Defining moments: Developing culturally responsive dispositions and teaching practices in early childhood preservice teachers. *Teaching and Teacher Education 24,* 316–329.

Kozol, J. (2005). *The shame of the nation: The restoration of apartheid schooling in America.* New York: Three Rivers Press.

Lin, M., Lake, V. E., & Rice, D. (2008). Teaching anti-bias curriculum in teacher education programs: What and how. *Teacher Education Quarterly, 35*(2), 187–200.

Nieto, S. (2002). *Language, culture, and teaching: Critical perspectives for a new century.* Mahwah, NJ: Erlbaum.

Risko, V. J., Roller, C. M., Cummins, C., Bean, R. M., Block, C. C., Anders, P. L., et al. (2008). A critical analysis of research on reading teacher education. *Reading Research Quarterly, 43*(3), 252–288.

Tatum, B. D. (1997). *Why are all the Black kids sitting together in the cafeteria? And other conversations about race.* New York: Basic Books.

CHAPTER 17

Socially Responsive Literacy Teaching in the Midst of a Scripted Curriculum

A Novice Teacher's Story

Kathryn S. Pegler

What happens when a preservice teacher graduates from a teacher education program that promotes culturally responsive teaching and winds up in a school with a scripted program that is in direct opposition to her educational philosophy? My doctoral-level research questions did not necessarily seek to answer this question; however, interestingly enough, that was the scenario each of the three participants in my study encountered when they obtained their first teaching positions. My study investigated the influence of a graduate literacy teacher education program that emphasized cultural responsiveness on first-year teachers. What my research illustrated was that each teacher reacted to their circumstances in unique ways.

One of the teachers was unable to insert her beliefs about teaching and learning into the classroom. Two of the teachers were able to negotiate the prescribed curriculum by enhancing their programs with meaningful and sophisticated literacy learning experiences. The results of each teacher's ability or inability to negotiate the curriculum ultimately had powerful consequences for the students in these classrooms and the teachers themselves. This chapter will focus on Rachael, a brave 23-year-old who allowed me to follow her into her classroom during her first year of teaching. Rachael, despite many obstacles, was able to successfully apply the tenets of culturally responsive literacy instruction in her urban classroom. An examination of Rachael's attitudes and practices can serve as a blueprint for other teachers in similar circumstances.

RACHAEL'S FIRST TEACHING POSITION

Rachael, like many first-year teachers, obtained a teaching position in a school environment that was very different from the one she attended. Growing up, Rachael did not have much experience with racial and linguistic diversity. She explained how the elementary and high schools she attended were "basically 95% White." She remembered "when the first African American students came through [her] elementary school, and the stir that it created because [the] school had always been completely Caucasian until the 4th grade."

As Rachael studied to become a teacher, she knew early on that she wanted to teach in a diverse school setting, stating, "I loved all my experiences in urban schools!" Rachael also enjoyed positive suburban field placements, but she felt she made more of an impact in the urban schools and that those schools positively shaped her as well. Rachael possessed what Nieto (2010) describes as a "sense of mission." This sense of mission is not an act of self-righteousness or rescuing others. Instead, it stems from a strong desire to teach diverse students to help ameliorate the discrepancy between the educational privileges granted to students in suburban schools, with the more limited educational opportunities afforded to students in urban and high poverty communities. Rachael explained:

> There are always teachers clamoring to get into good suburban schools, but I feel better going every day to a school that I think really needs me, and where I can really make a difference. It just feels right knowing that I am giving all that I can to students that might not be given all the opportunities that other children have.

Driven by this stance, Rachael pursued a teaching position in an urban school district and was offered a teaching position at a Catholic school located on the border of a large urban district.

Rachael's position entailed providing learning support in the areas of reading, writing, and math at a school that served students in grades kindergarten through 8, 91% of whom were students of color, including African Americans, Asian Americans, and Hispanics, from low socioeconomic backgrounds. Rachael instructed 19 students in grades 3 through 8 on a rotating basis. On Monday, she taught nine students in grades 3 through 5, and on Tuesday she taught 10 students in grades 6 through 8. So over a 2-week period, she saw each group for a total of 5 days. Rachael said most of her students resided in single-parent homes.

Rachael's classroom was representative of many resource rooms across the United States. For one, her room was tucked away out of sight in the basement of the school and away from the center and pulse of school activity. In addition, the students in Rachael's classroom consisted mainly of students of color and the boys outnumbered the girls, three to one. As such, her classroom mirrored special education designations that often fall along lines of race, class, and gender (Kozol, 2007). What was most worrisome to Rachael, however, was that many of her students were apathetic toward reading and writing.

Rachael took responsibility for her students' learning and progress through enacting many tenets of culturally responsive teaching. In just a few months, she gradually overcame her students' indifference and resistance toward literacy learning. She began to see that her students gained ownership of their literacy learning (Au, 1998, 2006).

RACHAEL'S BACKSTORY

Rachael's ability to enact beliefs about her own responsibility to teach and the importance of student empowerment had developed before she assumed her first teaching position. What initially started Rachael on this path was her 5-year teacher education program. One of the courses in the program stressed social equity teaching, specifically as it applied to literacy. Rachael learned to confront her own racism and ethnic biases while examining and becoming more open to other ethnic and cultural perspectives and realities. Rachael felt this course helped her develop positive attitudes and beliefs toward the students she served, especially when it came to learning about her students' funds of knowledge (Moll, Amanti, Neff, & Gonzalez, 2005) and her students' economic, social, and cultural reading capital (Compton-Lilly, 2007). In addition, the course provided the structure for Rachael to examine White privilege and racial identity development (Howard, 1999), structural racism, and other sociological factors impacting literacy achievement (Lazar, 2004), transformative curriculum design (Banks, 1994), relatioships between language and identity (Delpit & Dowdy, 2002), and the acceleration of children's literacy development while attending to children's sociocultural needs (Dozier, Johnston, & Rogers, 2006). Not only did Rachael read and respond in writing to the above cited research, but she engaged in active discussion, and wrote her own cultural autobiography that centered on her experiences of privilege and subordination (Milner, 2007). Rachael credited the course with not only challenging but also changing her assumptions about *students:*

I really did learn about examining what I thought about kids and what I thought about families with single-parent homes. The fact that none of these kids—maybe 75% of these kids—don't know their dad or don't know who their dad is. I guess when I first started college, living [in Smithville] that would have seemed shocking to me. And now, because [I know] that was an assumption, I know that I can't make judgments, and I don't anymore. At least, I don't think I do.

In addition, Rachael possessed firm beliefs about literacy learning and teaching. These beliefs influenced her instructional decisions and allowed her to assert her own authority to bring about changes that went against her teaching beliefs. Rachael's goal for literacy instruction was for her students to have ownership in their reading experiences and for them to recognize the value of literacy (Au, 1998, 2006). Rachael explained:

An important goal that I have for my students is that they be enthusiastic or motivated readers and writers. I want them to see that reading and writing can be good ways to pass time. I want them to learn that reading and writing don't only have to happen at school. One of my favorite moments throughout the week is when I'm reading out loud and stop at a critical point, and they yell because they don't want me to stop. Each time this happens, I have a glimmer of hope that they are starting to recognize the power that can happen when they read.

NEGOTIATING A SCRIPTED LITERACY PROGRAM

Rachael was required to provide decoding and comprehension instruction using the SRA Corrective Reading Program. The purpose of the SRA program is to correct motivational deficiencies and increase student skills through the use of scripted lessons that follow a fast-paced teaching guide. These lessons include reading stories with controlled vocabulary and contrived storylines in order to reinforce phonics patterns. Initially, Rachael praised the organization and explicitness of the program: "We're supposed to dedicate 45 minutes for each child to do SRA. It's very specific and outlined. Everything you are supposed to do. It's scripted, which is nice. The manual even tells you what to say if a student makes an error." What concerned Rachael most was the fact that she was required to use a much older edition of the program. Upon learning that the textbooks and comprehension workbooks were from 1995, Rachael stated, "I was just shocked! Reading instruction has changed so much in the last 13 years. How can you still be re-ordering the same books?" Rachael took initiative and inquired about the outdated books to another teacher. This teacher disagreed with Rachael and indicated that she did not believe the program had changed considerably. Rachael replied sarcastically, "You're right, it is exactly the same—let's hand out Dick and Jane!"

However, soon the ease of relying on the scripted program began to deeply trouble Rachael as it contradicted her beliefs about literacy learning and teaching. Rachael also started to realize there were social justice issues regarding the use of SRA, and she struggled over the issue of fairness and the idea that these low-level thinking programs were mainly used in classrooms of students of color from lower socioeconomic households. Rachael explained:

> As a first-year teacher, it's helpful just because it is so scripted that there really is no room for doubt. I know that I'm going to ask this question and then I'm going to ask this question. But it goes against what I learned for 5 years about how you teach reading. That reading instruction shouldn't be scripted, and it should be based on each student, and it should address higher levels (of thinking). And I know this doesn't. So I'm going okay, this is helping me right now, but it's not what I know is best. I feel kind of conflicted about it . . . but most other schools that I've been in—the urban schools or the high-poverty schools always have the very scripted programs. I know my mom teaches in [Smithville, a suburban school]. They don't use a program, they just have a curriculum and the teachers get to design around that . . . they get that extra leeway and almost faith. I'm kind of conflicted about using it, it's helpful now, but I know it's not the best, and I know it's not what the kids need to be getting, and I really know that it's going to bother me when I'm more set up and established as a teacher.

Rachael's internal conflict over the effects of using the program steadily grew, "It [SRA] just drives me nuts because it is just so predictable and so repetitive. I know that I get bored doing it, and I feel so bad for the kids because I know they must too."

In response, Rachael scrutinized her curriculum to find places where she could give her students an array of meaningful reading and writing experiences, and she was determined to match instruction to each child's unique literacy needs. Rachael made decisions about her students' reading abilities based on a variety of informal and formal assessments and then differentiated instruction through the use of small guided reading groups during which she taught her students the strategies and skills that good readers use during the course of real reading. Rachael explained:

> We're also doing a novel right now. We're doing *Number the Stars* with my older kids, and with the younger kids . . . right now, I'm doing Cam Jansen . . . and shorter stories with the lower kids. When I do guided reading with the younger students they enjoy it because we push the desks aside and put the rugs in a circle on the floor. Luckily, there have been many, many teachers in the room before me so I inherited quite a collection of materials that I still am sorting through, every now and then I find a gem.

Rachael also made time in her daily schedule to incorporate journal writing and the writing process approach where she incorporated mini-lessons and modeling to support students to ensure they gained access to basic skills and conventions as they wrote on their own (Delpit, 2006). Rachael explained the process:

> I do mini-lessons on writing, and I try to have them do journal writing as often as I can throughout the week. I want them to become accustomed to using writing more often; they were very reluctant from the beginning but now start the lessons much faster. I also have some books with extensive units on different forms of writing that have been helpful. The older students just completed the unit on factual recounts. I started by having them read an example of a Factual Recount and then I took the students through the process and steps until they wrote one themselves at the end. With the younger students, I just completed a unit on poetry writing that they really enjoyed.

In addition to guided reading and writing, Rachael provided students with daily independent reading time. Based on her belief that student interest is a way to help motivate reluctant readers, Rachael purchased many of these materials. "Early on, I asked what they would be interested in reading. I tried to go and get some sports books. I wanted to get some car magazines, but I would just have to censor so much of it because every ad had a girl half naked." Moreover, Rachael read aloud to her students. This, not only provided a model for her students, but it helped spark a desire for them to read. "I read *The Black Cat* with them, by Poe, and they were in awe, which was good. And they were like 'okay, can we read more?' I was like YES!!" From then on, Rachael built time every day to read aloud:

I try to use the block directly after lunch. I use this time because I have all the students and it is a good way to transition them back into the classroom. It is good because this was a block of time that I could never get what I needed done, but now the students know that this is the time to just come in and take a seat and get ready to listen. I try to read about 20 to 30 minutes every day.

Based on student reaction to her instructional practices, Rachael also began developing what Nieto (2010) calls "solidarity with and empathy for" her students. According to Nieto, these are not "sentimental emotions" but, rather, this is where teachers genuinely respect their students' cultural identities. This admiration insists upon maintaining high expectations for students. As this high regard for her students developed within Rachael, she decided she could no longer stand the negative effects the SRA reading program was having on her students; thus, she took further action. Rachael began restructuring her schedule; she reduced the amount of instructional time spent on SRA and increased the amount of time students spent engaged in meaningful literacy experiences:

I started the year by having the students complete as many as three SRA stories a week. I cut it down so that SRA is completed only as filler if the students finish their other work. I could see how much the students were resisting SRA and how much it was turning them off to reading. I have added more novel work and independent reading to the schedule and I do more DRTA's with literature because I know they appreciate and enjoy it more. I hear fewer groans from the students when I say take out your novel as opposed to take out your SRA books and I have seen a change in the viewpoints of most of my students when it comes to reading.

Rachael made these changes and then informed her supervisor. Rachael said, "I didn't discuss it with my supervisor before I did it, but we have talked about it since then. She was okay with my decision because I was replacing SRA with more authentic texts and related activities."

After consciously deciding to limit the SRA program, Rachael began to provide sophisticated literacy instruction that involved incorporating before-, during-, and after-reading strategies to actively involve her students in the reading process. For example, on the day I observed, Rachael stated that the purpose of the day's lesson was to engage her students in a higher-level thinking activity through the process of analyzing text in order to determine the cause and effect relationships in the story being read. Rachael began the lesson by instructing the students about cause and effect relationships. She provided examples, and then had the students share their own examples. Before reading the story, Rachael activated her students' background knowledge. A discussion took place about the book based on the title *If You Take a Mouse to the Movies.* The students shared their information about similar books they had read by the same author, as well as their knowledge about the structure, or how these stories unfold. Rachael set a purpose for the reading and told the students they would be looking for cause and effect relationships. During reading, the story was read in a variety of ways; students read out loud individually, students read together chorally, and Rachael read to the students. Moreover, periodically, Rachael stopped and had the students recap the story and briefly discuss some of the cause and effect relationships. During these stops, students made predictions about what they thought would happen next, as well as to confirm or disprove their prior predictions. All of these strategies helped to promote comprehension and student engagement during reading.

After reading, Rachael had the students discuss some of the cause and effect relationships with a partner. She then connected the reading to a purposeful writing activity. Students were going to make a cause and effect booklet. In order to make the booklet, students needed to know how to write a "why" question. Rachael modeled how to write a why question, then she provided guided practice as the students wrote why questions with her. Once Rachael was sure the students had the concept of writing a why question, she modeled how to make the booklet. The students were instructed to apply what they learned about cause and effect and writing why questions to analyze the story they had just read and to write questions for the other students to answer. Therefore, instead of Rachael questioning students to determine if students comprehended the story, the students demonstrated their learning by developing their own questions and asking each other; hence, Rachael turned over the ownership of learning to her students. Throughout this entire lesson, the students were engaged and actively involved, as Rachael implemented a variety of higher-level meaningful reading and writing experiences that incorporated skill instruction (Delpit, 2006).

Rachael's solidarity with and empathy for her students was also substantiated in her strong belief that all of her students were capable of attaining high levels of literacy even though many of her students lacked the motivation to read. Rachael refused to accept this mindset, and, instead, Rachael worked tirelessly to ameliorate this problem, stating:

> With the older kids, there is a definite weakness in desire. None of
> them, maybe three of them want to read, and I've actually bumped

that up. I've got maybe four or five now who want to read. I did Poe with them, and I did, I got this [a Dracula book] . . . and one of the boys who hated reading actually wanted to read it. He saw it, grabbed it, and ran away to read it.

Another issue that deeply troubled Rachael was her students' resignation that they were poor readers: "The older kids, I think some of them have resigned that they're bad readers, and have told me, 'Ms. [Rachael], I hate this. I'm not good at this. I don't need it.' I'm like, 'you don't *need* reading, what?'" Rachael rejected that attitude and committed herself to providing her students with more instruction. Rachael acknowledged that this confused some students who had previously been held to low expectations. Rachael explained:

My older students don't understand why I push them, when last year they were just let off the hook, and one student is extremely behind for her grade and in the past years, the school day consisted of putting her on simple Web sites or computer games, while the other students were addressed. She has been pushed through the school as a "pet"; she is incredibly sweet and affectionate and because of her personality, she was never pushed or been held to standards. I am happy to say that I push her and don't let her quit after giving me a sad smile. She is doing very well and I can see how proud she is of herself when she succeeds or even just puts her best into her work.

As the students became motivated, Rachael enjoyed the rewards of "hooking" the reluctant reader. In the following, Rachael described Jenna, a 7th-grade student:

Jenna started this year talking about how much she hated reading and how she could never find books that interested her but what I think happened was that she confused SRA with reading. She didn't seem to understand that reading didn't just mean reading SRA and then answering some repetitive questions. Since the beginning of the year I have watched Jenna develop more of an interest in reading, she is very into *Number the Stars* and the stories we read by Poe, but she still seemed reluctant to start a novel on her own. Then one day she showed up with a huge book. She brought me the first book in the series *Twilight* and asked if I thought she could read it—she seemed scared at the prospect. I told her that she should at least try it. . . . I was thrilled to see that the minute she finished her class work or had any down time that she would pull out *Twilight*, separate herself from the class, get comfy, and read. She finished it within a week. She is so proud of herself and is already starting the next in the series, *New Moon*. As an added bonus, the other girls in the class, who look up to Jenna, are now also interested in reading *Twilight* and some have even started it.

Rachael guided her students to attain the high bar she set and this had positive effects on her students' motivation and ownership regarding literacy experiences.

Another practice that Rachael enacted was inviting and acknowledging her students' out-of-school lives within the classroom. Rachael worked tirelessly to create a classroom community in which students were comfortable and shared stories about themselves. Rachael wanted her students to know that she knew them and cared about them. So during the first week of school, Rachael took the time to get to know her students. "I gave two inventories the first day, and I didn't just tuck them away. I use them and could talk about it with the kids so they knew that I was getting to know them." This approach seemed to put her students at ease, as they felt comfortable opening up and discussing their cultural backgrounds. This was surprising to Rachael because during Rachael's student teaching experience this was not typical; students did not talk about their racial identities. "Here, it's just like, they talk about it, they're like, 'Oh, what are you?' 'Oh, I'm half Black,' 'I'm half Mexican,' 'I'm half Spanish,' 'I'm half White.' I'm like, 'All right, that's great, let's talk about it.'"

With regard to classroom management, Rachael noted that the special education program followed "the school management policy, which is a point system. Points are given out for misbehavior and after a certain number of points the students have to attend detention." Rachael adopted this policy only when necessary and mainly for hallway behavior. In the classroom, Rachael let her students know from the beginning that "disrespect and rudeness would not be tolerated." To achieve this goal, Rachael did not incorporate a behavior system; instead she allowed students to engage in natural communication patterns. For instance, students often engaged in back and forth banter and laughter; however, when Rachael or other students were speaking, students were respectful and listening. I witnessed this as the class was discussing cause and effect relationships:

Rachael: How about cause, my alarm clock rang—effect, what would the effect be of your alarm clock ringing in the morning?

Damien: You fell out of the bed.
Students: [Laughter]
Rachael: Who else can think of one?
Lamar: If a train hit you, your legs are broken.
Isaac: Your arms *and* legs *and* body would be broken!
Students: [Laughter]

What was apparent in Rachael's classroom was that the students were engaged in the learning process, as they listened and participated in the lesson. The environment also showed that learning can be pleasurable. This was evident through the laughter and the singing that took place. For example, when the students got loud and spoke out all at once, Rachael handled the situation with quick wit that the students appreciated:

Rachael: Put the date at the top. What's today's date?
Students: [Yelling out all at once]
Rachael: I asked one question, and I got 20 different answers!
Lamar: Twenty different answers? There's only about five of us in here or
    seven?
Rachael: Well a couple of you gave four answers!
Students: [Laughter]
Rachael: So what's the date?
Lamar: Monday, January 12.

Laughter frequently occurred throughout the lesson, as the students gave examples of cause and effect relationships. Some of the examples were silly. However, Rachael allowed for this and as a result students would laugh and talk and then calm down as they participated and paid attention during the lesson. Toward the end of the lesson, Rachael asked the students if they knew the song about the monkeys jumping on the bed. The students identified the song and then determined what the causes and effects were in the song. As Rachael began passing out the books for the students to share, some of the students were singing the monkeys jumping on the bed song. Once all the students had their books and they were ready to proceed with the lesson, the students stopped singing and became engrossed in the reading of the story.

Lastly, Rachael was willing to look honestly at areas where she knew she was weak. For instance, some of Rachael's students were academically capable of being in the regular classroom; however, Rachael believed that due to their extreme behavior, such as throwing chairs or picking fights, they were placed in her classroom. Rachael doubted her own ability to help these students, but she made the decision to try and teach the students the appropriate behavior for success in the classroom anyway. Rachael explained:

> I'm like all right, we'll work on your behavior, we'll try, we'll work on that, but I don't know, I know some keys, some tools for working on behavior issues, but I studied reading and I studied just special [education] more on the learning issues and learning disabilities, I don't know—I know how to do some behavior plans and I know how to kind of try to modify some behaviors.

Rachael also voiced concern about the materials she was providing her students. Rachael knew she needed to find and add more diverse texts so that her students would be represented in the books that they read. She explained:

> I have been looking up different texts that would be more culturally relevant to my kids. There are several authors I have been looking into and one text in particular, *Call Me Maria*. I want books that focus on the life experiences of growing up Latino/a as they are. I enjoy reading classics with them and they enjoy them too, but I think they also need to be able to recognize themselves in books.

Toward the end of the study, Rachael reported that she felt better about how things were going in the classroom and in the school community. Rachael had positive experiences with parents at conferences, and students were recognizing that they could go to Rachael for help. This pleased Rachael:

> Many things are going well. I am getting faster at planning and preparing my lessons so I am not staying the long, long hours that I was in the beginning. I am also figuring out more each day what works for my students and what doesn't and also who I can go to in the school if I need something. I also feel that I am becoming a real part of the staff and, as a result, I am helping to fix some of the issues in the school. We also just finished our parent–teacher conferences and the majority of the parents seemed pleased with the work their children have been doing. Many were asking my advice on what books to read that were similar to the ones we read in class because they go home and talk about them. I have also been able to help several of my

students with their confidence levels and their self-esteem. I am very happy when they feel comfortable enough to come and talk to me about a problem they might be having.

Rachael's narrative illustrates what can happen in classrooms where teachers recognize that all students have unlimited potential and knowledge. This view directly influenced what Rachael did in her classroom to promote her students' literacy learning and the reflection she did outside the classroom to challenge her practices. Rachael recognized the harmful nature of the scripted program. Rachael negotiated the SRA program to a minor role in her classroom, while putting in rigorous exemplary reading and writing practices that motivated and engaged her students in higher-level thinking processes. She provided students with engaging books and time to read. In addition, she acted as a model by reading aloud daily. Her beliefs about all students' capabilities coupled with her practices and high expectations combined to help students reach their literacy potential. In addition, Rachael's story exemplifies the importance of recognizing the lives of students inside the classroom. Rachael repeatedly showed her students she cared about them and was concerned for them. All students were important, and Rachael strove to meet their needs culturally, emotionally, and academically. Rachael's recognition of students' lives fostered a culturally responsive classroom community that enjoyed laughter, singing, and literacy engagement.

CONCLUSION

Rachael's ability to implement culturally responsive literacy practices had positive, powerful outcomes for both Rachael and her students. As a result of Rachael's attitudes and practices, her students, many of whom had previously exhibited apathetic attitudes and behaviors toward literacy learning, displayed high levels of motivation, literacy engagement, and ownership. These are essential components for helping students to realize their literacy potential.

MAKE THIS HAPPEN IN YOUR CLASSROOM

- *Be a reflective practitioner.* It is possible that you can enact practices similar to Rachael. One essential procedure Rachael consistently implemented was critically reflecting upon her teaching and how it influenced her students and their experiences in the classroom. It was this reflection that allowed Rachael to change harmful practices while enacting more beneficial ones. Some questions that Rachael routinely asked and are important for all teachers to raise are:

1. What are my own personal attitudes and biases regarding my students and their culture, class, and gender?
2. How can I get to know my students better and learn about their background and personal experiences—e.g., informal inventories, phone calls, or visits home?
3. Do my students know that I care about them emotionally, socially, and academically?
4. Am I providing meaningful, relevant, and rigorous literacy experiences?
5. Do I incorporate before-, during-, and after-reading strategies that allow my students to develop reasons for reading and writing and foster active student engagement?
6. Am I connecting reading with meaningful writing processes while providing the skill instruction and guided practice necessary to ensure student success? (Delpit, 2006)
7. When and how do I model for students the enjoyment that comes from reading so students can recognize the inherent value of literacy?
8. How do I advocate for my students?
9. Do I ensure that reading materials are motivating and interesting to my students?
10. Do my students see mirrors of themselves in the stories we read?
11. Are my students able to witness the lives of others who are different from my students?
12. Do I examine and reflect daily on the effects that my teaching practices have on my students? Specifically, what are the areas I'm weak in and how can I challenge and change those practices to benefit my students?
13. Where else in my daily encounters with my students can I incorporate higher-level thinking processes?
14. Do I make sure that no matter what program I am using—even if it is scripted—that my students' background experiences are incorporated into each lesson? For instance, Rachael knew that her students' literacy endeavors must be rooted in their own personal experiences, so she found ways to incorporate natural communication and discourse patterns in the classroom including laughter and singing, demonstrating there is joy in learning.

- *Find out how other teachers create engaging classrooms.* One book that I have found very helpful is *Teach Our Children Well: Essential Strategies for Urban Classrooms* (Maniates, Doerr, & Golden, 2001). The title suggests that this book is for teachers in urban areas; however, the concrete, explicit strategies are appropriate for all teachers in all environments. This short book offers useful approaches to creating a respectful, student-friendly classroom, while also maintaining rigorous academic standards and active student engagement based on students' background experiences.

REFERENCES

Au, K. H., (1998). Social constructivism and the school literacy learning of students of diverse backgrounds. *Journal of Literacy Research, 30*(2), 297–319.

Au, K. H., (2006). *Multicultural issues and literacy achievement.* Mahwah, NJ: Erlbaum.

Banks, J. (1994). *An introduction to multicultural education.* Needham Heights, MA: Allyn and Bacon.

Compton-Lilly, C. (2007). The complexities of reading capital in two Puerto Rican families. *Reading Research Quarterly, 42*(1), 72–98.

Delpit, L. (2006). Lessons from teachers. *Journal of Teacher Education, 57*(3), 220–231.

Delpit, L., & Dowdy, J. K. (2002). *The skin that we speak: Thoughts and language and culture in the classroom.* New York: New Press.

Dozier, C., Johnston, P., & Rogers, R. (2006). *Critical literacy /critical teaching: Tools for preparing responsive teachers.* New York: Teachers College Press.

Howard, G. R. (1999). *We can't teach what we don't know: White teachers, multiracial schools.* New York: Teachers College Press.

Kozol, J. (2007). *Letters to a young teacher.* New York: Crown.

Lazar, A. (2004). *Learning to be literacy teachers in urban schools: Stories of growth and change.* Newark, DE: International Reading Association.

Maniates, H., Doerr, B., & Golden, M. (2001). *Teach our children well: Essential strategies for the urban classroom.* Portsmouth, NH: Heinemann.

Milner, H. R. (2007). Race, narrative inquiry, and self-study in curriculum and teacher education. *Education and Urban Society, 39*(4), 584–609.

Moll, L. C., Amanti, C., Neff, D., & Gonzalez, N. (2005). *Funds of knowledge for teaching: Using a qualitative approach to connect homes and classrooms.* Mahwah, NJ: Erlbaum.

Nieto, S. (2010). *Language, culture, and teaching: Critical perspectives* (2nd ed.). New York: Routledge.

CHAPTER 18

Becoming a Teacher for All Children

A Teacher's Story

Jiening Ruan and Brandi Gomez

Educating children from different cultural, ethnic, linguistic, academic, and socioeconomic backgrounds within the same classroom is the new reality for teachers. This reality can be both exciting and overwhelming. Teaching "other people's children" (Delpit, 2006) can be a challenge but also an opportunity. We know teachers who take up this challenge, and they blossom. In this chapter, the authors will introduce you to Bethany, a middle-class, European-American female teacher, and her incredible journey to become a teacher for all children. In her, we see a teacher who shows a true passion for teaching children from all backgrounds and a never-ending quest for culturally responsive instruction.

We understand that literacy learning is shaped by social, cultural, and linguistic factors and experiences (Ladson-Billings, 1994, 2001; Nieto, 2002; Vygotsky, 1962). In such a learning environment, students construct new knowledge and understanding by interacting with peers and knowledgeable adults (Vygotsky, 1978). As facilitators, teachers work to provide culturally meaningful learning experiences for their students to enhance their growth intellectually, emotionally, socially, and academically. We are firm supporters of culturally responsive teaching or culturally relevant teaching (Au, 2001; Gay, 2000; Ladson-Billings, 1994, 2001; Ruggiano Schmidt, 2002, 2003; Ruggiano Schmidt & Ma, 2006). Culturally responsive teaching involves using the cultural characteristics, experiences, and perspectives of diverse students to teach them more effectively (Gay, 2000). It emphasizes the importance of situating academic knowledge and skills within the lived experiences of students to make learning meaningful and relevant to them. Culturally responsive teachers are also mindful of the strengths each student brings to the classroom and seek to maximize their learning through valuing and building upon those strengths (Au, 2001). In this chapter, you will meet a teacher who is guided by these principles and read about the road she traveled, the lessons learned, and the teaching practices she has honed.

BETHANY'S STORY

Bethany grew up in a traditional European-American middle-class family in which both her parents and grandparents were still married to each other. Her mom and three of her grandparents were teachers. In Bethany's words, "Teaching is in my blood." She attended a mainstream elementary school in a middle-class suburb of San Antonio, Texas. San Antonio is a city influenced by many cultural communities, especially those affiliated with Mexican Americans, and this influence continues to impact her cooking and desire for life experiences that include multiple perspectives.

Bethany completed her undergraduate program at a small private university, outside of Austin, Texas, aiming to become a high school mathematics teacher. After her first semester and a class in special education, she realized that her true calling was elementary education, with an emphasis in special education. She wanted to be able to integrate special-needs students into her general education classroom and provide them with the least restrictive environment for success. Her teacher education preparation gave her the conviction that *every* child needs some instructional modifications and accommodations in order to be successful academically and socially.

Today, Bethany is into her 8th year of teaching and continues to maintain her enthusiasm. She had been teaching 1st and 2nd grades and now is in her first year of teaching 3rd grade. She is enjoying this new challenge and claims that her commitment to culturally responsive literacy teaching guides her to create a successful classroom environment.

From being a sheltered child in a White middle-class family to becoming a teacher respected by diverse groups of parents and students, Bethany's journey demonstrates a major transformation. The significant factors that prompted this transformation include her teaching experiences and an immersion trip to Guadalajara, Mexico, where she learned valuable lessons and gained critical insights.

FIRST YEAR TEACHING

Bethany has never forgotten that first year of teaching. At age 22, she walked into a first-grade classroom with only one Anglo-American student. The rest of her students were African American and Hispanic—and they knew poverty and discrimination. Her 6-year-old students told her, "I hate White people."

Bethany struggled to keep her students focused and involved academically, but a large number could only sit still for a few minutes. Determined to be a successful teacher, Bethany read professional books on how to motivate and engage students, participated in professional development opportunities, and sought help from more experienced teachers on her 1st-grade team. As a result, during that year, she discovered how to incorporate movement through songs and chants to help students make connections between their lives and learning. She also came to understand that she had a responsibility to respect and understand each student's experiences and draw from these understandings to help her students grow academically and socially.

LANGUAGE AND CULTURE IMMERSION
IN GUADALAJARA, MEXICO

Bethany fell in love with Joe, a second-generation Mexican American, and married him during her first year of teaching. Both Bethany and Joe were motivated to learn more about Mexican culture and gain stronger proficiency in the Spanish language. In particular, Bethany wanted to have first-hand experience in Mexican culture and also acquire the ability to speak Spanish fluently so that she could be more effective when working with her Hispanic students. This led Bethany and Joe to travel to Guadalajara, Mexico, for 5 weeks during the summer of 2008.

When Bethany and Joe arrived in Guadalajara, often called the "most Mexican of cities," she experienced culture shock. As a fair-skinned, blue-eyed blonde, she couldn't easily blend in among the local population. With a different physical appearance and very limited Spanish, Bethany recalled that she was way out of her comfort zone. However, this experience gave her a new perspective on what it means to "fit in," something she had taken for granted all of her life. While in Guadalajara, they lived with a traditional Mexican family—a cowboy father working at a ranch and a stay-home mom who took care of the family and created delicious food in her small kitchen. Because the hostess knew very little English, Bethany often found herself struggling to communicate to get her basic needs met. This eye-opening experience helped her understand what some students in her classroom would be feeling, whether they were nonnative English speakers, students who struggled with reading, or students with other special needs.

Over the course of their stay in Guadalajara, they learned to navigate the city using public transportation, to eat foods they would never have tried, and to communicate in Spanish. They attended a Spanish language school at which the teachers were allowed to speak *only* Spanish to the students. At the beginning, Bethany was lost much of the time in class and felt very frustrated. This feeling also was new for her, because she had never struggled with school. Fortunately, Bethany had a teacher who was not afraid of her anxiety. He did not allow her to give up when something was difficult, but pushed her to find different ways to express herself. Though the learning process was painstaking, she made great progress in Spanish due to the constant scaffolding and unending dedication of her teacher. The insights that Bethany gained through this struggle have proven invaluable in her subsequent years of teaching. She has gained true empathy for students who come from diverse cultural and linguistic backgrounds. She makes sure that all children feel welcome, but at the same time she pushes and guides them toward understanding.

CULTURALLY RESPONSIVE TEACHING: INSIDE BETHANY'S CLASSROOM

In this section, you'll read about the various instructional practices that Bethany implements in her classroom. These include setting the tone, setting high expectations, working with children who learn differently, and striving to meet the special needs of English language learners.

Setting the Tone

A major goal for Bethany every year is to cultivate an environment that every student feels safe in, knowing that they will be free from ridicule and that the chances they take will be met with support and encouragement from everyone, rather than judgment. They spend the first week of school establishing classroom rules and codes of conduct on how they want their friends to treat them and how they promise to treat their friends. She has four main questions, adapted from the training program Capturing Kids Hearts. Students' answers become the class rules, or "promises." These questions are "How do I want to be treated by my friends?" "How do I want to be treated by my teacher?" "How does my teacher want to be treated by me?" and "What can I do in case of conflict?" They spend one day answering each question, making sure that each child has input into what they brainstorm for their guiding principles. They are very specific concerning what it means to "be nice." What does it look like, feel like, and sound like? There is no confusion about what is expected.

Bethany firmly believes that the time invested in these discussions of classroom interactional rules establishes the tone for the whole year. Her students know that only encouraging words are allowed in their classroom, and they know *why* they only allow encouraging words. They talk about how they are a family working together to help make everyone better and that they have to work hard all year long in different ways to help each other grow. Establishing these expectations together gives the students a sense of ownership, and the students become the main enforcers of expectations, because they are *their* rules and expectations.

In a classroom of students with varying needs, when the environment is right, the students learn to recognize each other's efforts before Bethany can. For example, when one of her students, Mario, responded in English, the class would burst into spontaneous clapping. They were proud of his efforts and were excited to share his accomplishments. At the end of the day, the class meeting starts with a compliment circle, where students give specific compliments related to their day. Bethany thinks this recognition by peers is important to encourage hard work and accomplishments

Bethany promotes risk-taking behaviors in her classroom with the caveat that we never negatively criticize someone's effort. For example, she shares that she is a not a perfect speller. She then shows them how she helps herself, by sounding out words, asking help from friends, and using the dictionary. She always gives authentic examples and encourages each student to grow in their own areas of weakness.

Working with Children Who Learn Differently

This past year, Bethany had a student who was hearing impaired. He could not communicate with words and would often hit other students to get their attention or to try to communicate. She did not wait for the pull-out teacher to remedy this child's behavior. Bethany rallied her class to help this student develop appropriate communication techniques, in a supportive, but firm manner. Bethany provided him with various roles that were important to the functioning of the classroom. This helped integrate him into the classroom community and gave him responsibilities. His classmates saw him as someone with strengths and, therefore, attempted to help him with appropriate communication techniques. Halfway through the first term, this child, with a hearing impairment, became a positive member of the community.

Bethany has her own set of unique beliefs about students who struggle with schoolwork but do not qualify for pull-out services. She believes these students can become successful in society, because they know how to struggle. If they are given the right support, they can learn two lessons: how to persevere and how to master a difficult skill. The word *failure* is not used in Bethany's classroom. If the student has not learned the skill, she states that the skill is "still developing." She has math checklists, and when a student demonstrates mastery of a skill, it is checked off. This type of checklist allows her to pull small groups of students who may have missed a previous skill and reinforce with more direct instruction. Bethany incorporates small guided reading groups into daily instruction as well as small guided math groups, because she thinks the more direct, one-on-one time helps her quickly understand strengths and needs.

Working with English Language Learners

Last year, Bethany had a student, Mario, who had moved from Mexico days before the school year started. She felt nervous with such a huge responsibility, but she was thrilled with the challenge and diversity that Mario would lend to her classroom. By talking to Mario and his parents in Spanish, it became evident that he had emergent reading skills in Spanish. Therefore, she began the school year creating readers with him using concrete words he would need to use in the classroom, such as *boy, girl, pencil, door,* in both English and Spanish. Gradually, these readers became books that he would read independently and to his classmates. Students were excited to help him become more confident in reading and speaking in English.

Since mathematics is a subject area that is less dependent on English proficiency than reading or writing, Bethany made efforts to encourage Mario to answer math questions in class. The first words Mario felt comfortable saying aloud in class were numbers.

Writing was a challenge for Mario. For his first writing project, he wrote his assignment in Spanish and she translated it for him into English, but she highlighted common conventions in both English and Spanish, such as spaces between words and capitalizing words. By the end of the year, Mario was writing completely in English. Though the grammar was still developing, his writing was very much his own work and his own ideas. The transformation was incredible.

Setting High Standards and Providing Differentiated Instruction

Bethany sets high academic and social standards for her students, but she always differentiates instruction. One specific example is seen in the writing projects. Her students publish three to four written compositions per year. They create drafts, self-edit and peer-edit, confer with Bethany, finish their final drafts, and then publish. During writing conferences, students talk about their individual goals and teacher expectations. Bethany thinks that every child is capable of creating a piece of writing, though some will be more developed than others. Mario, who was new to English, did all of his writing projects and was an important contributor during writing workshop. In September, Mario wrote in Spanish and Bethany translated it for him into English. By doing this, he was able to demonstrate his literacy knowledge. This was a sign of respect and appreciation for his culture and background. She was also able to teach Mario the corresponding words in English that he already knew in Spanish. Bethany set high but realistic expectations for him.

Bethany is keenly aware of the struggles that English language learners experience. Even if they are proficient in social English, they may not be proficient in academic English. This year she is meeting daily and individually with two students in her classroom, both English language learners, in different stages of English acquisition. Not only is she able to individualize instruction, but she is also able to closely monitor learning strategies that are being used and developed and focus on some of these strategies during one-on-one reading lessons. Time is always a constraint, and finding time to meet with two students independently was difficult, but with structured planning and a set routine, Bethany is usually able to meet with her students individually. She uses visuals, hand gestures, and concrete, short sentences that are very clear and direct in order to communicate with all students. She is a big fan of using songs that repeat phrases and incorporate high-frequency words so that her English language learners hear new words often. She encourages movements or drawing to demonstrate understanding. Bethany has discovered that many of the teaching strategies she uses for English language learners have benefits for all the students in her class.

Bethany realizes that students who are advanced in content areas may have difficulties reading grade-level texts but are capable of much more critical thinking. One way that she addresses this problem is by using literature circles, through which students develop critical thinking skills by evaluating texts and responding thoughtfully. Bethany models in each literature circle several thoughtful responses, so that students have a secure idea of what she expects. Then her students are expected to read the agreed-upon assignment before each circle meeting. Students also keep a journal, in which they record daily responses to their readings. Students share their responses and respond to each other's responses. This analysis of literature is often thought to be above 2nd-grade abilities, but by the end of the year, most students are engaged in thoughtful discussions.

Embracing Different Cultures Through the Use of Children's Literature

Bethany makes conscious efforts to introduce her students to different cultures. She incorporates literature from a variety of diverse ethnic and linguistic backgrounds to reinforce reading skills as well as to help her students gain an expanded understanding of our diverse world community. *The Keeping Quilt* was one book that her students enjoyed reading. She and her students discussed how they all had special things that had been passed down in their families from one generation to another. They used this text to examine how cultures may have different celebrations and traditions, but at heart, they all shared the same feelings of wanting to be connected to their families. They concluded that people from different cultures may have many similarities.

Because the majority of her ethnically diverse students are Spanish speaking, Bethany tends to use more literature reflecting that background. For example, the book *Gracias, the Thanksgiving Turkey* enables her students to build on their schema of Thanksgiving, while gaining a new perspective of a Spanish-speaking child while learning Spanish words in the text. It allowed her English-speaking students to infer meanings and provided opportunities for her Spanish-speaking children to demonstrate their expertise.

Bethany uses literature reflectively, not only of cultures that are represented in the school community but also of other parts of the world in order to make the world a more accessible place to all students in her classroom. She incorporates folktales and legends from different cultures, such as books by Tomie dePaola who brings culturally diverse folktales to life through *The Legend of the Poinsettia, The Legend of the Bluebonnet, The Legend of the Indian Paintbrush,* and *Patrick: Patron Saint of Ireland.* Through the use of these legends and folktales, students begin to develop an open-mindedness of the world around them. She also introduces the works of Patricia Polacco, believing that the autobiographical nature of her writing, with her Russian ancestry playing a dominate role in her storylines, provides opportunities for her students to see that there are more similarities than differences between their own and others' cultures. Patricia writes about her *babushka,* and her students are able to identify that as her grandmother through accessing their schema and making inferences. Multicultural children's literature provides her students not only opportunities to reinforce their reading skills but also a window into different cultures.

Teaching Diversity Through Real-Life Events

During the recent tragedy of the earthquake in Haiti, Bethany and her students talked about the differences and similarities between going to school in the United States and going to school in Haiti. A student at their school came from Haiti and has some family members living in Haiti. The school undertook an outreach project to raise money to help his family in Haiti. In her classroom, Bethany and her students brainstormed ways that they could earn money to help support this family, and she tried to emphasize that the students' hard work would reach further than they could imagine.

In 2009, Bethany made a personal trip to the historic inauguration of President Barack Obama in Washington, D.C. She felt that this was an incredible historical moment, regardless of personal political viewpoints, and the students in her classroom were old enough that they would remember this event for their lifetime. She hoped to make it even more memorable for them to be able to say that their own teacher was there in the crowd during that moment. She embraced the teachable moments she was presented with at this event but was cautious because she was aware that many of the parents of students in her classroom did not vote for President Obama. She carefully addressed the historic aspect of the inauguration, by emphasizing that in only 60 years, America went from segregated water fountains to an African American president. With the emotion and politics removed, they examined the event and what it meant historically for our nation.

Connecting with Parents

Bethany views parents as important partners in children's education. To Bethany, the biggest threat to prejudice is knowledge, so she tries to bring in experts in various cultures and languages to help the students gain a broader knowledge of the world and to celebrate differences rather than be afraid of them. She invited parents to come to her classroom to talk about celebrations in their respective cultures so that all students could feel proud of their own cultural heritage. Another successful strategy that Bethany has used to get parents involved is incorporating student-led conferences in each spring semester. Bethany and her students work together to develop a conference plan, and at the conference time, she steps aside and the students explain to the parents the learning that has been going on in their classroom, their own successes, and their personal areas needing improvement. The process of student-led conferences gives the students a deeper insight into their own learning, empowers students to take ownership of their learning, and engages parents in a positive experience in the classroom, where they are able to see their child shine and see them as the experts in their own education.

Recently, Bethany also involved parents in writing groups. Twice a week, parent volunteers came into her classroom and supervised students as the students continued to work through the writing process on projects that they had begun. This process has been very important for the students, who are able to proceed through the writing process more confidently, having more adults available to assist. It also gave parents a window into the classroom. The parents have been awed at the quality of work that 3rd-grade students are able to produce.

LESSONS LEARNED FROM BETHANY'S PRACTICES

Bethany's teaching reflects several aspects of culturally responsive pedagogy (Au, 2001; Gay, 2000; Ladson-Billings; 1994, 2001; Ruggiano Schmidt & Ma, 2008). First, Bethany and her students create a supportive, encouraging community where all feel confident to take chances. They hold each other accountable and build each other up for more success. They help each other celebrate achievements.

Bethany believes that all students can learn and resists the practice of labeling children. To her, giving students a label only identifies their weaknesses and does nothing to highlight their strengths. She views each student as an individual with unique strengths and needs. When students walk into her classroom, she wants to highlight their strengths and build on them to further advance their learning. Bethany believes that it is a mistake for teachers to discount the knowledge that students of diverse cultures bring with them into a classroom. Accessing the "funds of knowledge" (Moll, Amanti, Neff, & Gonzalez, 1992) they bring with them makes their learning experience more successful, as well as enriches the experience of the other students in the classroom.

Bethany sets her expectations high for each student, but the expectations are also individualized. She is a firm believer in pushing students to do their best in everything, but she always reassures them that she will never hold them accountable for something they cannot do. It is important to set achievable goals with students throughout the year, so that they can see their success and celebrate growth.

Other keys to success that Bethany holds include respecting and honoring parents' roles in their children's education and actively seeking opportunities to get them involved in her classroom. She helps students make connections between home, school, and community so that learning is relevant and meaningful to the students. She understands that her students have different learning styles and makes conscious efforts to accommodate them. She provides differentiated instruction to her diverse learners through small-group and individualized instruction. She also promotes among her students a respect and an appreciation for diversity through using multicultural children's books.

In assessing the impact of culturally responsive teaching, Bethany believes that all of her students, including mainstream and ELLs and students with special learning needs, benefit from such practices. Understanding the limitations of formal assessments, Bethany uses a mix of formative and summative as well as formal and informal assessments throughout the year to help her to document and monitor student progress. She places great value on the information she obtains from informal assessments such as observations, conversations and discussions, student-generated projects, reading response journals, writing samples, and reading logs. She constantly uses assessment results to keep her informed of where each student is along the development continuum and the amount of progress each student makes. She then revises and sets new goals for each student. Such an approach has proven to be very effective, and she has witnessed marked progress in all her students, especially culturally diverse students. Through her students' products, feedback from the parents, formal and informal assessments of her students, and student evaluations of their own learning, Bethany believes that her students have greatly benefited from culturally responsive teaching practices. Her students are motivated to learn because all of them have experienced success and are proud of their own successes and the successes of their classmates.

CONCLUSION

Reflecting on her journey from being a novice teacher to becoming a culturally responsive teacher, Bethany thinks that the biggest differences between who she was then and who she is now lie in her understanding of what culturally responsive teaching is about, and how specifically to show respect to her students and also gain respect from them. When she first walked into her classroom during her first year teaching, she naïvely thought that by incorporating student jargon into her speech, she could make all of her culturally diverse students feel comfortable and welcome. She soon found out that this approach did not work. The students did not take her seriously, and she was never able to gain the respect she needed from her students. As a culturally responsive teacher, she now makes a great effort to show all of her students respect by acknowledging who they are. To model this, she does not change who she is or the way she speaks with them. Her classroom is a community of mutual respect, and she has been successful at fostering an environment where differences are respected and every student is expected to be successful.

MAKE IT HAPPEN IN YOUR CLASSROOM

- Help students develop a positive cultural identity by acknowledging their achievements.
- Create a learning community in which students hold each other accountable and also support each other.
- Make learning meaningful and relevant by connecting learning activities to students' home and community experiences.
- Make efforts to learn about cultures and languages represented in your classroom.
- Maintain an open line of communication between you and the parents and get them involved in their children's learning.
- Use children's literature that reflects and validates the cultural heritage and experiences of all students, especially students whose backgrounds are not that of majority White European Americans from the United States.
- Use instructional activities that accommodate diverse learning and interaction styles.
- Participate in professional development opportunities that increase your knowledge and skills for culturally responsive teaching.

NOTE

Bethany's story is based on the true story of Brandi Gomez, the second author of this article.

REFERENCES

Au, K. H. (2001, July/August). Culturally responsive instruction as a dimension of new literacies. *Reading Online, 5*(1). Retrieved April, 10, 2010, from http://www.read-ingonline.org/newliteracies/lit_index.asp?HREF=au/index.html

Delpit, L. (2006). *Other peoples' children: Updated edition.* New York: New Press.

Gay, G. (2000). *Culturally responsive teaching: Theory, research, and practice.* New York: Teachers College Press.

Ladson-Billings, G. (1994). *The dreamkeepers: Successful teachers for African American children.* San Francisco: Jossey-Bass.

Ladson-Billings, G. (2001). *Crossing over to Canaan: The journey of new teachers in diverse classrooms.* San Francisco: Jossey-Bass.

Moll, L. C., Amanti, C., Neff, D., & Gonzalez, N. (1992). Funds of knowledge for teaching: Using a qualitative approach to connect homes and classrooms. *Theory into Practice, 31*(2), 132–141.

Nieto, S. (2002). *Language, culture, and teaching: Critical perspectives for a new century.* Mahwah, NJ: Erlbaum.

Ruggiano Schmidt, P., & Ma, W. (2006). *50 Literacy strategies for culturally responsive teaching (K–8).* Thousand Oaks, CA: Corwin Press.

Vygotsky, L. S. (1962). *Thought and language.* Cambridge, MA: MIT Press.

Vygotsky, L. S. (1978). Mind and society. Cambridge, MA: Harvard University Press

Reflective Practice and Evaluation

As you develop your culturally responsive teaching, reflect on your progress and evaluate yourself. This will help you move forward on this positive journey toward meeting the needs of your students from diverse linguistic, cultural, and economic backgrounds.

Becoming a culturally responsive teacher	I tried the suggestion.	I am working on it.	It was successful.	I made modifications.
Preparing Myself				
I wrote my autobiography.				
I interviewed a parent.				
I completed a cross-cultural analysis related to the parent.				
I am reading about culturally relevant or culturally responsive teaching.				
I am requesting staff development and/or college credit for culturally responsive learning.				
Getting to Know Families and Communities				
I know about the diverse linguistic, economic, and cultural backgrounds of the families of my children.				

I call my parents and tell them something positive about their child.				
I invite family and community members to share their talents, interests, and/or cultural practices in my classroom.				
I can be seen in my students' communities—at the recreation center, place of worship, park, or grocery or drug store.				

Centering Students in the Curriculum and Classroom

I use my students' languages in my classroom.				
I have used literature that my students can relate to themselves.				
I use the arts (music, art, theater) to explore cultures in my classroom.				
I use relevant literature that connects to content areas.				
I allow my students to work in pairs when they are learning new concepts.				
I am learning to design culturally responsive lessons.				

Assessing My Progress

I have high expectations for my students because I scaffold their learning.				
My families see me as an equal partner in the education of their children.				
The families and students trust me.				

About the Contributors

JIM ANDERSON is a professor in the Department of Language and Literacy Education at the University of British Columbia where he teaches and researches early literacy and family literacy.

ROSANNE BARBACANO is a grade 2 teacher in Lexington Public Schools in Massachusetts. She is currently on the English Language Arts Curriculum Review Committee and focuses on teaching and reaching all learners through many diverse cross-curricular methods and techniques.

AMELIA COLEMAN BROWN is the principal of the William D. Kelley Elementary School in Philadelphia and the Co-coordinator of Professional Development for the Philadelphia Writing Project. She has worked as a vice principal, a classroom teacher, an academic coach, and continues to work as a teacher consultant for the Philadelphia Writing Project.

JULIE COPPOLA is an assistant professor of education at Boston University, where she teaches courses in first and second language and literacy development and directs the teacher education programs in Bilingual Education and Teaching English as a Second Language (ESL).

TANJA COSENTINO has been an ESL, ELA, and social studies alternative education teacher for the last 7 years. She enjoys inspiring young people to achieve emotionally and academically.

PATRICIA A. EDWARDS is Distinguished Professor of Language and Literacy in the Department of Teacher Education and a Senior University Outreach Fellow at Michigan State University. Her publications are rich with evidence and insights into issues of culture, identity, equity, and power that affect families and schools.

ERNIE ESTRADA has taught mathematics for the last 30 years at Everett High School in Lansing, Michigan.

JUNE ESTRADA has taught social science for the last 15 years at Everett High School in Lansing, Michigan.

JAMIE GARTNER is in her third year of teaching English language arts in the Syracuse City School District. She earned her bachelor's degree from Le Moyne College in secondary English Education with a dual certification in Special Education and is currently pursuing her master's degree at Syracuse University in Literacy Education.

BRANDI GOMEZ teaches third grade at Truman Elementary School in Norman, Oklahoma and is currently pursuing a master's degree in Reading Education at the University of Oklahoma. She has worked with ethnically, linguistically, and economically diverse students, as well as students with special needs in her classrooms.

LEE GUNDERSON is a professor of language and literacy education at the University of British Columbia, where he teaches both undergraduate and graduate courses in second language reading, language acquisition, literacy acquisition, and teacher education. He has been a revered elementary teacher, principal and outstanding researcher leader in the area of immigrant English literacy development.

HARRY HUGHES is principal of an elementary school within the District of Columbia Public Schools. In his many years as an educator and teacher leader, He has been able to garner tremendous academic outcomes from the hardest to reach population of students.

JULIE K. KIDD is an associate professor in the College of Education and Human Development at George Mason University. She is the Coordinator of the Early Childhood Program and was previously a classroom teacher and reading specialist.

GURKAN KOSE has taught math and coached mathematics olympiad teams in public schools for 5 years. He is also a part-time doctoral student in Mathematics Education at Syracuse University and an active member of the Northern New Jersey Lesson Study Group at William Paterson University.

ALTHIER M. LAZAR is a professor of education and department chair in the Teacher Education Department at Saint Joseph's University. Her research focuses on preparing teachers to serve children in culturally nondominant communities.

MARYELLEN LEELMAN is a speech and language pathologist in the Lexington Public Schools in Massachusetts and a doctoral candidate at Boston University's School of Education in Literacy and Language, Counseling and Development. She has worked in elementary public schools as a certified speech, language, and hearing pathologist since 1981.

GUOFANG LI is an associate professor in the Department of Teacher Education at Michigan State University. She specializes in ESL/ELL/EFL education, family and community literacy, and Asian American education. She has conducted research in these areas in international settings including China, Canada, and the United States.

MARIO LOPEZ-GOPAR is an associate professor in the Faculty of Languages of Benito Juarez Autonomous University of Oaxaca. His Ph.D. thesis was awarded both the 2009 AERA Second Language Research Dissertation Award and the 2009 OISE Outstanding Thesis of the Year Award.

KRISTIN R. LUEBBERT is a middle grades teacher and reading specialist in the School District of Philadelphia. She has taught 7th- and 8th-grade reading and social studies at the Bache-Martin School in the Fairmount neighborhood for 9 years.

FIONA MORRISON is co-creator with Jim Anderson of the Parents as Literacy Supporters (PALS) Program. She is a teacher facilitator in the program with a background in early childhood education.

HEIDI OLIVER is an assistant professor in the Department of Education, University of the District of Columbia. She is a native Washingtonian committed to the renewal of education and development for traditionally marginalized children and youth.

KATHRYN S. PEGLER is an assistant professor of education at Neumann University, where she teaches undergraduate and graduate-level reading courses. She has taught in both private and public schools as a 1st-grade teacher and a reading specialist.

CRYSTAL PONTO has been an English and Global Studies alternative education teacher for 14 years. Her experience teaching reluctant learners has provided her with the talents necessary to teach present and future educators how to create successful classroom environments.

TARA RANZY is the sole proprietor of The School of Life (SOL): Life Coaching Workshops for Educators. She has worked as an educator in the city of Philadelphia for more than 10 years and currently serves as the founding 6th-grade chair, dean, and 6th-grade writing teacher at KIPP West Philadelphia Preparatory Charter School in Philadelphia.

FERNANDO RODRIGUEZ is studying for his master's degree in secondary English and a certification for Teaching English to Speakers of Other Languages at Le Moyne College in Syracuse, New York.

JIENING RUAN is an associate professor of Literacy/Reading Education and Chair of the Reading Specialist Certification Program at the University of Oklahoma. Her research interests include literacy development of diverse student populations in the United States as well as in international contexts.

PATRICIA RUGGIANO SCHMIDT is a professor of Literacy Education at Le Moyne College in Syracuse, New York. Her research examines preservice and inservice preparation for culturally responsive teaching in elementary and secondary classrooms. In the 2010–2011 school year, she became principal of Cathedral Academy at Pompei, an urban international school in the Roman Catholic tradition.

KEVIN SALAMONE earned a master's degree in Education from Le Moyne College and currently teaches Secondary English Language Arts for 7th and 8th grades at Roberts School in Syracuse, New York.

LAURA SANDRONI graduated with a Master of Science in Education from Le Moyne College in May 2010. She teaches English at Jamesville-Dewitt High School in New York State.

SUNITA SINGH is an assistant professor of Education at Le Moyne College in Syracuse. Her research explores ways in which teachers can be supported to provide developmentally appropriate literacy instruction to all children, especially in classrooms that are culturally and linguistically diverse.

JENNIFER D. TURNER is an associate professor in Reading Education at the University of Maryland, College Park. Her scholarship centers on effective reading teachers and teaching for African American elementary students, and preparing elementary reading teachers for diversity.

Index